COURTING POWER

GARLAND STUDIES IN MEDIEVAL LITERATURE
VOLUME 17
GARLAND REFERENCE LIBRARY OF THE HUMANITIES
VOLUME 2095

Garland Studies in Medieval Literature

Paul E. Szarmach and Christopher Kleinhenz
General Editors

COURTING POWER
PERSUASION AND POLITICS
IN THE EARLY THIRTEENTH CENTURY

LAURIE SHEPARD

GARLAND PUBLISHING, INC.
A MEMBER OF THE TAYLOR & FRANCIS GROUP
NEW YORK AND LONDON
1999

Library of Congress Cataloging-in-Publication Data

Courting power / persuasion and politics in the early thirteenth century by
    Laurie Shepard.
            p.   cm. — (Garland studies in medieval literature ; v. 17)
    (Garland reference library of the humanities ; v. 2095)
        Includes bibliographical references and index.
        ISBN 0-8153-3122-3 (alk. paper)
        1. Latin Letters, Medieval and modern—History and criticism.   2. Per-
    suasion (Rhetoric)—Political aspects—History—To 1500.   3. Power (Social
    sciences)—Europe—History—To 1500.   4. Europe—Politics and govern-
    ment—476–1492.   5. Letter writing, Latin—History—To 1500.   I. Title.
    II. Series.   III. Series: Garland reference library of the humanities ; vol.
    2095.
    PA8089.S34   1999
    876'.0309—dc21   98–45426
                                                                          CIP

Printed on acid-free, 250-year-life paper
Manufactured in the United States of America

To my teacher, Maria Picchio Simonelli, with love and gratitude.

Contents

General Editors' Foreword

Garland Studies in Medieval Literature (GSML) is a series of interpretative and analytic studies of the Western European literatures of the Middle Ages. It includes both outstanding recent dissertations and book-length studies, giving junior scholars and their senior colleagues the opportunity to publish their research.

In accordance with GSML policy the general editors have sought to welcome submissions representing any of the various schools of criticism and interpretation. Western medieval literature, with its broad historical span, multiplicity, and complexity of language and literary tradition, and special problems of textual transmission and preservation as well as varying historical contexts, is both forbidding and inviting to scholars. It continues to offer rich materials for virtually every kind of literary approach that maintains a historical dimension. In establishing a series in an eclectic literature, the editors acknowledge and respect the variety of texts and textual possibilities and the "resisting reality" that confronts medievalists in several forms: on parchment, in mortar, or through icon. It is no mere imitative fallacy to be eclectic, empirical, and pragmatic in the face of this varied literary tradition that has so far defied easy formulation. The cultural landscape of the twentieth century is littered with the debris of broken monomyths predicated on the Middle Ages, the autocratic Church and the Dark Ages, for example, or conversely, the romanticized versions of love and chivalry.

The openness of the series means in turn that scholars, and particularly beginning scholars, need not pass an *a priori* test of "correctness" in their ideology, method, or critical position. The studies published in GSML must be true to their premises, complete with their articulated limits, and accessible to a multiple readership. Each study will advance the knowledge of the literature under discussion, opening it up for further consideration and creating intellectual value. It is also hoped that each volume, while bridging the gap between contemporary perspective and past reality, will make old texts new again. In this way the literature will remain primary, the method secondary.

Although today the term "rhetoric" often has negative connotations, suggesting a less than honest representation of the fact in a particular situation, in the Middle Ages it was a highly desired and prized commodity in the extensive commerce of words. The ability to persuade and move someone to action through speech or written words was a great gift, one the practitioners of this art put to excellent use in their positions in both ecclesiastical and secular institutions.

In *Courting Power,* the seventeenth volume of this series, Laurie Shepard examines the development of epistolary rhetoric in a particularly rich period of its history, the early thirteenth century. The correspondence between the imperial chancery of Frederick II and the papacies of Innocent III, Honorius III, and Gregory IX is remarkable for the picture it presents of the relationship between these formidable institutions and personalities. In the first part of the book Shepard focuses on the general shape and practice of the *ars dictaminis* in this period as observed in the manuals, as well as the impact of letters on their audience(s) and a history of the relationship between pope and emperor in the first half of the thirteenth century. In the second and third parts of this study she examines, respectively, the epistolary production of the papacy and the empire, seen both in terms of their increasingly hostile dynamic and against the backdrop of major cultural events and intellectual interests of the age. As Shepard notes,

> The papal-imperial exchange reveals how medieval epistolary persuasion, so well adapted to the mentality associated with Latin Christendom in the late twelfth and early thirteenth centuries, maintained its validity by transforming itself. In theory and in practice, epistolary persuasion struck out on a new course in certain milieus, the consequence of intractable political problems, more sophisticated legal and ideological discourses, a nascent but powerful idea about human society governed by laws perceptible to the human intellect, and the chancellors' recognition of a new European intellectual elite. The vigor of rhetorical persuasion may be read as a sign of confidence in the potential for the rational resolution of

conflict. The time and thought dedicated to persuasion in both the papal and imperial chanceries was at once an expression of hostility and of the attempt to define communality in an increasingly complex political situation. It reasserts the importance of rhetorical persuasion in the political arena of Latin Christendom, and it highlights the desire to come to a meeting of minds and to avoid the use of harsher measures, especially the spilling of blood.

The editors are happy to welcome this volume to the series. They furthermore wish to express their appreciation to Dr. Shepard for her cooperation and collegiality.

Christopher Kleinhenz   Paul E. Szarmach
University of Wisconsin-Madison   Western Michigan University

Preface

A major battle of words took place in the first half of the thirteenth century. At issue were competing visions of Christendom. The combatants conveyed an urgent desire to achieve satisfactory accommodation on points of difference; their letters jubilantly celebrated the cooperation and affection that bound them, and in periods of crisis they bristled with hostility. This book explores the language of persuasion in those letters, composed at the papal and imperial chanceries, and the new paradigm of persuasion which emerged when the vision of Christendom that defined the relationship became controversial.

The challenge to traditional persuasion crystallized in the letters of Frederick II, Holy Roman Emperor from 1220 to 1250. While conventional epistolary exchanges aspired to reinforce the harmony between writer and addressee, and responded to discord with cajoling, lamentation, or censure, the new imperial paradigm became the means to respond to controversy. Imperial letters of the 1220s and 1230s focused on the point of contention between the parties, and did not reduce it to a mere accident to be rectified in the light of an eternal or commonly held truth. The historical circumstances of a controversial event became an integral part of the strategy to persuade the addressee.

Scholars have described the ornate language of the letters produced at the papal and imperial chanceries, interpreted the political ideas, and traced the sources of both. This book examines epistolary rhetoric as an act of communication, defined and contoured by a number of factors: well established generic expectations, the culture of the writer, his perception of the public being addressed, and the contents of the message. It chronicles the development of a new paradigm of persuasion, and explores possible reasons for the development. I use the term "persuasion" to refer to the essential function of epistolary rhetoric, an art of engagement that aims at attaining the adherence of a particular public on an issue at a precise time. Within the framework of the epistle, pope and emperor sought power by courting the minds and hearts of prominent men of Latin Christendom, and to that end the chancellors of both camps employed vastly different arguments and interpretations of events for different publics.

Facts were occasionally sacrificed to the logic or passion of an appeal, as in the case of a 1227 papal encyclical announcing the excommunication of the emperor. For the present study the inaccurate report of legal violations that was leveled against Frederick is as important as the avalanche of words dedicated to the arousal of public indignation at the emperor's immoral nature—the reason for God's denial of Christian aspirations in the Holy Land according to Pope Gregory. The letter moves us to probe the Roman chancery's perception of Christian princes and prelates on whom it depended if Frederick were to be cast from the community of Christians. It raises questions about the relationship between conviction and persuasion in the period. Was legal excommunication not sufficient to bring a ruler to his knees? In the light of the pope's moral ascendancy, did lesser beings have the right to interpret events differently and question the premises of the papal interpretation of the facts? Was there a public for Frederick's letter of self-defense and his countercharge that Christians failed in the Holy Land because of the inept military leadership provided by the church?

Other more general questions emerge from the reading of the letters of pope and emperor. To what extent should the traditional epistolary appeal, based on harmony between parties, be viewed as an ideological instrument designed to gloss over dissension and reaffirm social and spiritual order? How did the traditional letter function in cases of intractable conflict? Did the prestigious prose style developed at the Roman chancery become endowed with a symbolic significance that cast competing discourses not merely as inferior, but as inappropriate or even heretical? How did one oppose the persuasive language of Rome? How dangerous to the unity of Christendom were rhetorical arguments rooted not in the poetic imagination or scholarly lucubration, but in partisan accounts of events?

This book examines epistolary persuasion as a porous discipline, most definitely cognizant of its own traditions, but receptive to the influence of developments in other spheres of intellectual activity as well—whether spiritual, legal, scientific, or political. For example, canon law was one of the powerful agents that galvanized and transformed Christian society in the early thirteenth century, and the pervasive influence of legal thought must be recognized in order to understand the development of epistolary persuasion. At a very fundamental level, canon law interpreted events, political or otherwise, in relation to moral categories, which signified the extreme difficulty of establishing a language at the papal chancery that explored the nature of conflict. Appeals dealing with conflict included statements of the law that were accompanied by jeremiads or condemnations, dominated by antithetical expressions of expectation and disappointment, good and evil, and by exclamations of joy, pain, deception, or shock.

The confluence of the language of law and the prestigious prose style employed at the papal chancery, known as the *stilus supremus,* or elevated prose style, is also pertinent. Roman prose, characterized by elaborate patterns of verbal, phonic, and rhythmic ornament, and laden with Biblical citations, figured prominently in traditional epistolary persuasion because it conveyed honor and respect for an addressee and solemn celebration of the status quo. The Biblical passages that endowed the elevated prose style with grace and grandeur were often encoded in canon law, and even banal metaphors like "nurturing mother" functioned as legal terms in papal letters. Roman letters resounded not only with the love of the holy father and the Roman vision of a hierarchical, hierocratic Christian society, but also with the conviction of the law.

The first part of this book includes three introductory chapters. Chapter 1 focuses on the attention and thought given to effective persuasive strategy in twelfth- and thirteenth-century manuals of letter-writing, which forecast the evolution in persuasive modes employed by papal and especially imperial chancellors. In manuals composed in the early and middle years of the twelfth century, letter-writers were advised to put the addressee in a compliant frame of mind with affectionate, flattering words, and to open letters with an interpretive principle, abstracted from the particulars, in order to guide the addressee to a desired end. Advice on the issue of interest to the two parties was limited to brevity and clarity. However, by the final decades of the twelfth century, manuals began to recommend that the specific circumstances pertinent to the issue at hand might be important to the overall persuasive strategy of the letter. This precept was well established in early thirteenth-century manuals. Chapter 2 examines the reception of the letters. Evidence of how the public reacted to competing papal and imperial appeals, and signs of the value of rhetorical persuasion in relation to other forms of argument are considered. The third chapter, almost an appendix to the book, provides a cursory account of the historical relationship between pope and emperor in the first half of the thirteenth century that is useful to understand the nature of the conflict that arose. The reader who is not familiar with the history of the period may choose to read Chapter 3 before Chapter 2. When the content of a quoted passage is more pertinent to the discussion than the language, Latin texts are included in the English translation only in Part 1. In the remainder of the book, all texts are in the original Latin with English translations. The translations are my own unless otherwise noted. Edited Latin texts are faithfully represented, leading to some inconsistencies in orthography and capitalization.

The focus of Part 2 is the production of the chanceries of popes Innocent III (1198-1216), Honorius III (1216-1227) and Gregory IX (1227-1241). Papal epistolary prose was the most prestigious language of the period, and Chapter 4 treats the brilliant standard associated with the chancery of Innocent III. Innocent recast epistolary prose to express his vision of pope as keystone of the Christian social edifice. Verbal figures reinforced his concept of a harmonious society governed by the pope and bound by love and law. Innocent's mastery of a discourse of power determined the challenge that secular rulers faced as they sought to manipulate the elevated prose style to assert alternative political visions. His successors, Honorius III (discussed in Chapter 5) and Gregory IX (Chapter 6), did not exercise the same stylistic originality as Innocent, and the power they communicated was less personal and more traditional. Honorius's letters offered spiritual interpretations of events, and appealed to the reason and the conscience of the emperor by alluding to recent historical events. In Gregory's letters, a sense of enmity toward the emperor, and fear of the harm that Frederick's ambition and mendacity might produce, swept up and scattered the facts—except in those passages where canon law determines the procedure. In the case of all three popes the profound interpenetration of law and epistolary persuasion is evident. The discussion of papal letters (like that of imperial letters in Part 3), is representative of the production of the chanceries, but by no means exhaustive. Letters have been chosen because they illustrate certain rhetorical trends, not on the basis of their historical importance.

Part 3 of the book analyzes the evolution of imperial epistolary persuasion between 1220 and 1239. Chapter 7 discusses the years that followed Frederick's Roman coronation, when the chancery's embrace of the language and ideology of the papacy, a discourse of love, gratitude, and obedience conveyed by celebratory verbal ornament and solemn invocations of Biblical verse, gradually weakened, and imperial epistolary persuasion was honed into a polemical instrument. The new paradigm of persuasion emerged in the second half of the 1220s and matured in the 1230s. The narration, that part of the letter that presents the complaint, looked and functioned differently than it did in traditional epistolary rhetoric. There was an insistent focus on the issue at stake; it was not eclipsed as a mere obstacle to harmony and concord between the correspondents. Contingent circumstances of events became determinant causes of imperial policies.

The imperial chancery was driven to define a new language of persuasion by the success of the Roman church's legal and administrative reforms. In situations of fundamental disagreement that pitted traditional royal prerogatives against those born of Rome's recent institutional achievements, princes were compelled to define a response. Rome spoke in the prestigious, loving, all-embracing voice that was fortified by law, but how did the prince defend his rights without incurring the charge of contumacy?

Another explanation for the genesis of the new approach to persuasion, difficult to prove but worth exploring, especially in relation to the production of the Frederican chancery and the elite public of the early thirteenth century, is the recovery of the Aristotelian science of nature, and its influence on the perception, description, and rationalization of human affairs. This idea is examined in the eighth chapter, where I argue that the imperial rhetoric of the 1230s represents a primitive manifestation of the epistemological impact of Aristotelian texts of natural philosophy. Michael Scot, chief astrologer and scientist at the imperial court, was the most prolific translator of the non-logical, "new Aristotle" in the 1220s and 1230s, a corpus that was still being absorbed into the more progressive university curriculums. Significant parallels between the inductive arguments of the imperial court and those offered by the Aristotelian biological texts are discernible. More generally, the chancery exploited the fault line opened by Aristotelian works between the spiritual and eternal, and the natural and temporal. It claimed for itself a discourse comprehensible to the mind and senses, and offered a vision of society shaped by human need and intellect that was discontinuous from the papal vision of Christian society governed by a transcendent code. It implicitly challenged the essential, necessary character of providential history. Imperial letters presented events in historical terms, and emphasized causality accessible to the human mind. The analysis of events systematically undermined the premises of the traditional epistolary appeal. Although the latter by no means disappeared from either chancery, and in fact remained the dominant epistolary code for centuries, the alternative is historically important because it rationalizes the challenging of authority, the very phenomenon that traditional epistolary rhetoric was designed to exclude. The correspondence of the 1230s changed the relationship between the papacy and empire, at least at the level of public perception, a determinant element for the selection of a rhetorical strategy. By 1239, Pope Gregory no longer assumed that he could effectively influence Christian princes solely on the basis of his divinely ordained authority, as Pope Innocent had believed earlier in the century. He elected, instead, to defend himself and his actions in order to persuade Christendom to support his policies.

The final chapter of the book examines the language of extreme hostility of 1239, at the point when the potential for exchange and the "meeting of minds" ceased to exist. Persuasion presupposes the possibility of intellectual contact between the orator and the public. The end of the fourth decade of the thirteenth century offers a convenient point of closure for the present study because of the mutual animosity of the leaders in question, and the tendency for the correspondence to take the form of blatant partisan attacks. The emperor called for a council to sit in judgment of the "heretic" Pope Gregory IX, while the policies and words of popes Gregory IX and his successor, Innocent IV, disclosed their conviction that further concessions to Frederick imperiled Christendom. The possibility of a shared language premised on a vision of Christendom where Frederick or one of his descendants played a role had vanished. Frederick spent his final years in open rebellion against the papacy.

The papal-imperial exchange reveals how medieval epistolary persuasion, so well adapted to the mentality associated with Latin Christendom in the late twelfth and early thirteenth centuries, maintained its validity by transforming itself. In theory and in practice, epistolary persuasion struck out on a new course in certain milieus, the consequence of intractable political problems, more sophisticated legal and ideological languages, a nascent but powerful idea about human society governed by laws perceptible to the human intellect, and the chancellors' recognition of a new European intellectual elite. The vigor of rhetorical persuasion may be read as a sign of confidence in the potential for the rational resolution of conflict. The time and thought dedicated to persuasion in both the papal and imperial chanceries was at once an expression of hostility and of the attempt to define communality in an increasingly complex political situation. It highlights the desire to come to a meeting of minds and to avoid the use of harsher measures, especially the spilling of blood.

Acknowledgments

I have relied on the patience of friends, colleagues, and family over the years, and I would like to express my gratitude to them. Maria Picchio Simonelli, to whom this book is dedicated, first taught me to admire the terrible brilliance of the *ultimo imperadore degli Romani*, and she opened up a world to me.

Others have read chapters and helped me to resolve problems, and I would like to extend my thanks. No one has been as supportive as my friend, Matilda Bruckner. My thanks to Dwayne Carpenter, Scott Westrem and Professor Martin Camargo, who generously assisted me from near and far. I would also like to thank Professor Chris Kleinhenz for his patience and encouragement over the years, and scholars at Boston College and elsewhere who have engaged in lively debate, and helped to clarify issues—Steven Brown, Michael Connolly, Richard Kay, Robert Levine, John Lomax, Arthur Madigan, and Camille Vappi.

I feel especially indebted to Cristiana Fordyce and Mark Stansbury, who read this work and grappled with the Latin with me, and also Ombretta Frau and Elena Ivanova.

My family has been extremely patient (and impatient). I am grateful to my father, Lawrence, for all of his help, and my brother, Dan. Most of all I need and wish to thank Oscar, Tommy and Louie, because you gave me the courage to complete this project.

I have received publishers' permission to reprint passages from the following works:

Alessio, Gian Carlo. Ed. *Bene Florentini Candelabrum.* Padova: Antenore, 1983.

Ehler, Sidney Z. and John B. Morrall. Trans. *Church and State through the Centuries: Collection of Historic Documents with Commentaries.* Westminster: Newman Press, 1954.

Powell, James M. Ed. and Trans. *The "Liber Augustalis" or "Constitutiones of Melfi" Promulgated by the Emperor Frederick II for the Kingdom of Sicily in 1231.* Syracuse: Syracuse University Press, 1971.

Van Cleve, Thomas Curtis. *The Emperor Frederick II of Hohenstaufen, Immutator Mundi.* Oxford: Clarendon Press, 1972.

PART 1

Background to the Question

CHAPTER 1

Framing the Facts in Medieval Epistolary Theory

Letters written in the early thirteenth century may strike modern readers as rambling and unfocused. The language is laced with ornaments and Biblical phrases, and the issue that provoked a letter in the first place, whether a petition for money or a threat of punishment, is submerged by an elaborate greeting accompanied by expressions of the writer's humility and his esteem for the addressee. The issue at hand is introduced in the light of a general principle and is recounted with few details. The writer resists coming to the point and once it has been touched upon, he beats a hasty retreat and concludes the letter. All this may be explained by the fact that the chief persuasive strategy in medieval epistolography was to put the addressee in a compliant frame of mind and thereby to achieve a harmony of wills between the writer and the recipient.[1] Affectionate, flattering words and a guiding principle were generally presumed to be sufficient to persuade the addressee to respond to a situation appropriately, and persuasion was the essential function of epistolary rhetoric. This book explores traditional epistolary rhetoric premised on harmony, as it was practiced by the papal and imperial chanceries in the early thirteenth century, as well as the persuasive strategies that evolved to embrace conflict when the vision of Christendom that defined the papal-imperial relationship became controversial.

The epistle, adopted for the promulgation and distribution of imperial edicts in the second century A.D., and perpetuated by the ecclesiastical and royal courts of medieval Europe, was the object of detailed instruction in the twelfth and thirteenth centuries. According to medieval theorists, letters were texts that expressed the will of an absent writer.[2] But the letters produced at the papal and other Latin chanceries were not merely epistolary decrees: they were persuasive, rhetorical documents expressing the will of the writer and endeavoring to gain the acquiescence of the addressee.[3] Despite the very significant differences between ancient oratory and medieval epistolography, the appropriation of the nomenclature and structure of the oration put the letter squarely in the tradition of ancient rhetoric and invigorated it with the essential persuasive function of oratory. Letters, like orations, were usually not private or intimate documents but composed for public circulation. Certainly the writers of the political documents discussed in this book envisioned a more numerous public than that indicated by the greeting, and in some cases the letters were intended to be read before large audiences.

In this introductory chapter I shall explore the extent to which textbooks of epistolography of the twelfth and thirteenth centuries instruct and reflect the persuasive strategies found in the papal-imperial correspondence of the third and fourth decades of the thirteenth century. Janet Martin notes that "the manuals are an imperfect guide to existing practice," and that it is difficult to determine how influential they actually were to epistolary practice.[4] But for the purposes of the present study, even a flawed mirror is useful because it shows that the textbooks already instructed both the strategies of persuasion associated with the rhetoric of harmony and key elements of a new paradigm of persuasion.

The manuals taught efficacy, whether the writer was requesting money, praising a patron, or denouncing a scoundrel. The two principal features of the manuals are the instruction of *dispositio,* with descriptions of the arrangement and function of the parts of a letter, and *elocutio,* with discussions of phonic and verbal ornaments as well as the correct construction, conjunction, and subordination of clauses. Another regular feature is an appendix of model letters and parts of letters, offered for imitation. The manuals were at once conservative and innovative: competition among the authors encouraged the adaptation or even wholesale pirating of any passage that proved useful to students.[5]

The evolution of the *artes dictandi,* or manuals of composition with a particular emphasis on letter-writing,[6] may be divided into three periods.[7] The center of innovation moves from Bologna to the Loire

Valley—Blois, Meung, Orléans and Tours—then back to Bologna. An initial phase, from 1100 to 1150, is characterized by the emergence of pragmatic *artes dictandi* that allowed functionally literate clerics and lay secretaries to compose letters and documents that were sufficiently correct to meet the burgeoning needs of both the ecclesiastical bureaucracies and the dynamic northern Italian city-states. In the same period in France, the traditional discipline of rhetoric was instructed by grammarians steeped in the study of ancient literature. During the second half of the twelfth century French textbooks began to adopt the Bolognese schematic approach, without always eliminating discussions of ancient poetics.[8] French manuals were the first to include explanations of the *cursus,* or rhythmic prose cadence in vogue at the pontifical chancery, and this soon became a standard feature of the genre.[9] From France, the epistolary manuals spread throughout Europe, but the center of innovation returned to Bologna. There, in the thirteenth century, epistolography was taught as part of a more systematic discussion of ancient and medieval rhetoric. However, such comprehensive textbooks remained the exception; most resembled the pragmatic *artes dictandi* of the earlier period.

Alberic, a monk at the monastery of Montecassino in the third quarter of the eleventh century, was the first teacher to provide instruction based on a division of the epistle into parts and descriptions of each part in terms of its function.[10] He borrowed both the nomenclature and functions from the ancient oration, and added the epistolary greeting to them. But Alberic never treated epistolography as a subject detached from prose composition or rhetoric.[11] New in Bologna in the twelfth century were manuals that focused almost exclusively on rules of letter-writing. The Bolognese manuals were tailored to the needs of secretaries and bureaucrats, and armed with an *ars dictandi,* a minimally literate man was able to compose a respectable epistolary document. The theoretical exposition of rhetoric that had long been practiced in the monasteries (illustrated in texts like Alberic's *Flores Rhetorici*) was streamlined by urban *dictatores,* or professors of rhetoric, in the name of *utilitas.* The very first extant Bolognese manual is the *Praecepta Dictaminum* of Adalbert Samaritanus, which is known in three redactions composed between 1111 and 1118. Adalbert uses the verb *enucleare* to describe the process of extracting epistolographic doctrine from the "compendiosam traditionem."[12] Theory is never completely eliminated in the urban manuals, but the goal is nearly achieved in the influential, anonymous 1135 *Rationes Dictandi.*

This chapter will focus on the instruction of strategies to present and frame the issue that provoked the letter in the first place, one of several topics regularly included in the manuals. The narration (narratio) is the part of the letter that recounts the issue, and its definition and relation to the other parts of the letter shed light on the evolution of epistolographic persuasive strategies. Of particular importance is the dialectic between the narration and the exordium of the letter, which presents the general, interpretive principle. In a tradition dating back to Antiquity, the three qualities associated with an effective narration are clarity, brevity, and plausibility.[13] Noting the lack of prominence attached to the narration in the Middle Ages, Faulhaber remarked that letters function like "a sort of enthymemic argument from authority, with the exordium serving as the major premise, the *narratio* as the minor premise, and the *petitio* as the conclusion."[14] A shift in the relative importance of major and minor premises that occurs in some letters in the early thirteenth century, signaling a new persuasive strategy formulated in response to political and cultural developments, is documented in this book. In these letters the narration, or minor premise, is not concise and shorn of all detail, but long and nuanced, with an emphasis on contingent circumstances to explain and justify actions. Rather than privileging the general principle and resonant harmony that bind the recipient to the writer, these letters posit persuasion in the presentation of the specific contingencies of an event. The same redimensioning of the parts of the letter is evident in thirteenth-century manuals of epistolography. While early twelfth-century texts limit advice for effective narrations to brevity and credibility, thirteenth-century manuals list numerous strategies to compose an effective narration, and add that there are as many different kinds of narrations as there are letter-writers. In the *Candelabrum,* composed in the 1220s, Bene of Florence reduces the exordium to a "preamble" to the narration [4.1.2].

The definition and instruction of the narration in representative textbooks illustrate the transformation of the doctrine in the course of the three periods that define the evolution of the *artes dictandi.* The manuals surveyed in this chapter include Hugh the Canon's *Rationes Dictandi* from Bologna, one of the oldest extant texts dated between 1119 and 1124; an influential anonymous textbook also known as the

Rationes Dictandi, composed around 1135 in Bologna; several French manuals from the final decades of the twelfth century entitled *Dictamen Bernardi,* the *Libellus de Arte Dictandi Rhetorice,* and the *Ars Dictandi Aurelianensis;* a Bolognese *Summa de Arte Dictandi* attributed to Geoffrey of Vinsauf and dated between 1188 and 1190, and two works from Bologna in the 1220s, Guido Faba's *Summa Dictaminis* and Bene of Florence's *Candelabrum.* These last two are contemporaneous with the papal and imperial documents examined in later chapters.

The canon Hugh, a contemporary of the previously mentioned lay professor of rhetoric, Adalbert, criticizes the latter for teaching epistolary composition as a discipline disassociated from the traditional monastic curriculum, and praises the teaching of the monk Alberic, regretting only that the latter never composed a tract on epistolography.[15] Unlike Adalbert, Hugh adopts Alberic's innovative application of the nomenclature and functions of the parts of the oration to the letter. His description of the parts reproduces the standard instruction of the oration established by Cassiodorus and the glossators of the *De Inventione.* In paragraph 8 Hugh writes,

Est vero exordium secundum tullianam diffinitionem oratio idonee conparans animum auditoris ad reliquam dictionem. Narratio quidem est rei geste vel quasi geste explanatio. Est autem conclusio totius orationis exitus sive determinatio.

And the exordium is, according to the Ciceronian division, the speech appropriately preparing the spirit of the listener for the rest of the talk. The narration is an explanation of, or similar to, the event. The peroration is the end or conclusion of the entire speech.

Hugh's manual actually opens with a detailed treatment of the greeting (salutatio), the only part of the letter that was not a feature of the ancient oration. Its role in the letter was fundamental because, as Faulhaber notes, "in the highly structured society of the Middle Ages these relationships [between sender and addressee] were of utmost importance and their proper expression crucial to the accomplishment of the sender's desires."[16] Hugh offers a set of greetings with variants arranged according to the social status of the correspondents, "not suggestions for rhetorical invention," according to Murphy, "but . . . instead models for copying."[17] Also included are seventeen model letters and parts of letters, eliminating the need for the inexperienced secretary to invent: he merely had to learn to apply the models appropriately.

In paragraph 13, Hugh presents a set of abstract "schemes" for framing different kinds of issues (modos epistolarum), which offers insight into Hugh's conception of the subordination of the particular issue that requires attention to the guiding principle. Effectiveness depends on the general nature of the problem at hand, and not on the specific contingencies. Hugh treats the specifics as merely accidental and requiring redefinition within an abstract, logical, or paralogical scheme; they are irrelevant to the process of epistolary invention, and not invoked to persuade the addressee to adopt a particular course of action. For example, a child's successful entreaty for money does not depend on his age, character, friends, fortune, or the precarious situation in which he finds himself, but on the natural imperative that a parent love and nurture offspring.

> Et est primus naturalis, a natura principium sumens. ad patrem scilicet. Lege nature et iure paterno cogitur quisque ex se natum diligere, ac a brutis exemplum sumere, que ad tempus fetus proprios elactant et nutriunt, quasi ratione discernerent. Decet igitur vos me vestrum filium in amore annectere, et sic mihi paternum auxilium dirigere. . . .

> And it is natural, first, to take our opening from nature. Thus to a father: by the law of nature and paternity, a man is compelled to love whoever is born to him, as we can surmise from the example of beasts, who nourish their own from birth, as if they discerned rationally. It is right, therefore, that you be bound to me, your son, with love, and that you direct paternal assistance to me.

In other *modos,* abstract relationships like analogy are cited as effective frames for the particular. Analogy is reinforced, in the following example, by a charged reminder of the social and personal superiority of the petitioned.

> Per simplicem similitudinem. Ad pastorem vel patrem vel consules conclusione parum variata. Sicut filii patribus, oves pastoribus, cives consulibus subesse, sic patres amare, pastores gubernare, consules

> defendere coguntur, ut utrobique nature et officii legibus decenter observatis laude eximia dignum habeatur quia ratione vivatur. Ergo pastor egregie, me gubernare et regere vos non pigeat, quatenus mea parvitas omni tempore vobis subesse et servire gestiat.

> By a simple analogy. To the pastor or father or consul with the conclusion of the pair varied. As sons are compelled to be subordinate to fathers, sheep to the shepherds, citizens to consuls, so in order that both the laws of nature and of duty be fittingly observed, fathers are bound to love, the shepherds to guide and the consuls to defend, so that, having lived rationally, one is deemed worthy with the greatest praise. Therefore inasmuch as my insignificance is beneath you and I eagerly desire to serve you for all time, let the shepherd not be ashamed to govern me and rule me absolutely.

Other cases are more abstract. Grammatical figures are suggested to impose symmetry and to support moral rigor: "Comparativa seu qantitativa. Quanto corpore splendidor, mente sagatior, tanto debes cunctis esse subiectior et in dei servitio promptior" [Comparative or quantitative. To the extent that you are more splendid in body, wiser in mind, so you should be more humble to all and more prompt to serve God], or to add refinement: "Et est primus, ubi nullum verbum preter primam personam indicativi et singularis numero ponimus, hoc modo . . . ," [and the first (case) is where we use no verb except in the first person singular indicative . . .]. The ancient doctrine of rhetorical invention has been reduced to rudimentary rules for the generalization, abstraction, or formalization of the particular.

In spite of the canon's insistence that the *ars dictandi* be taught as an integral part of the monastic curriculum, early manuals like Hugh's represent a milestone in the transfer of public administration from the monastery to the marketplace. It is in a sense a "technological" innovation, an instrument that allowed modestly educated laymen to produce acceptable petitions and official documents, and it broke the traditional dependence of secular rulers on clerics. A century after Hugh, the Emperor Frederick II established a school in Naples to train lay bureaucrats to serve his kingdom, and in Bologna Guido Faba taught oratorical and dictaminal techniques to the new urban leaders, merchants, and notaries, in both Latin and the vernacular.

The anonymous Bolognese *Rationes Dictandi* of 1135 was extremely influential and exemplifies the structure and scope of the *ars dictandi* genre that spread throughout Europe.[18] It is short, elementary, and pragmatic. The limits of the manual are specified by its author, who insists that effective epistolographic composition is born of experience, not rules, and so "we are contenting ourselves in this book with providing some basic skills for the untrained." I will describe the whole manual to give the reader unfamiliar with the *artes dictandi* a sense of the genre. The instruction of epistolography is prefaced by a minimal list of definitions pertaining to composition in general, with a fundamental distinction established between poetic and prose composition.[19] Then the author launches into a discussion of the letter and its five parts. Persuasive efficacy is posited in the balance of structure and tone. The goodwill of the letter's recipient is the single most important element to achieve one's end and the anonymous author of the *Rationes Dictandi* explains how the appropriate composition of each part of the epistle promotes this end.

The discussion of the greeting or *salutatio* takes up about a third of the manual. The author states that "very often the largest part of securing the goodwill is in the course of the salutation itself." The greeting acknowledges the addressee's rank and importance, with attendant expressions of admiration and affection. The order of the names of the writer and the addressee in the greeting, and the appropriate and flattering qualifiers are determined by the relative rank and estate of the correspondents and the subject matter of the epistle. The author illustrates his doctrine with examples that must have seemed, in some cases, ambitious to the novice: "The Pope's Universal Salutation," "The Emperor's Salutation to All Men," "Greetings of Lords to Guilty and Offensive Subjects," and the "Greetings of Delinquent Sons to Their Parents." He also includes instruction on noun declension necessary for grammatically correct greetings. The greeting was so fundamental to epistolary protocol that even rudimentary texts like the *Rationes Dictandi* explain it in detail, establishing, for example, the distinction between clerical and secular expressions of submission. In the case of correspondence between clerics, the qualities recommended to ingratiate the writer include "obedientiam, reverentiam, subiectionem, devotionem, famulatum, famulamen" (obedience, reverence, subjugation, devotion, bondage, serving). In secular letters, however, terms like *reverentiam* and *obedientiam* are not suitable: "Cum in secularibus personis subditi ad dominos salutem pronuntiant, non utique 'reverentiam' nec 'obedientiam' dicant, set 'servitium,' 'obsequium,' 'servitutem,' 'fidelitatem,' 'subiectionem,' et similia" [When secular subordinates write a salutation to their lords, they should not under any circumstances say "veneration" or "obedience," they should say instead "service," "compliance," "servitude," "loyalty," "subordination" and the like]. Certain words appear to have assumed an almost ritual quality, and the omission or inclusion of phrases transcends mere protocol or the effort of the writer to ingratiate or offend the addressee.[20] The tone of the letters and the inclusion of formulas of courtesy become issues of contention in some of the more polemical documents examined in this book.

In the anonymous 1135 *Rationes Dictandi,* the *captatio benevolentiae* or "securing of goodwill" follows the greeting. It is again intended to flatter the recipient by the expression of benevolence and praise. In other manuals the discussion of the *captatio benevolentiae* is replaced by a description of the exordium, usually a Biblical or proverbial statement, or a maxim from law or logic, which establishes a general principle to guide the recipient's response to the writer's petition. But the two approaches are not always clearly distinguished in the *artes,* and even the sample letters of the *Rationes Dictandi* appear to illustrate exordia.

The instruction of the remainder of the letter is concise. The standard advice concerning the narration, the focus of this chapter, is brevity and plausibility. The 1135 Bolognese text simply states that events should be disclosed in a clear and orderly fashion so that "the materials seem to present themselves" [Narratio vero expositio est rerum gestarum vel ut potius se geri videbuntur]. Two other qualifications are added to the discussion of the narration. The *Rationes Dictandi* distinguishes between the "simple narration," focused on a single issue, and a "composed narration" that raises more than one issue. Temporality is presented as an intrinsic feature of the narration: "Furthermore, some narrations are written about the past, others about the present, and still others about the future" [Item narratio alia fit de preterito, alia de presenti, alia de futuro]. The importance of this last point is highlighted later in the century when Geoffrey of Vinsauf juxtaposes the instruction of the epistolary narration with the Ciceronian definition of a rhetorical narration, and contrasts the timeless and eternal quality he associates with Cicero to the immediacy and urgency of the epistolary appeal.[21] In the anonymous 1235 manual, the manipulation of verb tenses is one of the essential lessons to be mastered by the novice secretary, and in the second part of the *Rationes Dictandi* the grammar of temporality is explained under the rubric "modo tractandi in singulis narrationibus."[22]

The fourth part of the letter is the petition (petitio), in which a request is made or an order issued. Nine categories of petitions are specified ("supplicatory or didactic or menacing or exhortative or hortatory or admonitory or advisory or reproving or even merely direct"). The author states that in clerical and lay documents of an official nature, the focus of this book, menacing petitions (comminationes) are most frequent because of the common use of threats in the exercise of power. Finally we read that letters should close with a conclusion or peroration that synthesizes and reiterates the main points. The 1135 Bolognese manual also offers guidance for varying the length of letters; any part may be omitted when unnecessary, given the subject matter and the relation of the writer to the addressee. The precepts and examples contained in the *Rationes Dictandi* are minimal, straightforward, and reductive.

A decade later, Bernard of Bologna (or Faenza or Romagna), a professor of grammar at Bologna, wrote a *Summa Dictaminum* that borrows a great deal from the anonymous 1135 *Rationes Dictandi*. The *Summa,* which is known to have reached France by 1160, is extant in two redactions composed in Italy between 1144 and 1153, and in a later French redaction that can be recognized as the "nucleus of most discussions of dictamen composed in both France and England during the late twelfth and thirteenth centuries."[23] In the description of the narration, the French redaction essentially retains the doctrine of the 1135 *Rationes Dictandi:* "Narratio est rerum gestarum vel prout gestarum expositio. Narrationum alia simplex, alia composita. Simplex quando de uno agitur officio, composita quando plura continet officia" [The narration is an account of the facts or like the facts. Some narrations (are) simple, others complex. A narration that is complete with the recounting of a single matter is simple. A narration is complex in which several matters are recounted].[24]

Bernard and the Bolognese tradition are combined with large tracts on poetics, the fruit of a renewal of the study of ancient poets at the schools of the Loire Valley in the twelfth century, in two French texts from the early 1180s. While most of the material concerned with letter-writing is drawn from Bernard's *Summa Dictaminum,* the description of the narration is an exception. In one of the texts, the *Libellus de Arte Dictandi Rhetorice,* the narration passage opens with the standard instruction, then interpolates two phrases. The first (ne sacietatem pariat auditori superflua verborum multitudo) is apparently lifted from a contemporary text composed at a school of the Loire Valley and known by its incipit, *Floribus Rhetoricis.*[25] The second element in the text's description of the narration that cannot be traced to Bernard's *Summa Dictaminum* is in fact more important to the present discussion. In the passage cited below, *probabilis,* a characteristic associated with the narration since Antiquity, is identified with the potential for effective deception (ne manifeste falsitatis possit accusari), in a letter. The entire passage reads:

> Nunc de narracione dicendum est, que brevis esse debet et delucida. Brevis ne sacietatem pariat auditori superflua verborum multitudo; dilucida quidem et serena ne verborum obscuritate mittentis intencio corrumpatur. Ceterum probabilis esse debet ne manifeste falsitatis possit accusari.

> Now of the narration it must be said that it should be brief and clear. Brief lest there seem a superfluous number of words to the educated listeners; and clear and measured lest the intention of the sender be corrupted by the obscurity of the words. But besides it must be plausible to avoid the possibility of being accused of manifest falsehood.

It is difficult to evaluate the final caveat, but it probably reflects the French masters' understanding of ancient oratorical theory.[26] An Orléans manual states the implications of *probabilis* more baldly. The *Ars Dictandi Aurelianensis* reads:

> Narracio est rerum gestarum vel prout gestarum explanacio. prout gestarum dixi, quia in epistola licet nos quandoque mentiri.[27]

> The narration is the explanation of the facts or just like the facts. "Just like the facts" is said because in a letter it is sometimes appropriate for us to deceive.

A third French text with a similar description of the narration was composed by Bernard Silvestris, and it dates from the end of the twelfth century. Bernard writes:

> Narracio est expositio sive explanacio rerum gestarum vel prout gestarum. Rerum gestarum dico quia quandoque res geste narrantur. Prout gestarum dico, quia quandoque non rese geste, sed prout geste recitantur, quia bene licet quandoque in narracione mentiri.[28]

> The narration is the setting out or explanation of what has happened or like what has happened. I say "of what has happened" becomes sometimes what took place is narrated. I say "like what has happened" because sometimes not the events but something similar is recited, since it is fitting, at times, to deceive in a narration.

When the traditional medieval reading of *probabilis* as "plausible" is replaced by one that explicitly alludes to the utility of deceit, the status of the narration changes within the letter. The notion that a false statement of events might contribute more to the efficacy of the petition than a straightforward account, and that it is occasionally useful to manipulate the issue that has prompted the letter in the interest of effect, destabilizes the traditional medieval approach to persuasion. The focus of invention can no longer be understood as the identification of a principle that will guide the reader to understand the accidents of time that are briefly and succinctly recounted in the narration. The orchestration or falsification of those accidents reduces the integrity and authority of the exordium, now, at least potentially, a principle selected to account for a useful lie.

Christians had always understood the dangers of rhetorical persuasion, but they regarded it as necessary because the arsenal of the preachers of Truth had to match and surpass that of the pagan purveyors of falsehood.[29] In *De Doctrina Christiana,* Augustine truncates the millennial old triad of attributes associated with the narration (brevis, dilucida, and veri simili in *Ad Herennium;* brevis, aperta, and probabilis in *De Inventione*).[30] Rejecting mere plausibility, Augustine's *De Mendacio,* Chapter 10, warns that deliberate deception on the part of clerics would undermine the entire ecclesiastical institution.[31] In the *Etymologiae,* Isidore (ca. 560-636) relies on Cassiodorus for rhetorical lore, but the Bishop of Seville rejects *ex silentio* Cassiodorus's definition of the narration as "rerum gestarum aut ut gestarum expositio" (an account of the events or very like the events) [2.2.9].[32] Doubtless following Augustine, Isidore writes that Christian rhetoric excludes the merely plausible, at least in theory: "According to the art of rhetoric an oration is divided into four parts: the introduction, the narration, the argument, the conclusion. The first captures the attention of the audience; the second sets forth the facts [secunda res gestas explicat]; the third wins assent by offering proof, the fourth ties up all the threads of the speech."[33] Bolognese texts like the 1135 *Rationes Dictandi* tacitly reflect this Christian conception of the narration and rhetorical persuasion. I have not been able to discover any manuals that describe or recommend a mendacious narration of events that predate the three French *artes*.

Nevertheless, Christian embarrassment with the merely "plausible" nature of rhetoric, and more specifically, the papal chancery's preoccupation with the integrity of its dealings, is alive and well in the twelfth and thirteenth centuries, and the documents of Pope Innocent III (1197-1215) frequently close with the formula "nullis litteris veritati et justitiae praejudicantibus a sede apostolica impetratis (no letters obtained from the Apostolic See [being] prejudicial to the truth or to justice).[34] Despite Innocent's professions of concern, his last chancellor, the Cardinal Thomas of Capua, who was also chief chancellor under Innocent's successor Honorius III, states in paragraph 22 of his authoritative *Ars Dictandi* that the narration ought to recount the facts, or offer an account that is plausible, though not necessarily true.

> Narrationem exordio sine medio complectendo [sed] ut congruit res gestas vel ea, que geri posse videbuntur, cum diligentia exponamus; que quidem expositio debet esse brevis, probabilis et aperta, ut si de Troiana ruina loqui volumus, non ab ovo gemmino initium capiamus sed a raptu Helene, que causa exstitit procul dubio destructionis; "aperta" si ordinem rerum gestarum servaverimus, "probabilis" erit, si tempus et locum ostendimus, ad rem facientia semper vere vel saltem verisimiliter explicantes.[35]

> The narration [must be] connected to the exordium without anything intervening, so that it corresponds to the events or to what seems possibly to have taken place. Let us explain carefully: in fact the account should be brief, plausible, and clear, so that when we wish to

speak of the ruin of Troy, we do not start from the twin egg but from
the rape of Helen, which stands out beyond doubt as the cause of the
destruction; "open" if we were to retain the order of the events, it will
be "plausible" if we tell the time and the place, always explaining
either what truly happened or at least what seems likely.

In another passage of the same textbook, however, Thomas sternly
rejects the substitution of conjecture for fact in the narration at the
Roman chancery.[36] Rhetorical persuasion, rooted in plausibility and not
necessarily in truth, is a matter of great concern to papal chancellors of
the period. The problem comes up repeatedly in the letters examined in
this book.

Preserved in three German manuscripts, the *Summa de Arte
Dictandi* was written in Bologna between 1188 and 1190 and is
attributed to the innovative master Geoffrey of Vinsauf.[37] The *Summa*
does not simply juxtapose the pragmatic, persuasive tradition of
Bologna and the literary experience of France; it integrates the
fundamental functions of the *ars dictandi* championed by the Italian
dictatores and the poetics reclaimed by the French traditions, and
focuses both on the immediacy of the letter and the need to elevate the
language of the narration above the brief, clear, and artless.

A twenty-hexameter prolog opens the text, the definition of the
parts of the letter and examples follow, and a brief discussion of
common faults associated with the epistolary genre concludes the
manual. Instruction of the greeting is again featured, not only because
the formulas necessary to master medieval epistolary protocol are
numerous, but "maxime cum salutatis affectus . . . totum epistole
pendet edificium" (especially because the whole construction of the
letter depends on the sentiments of the greeting). The description of the
exordium is also elaborate, with the recommendation that proverbs or
axioms drawn from custom or nature be used. Numerous examples are
provided, according to the subject matter of the letter.

Geoffrey, in keeping with tradition, does not hesitate to remind his
readers that an affectionate greeting will make or break an epistolary
appeal; similarly, his instruction of the exordium, that part of the letter
built upon common beliefs or eternal and universal principles, is not
original. It is the narration that departs from the traditional advice of
clarity, brevity, and plausibility, and instead reproposes the accidents of
time as the object of a new amplification. Geoffrey calls attention to the

narration by making it the focus of invention, and a crucial component of the overall persuasive appeal of the letter.

The text of the *Summa* juxtaposes and distinguishes the dictaminal narration and the rhetorical narration.

> Est narratio rethoris et est narratio dictatoris. Narratio rethoris tantum res gestas vel quasi gestas prosequitur; narratio dictatoris facta vel ficta exprimit circa presens, preteritum et futurum. Non enim epistolantis est ut tantum preterita sue narrationis ducant curriculum, set etiam de futuris et presentibus negotiis suam narrationem intexat, maxime cum salutatis affectus, a quo totum epistole pendet edificium, nunc de presentibus deliberet, nunc ad preterita redeat, nunc extendat sollicitudinem ad futura. [3.1]

> There is the narration of the orator and the narration of the *dictator*. The narration of the orator merely follows the deeds or something like the deeds; the narration of the *dictator* expresses facts or falsehoods about the present, past, and future. In fact, it is not so much past events that command the course of the letter-writing, but [the writer] should weave his narration around future and present matters, especially with an affectionate greeting [on which the epistolary edifice depends], at times deliberating on current matters, at times reverting to past events, at times turning to his concerns about the future.

The distinction hinges on the temporal dimension and the persuasive intention of the letter. Although the temporal dimension of the epistolary narration had been mentioned in the manuals from the time of the 1135 *Rationes Dictandi,* it becomes a defining characteristic of the genre in Geoffrey's discussion. Geoffrey's notions of temporality are rooted in the different ends of the orator and the *dictator:* the letter deliberates on the here and now, and aims at promoting a certain response in the addressee. The letter-writer expresses facts to influence the outcome of events, and the verb *exprimit* used by Geoffrey to describe the narration of the letter contrasts neatly with *prosequitur* of the oration narration, a deponent verb conveying passive adherence to the events as they present themselves. The space left by the monumental ancient discipline has been filled by the immediacy and urgency of the *ars dictandi*. Ancient oratory, its very authority founded upon its detachment from the present age, was intended to yield moral edification, but not immediate and salutary action.

Geoffrey advises that the narration open with a joyful and authoritative statement in order to unite the minds of the public. In keeping with the ancient doctrine of forensic invention, he writes that this should proceed from the situation in life (fortune, affect, fame, habits, and associates) of those involved in the events being recounted. There are as many kinds of narrations as there are writers of letters [Narrationum multiformis est forma. Totus enim narrationis modus est, quotus dictatorum numerus]. What is accidental, temporal and contingent is valorized and becomes essential to the persuasive efficacy of the letter. Geoffrey teaches that the letter is an instrument designed to prevail over events as they present themselves.

Works by two of the most famous Bolognese masters of rhetoric of the first half of the thirteenth century, the *Candelabrum*[38] and the *Summa Dictaminis,*[39] give a sense of the development of dictaminal theory in the third period. Bene of Florence (fl. 1220-1240) compiled the *Candelabrum* between 1221 and 1226, and the text has been described as the most complete discussion of dictaminal lore of the period,[40] although the different traditions are not always integrated, resulting in frequent repetition and occasional contradiction. Guido Faba (ca. 1190-ca. 1243), composed the *Summa Dictaminis* in 1228 or 1229, and it became a text of such great authority that it did not suffer the fate of most manuals—dismemberment and pillage of useful passages—but survived "intact through nearly two centuries of use throughout Europe."[41] In addition to the *Summa,* Guido wrote seven collections of model letters, parts of letters, and speeches. His *Arenge* was composed of exordia intended for letters and speeches by civic leaders and a later redaction includes entire speeches. The *Gemma Purpurea* is a collection of epistolary exordia in both Latin and the vernacular. The *Parlamenta et Epistole,* as the title promises, provides both epistolary and oratorical models, in the vernacular and in Latin.

The list of titles attributed to Guido suggests that the early thirteenth-century Bolognese professors of rhetoric did not address themselves exclusively to undergraduates; just as the twelfth-century manuals facilitated the business of lay bureaucracies, the *dictatores* promoted civic education in the city-states of northern Italy. Bologna has been described as the "key city" in the development of popular government in the northern Italy, where interclass strife led by men like the merchant Urseppo dei Toschi renewed the social and political structures.[42] The merchant needed to learn the language of the public administrator and civic leader, a language that was correct and persuasive, and that could move others to action. While Boncompagno, a generation before Guido, rants against popular orators who spread lies and use deceptive modes of persuasion,[43] Guido Faba is the first teacher of the *ars dictaminis* to provide oratorical and epistolary models in both Latin and the vernacular.

Guido is considered the most accessible and effective teacher of the dictaminal art. As he himself declares in a sample exordium of paragraph 69 of the *Summa Dictaminis,* "Magister Guido ubique diligitur quia sua dictamina comprobantur" [Master Guido is loved everywhere because his rules of composition are valued]. The *Summa Dictaminis* is straightforward and illustrated with numerous models for each part of the letter.

The dangers attendant upon the writing of an effective narration appear early on in the *Summa.* Paragraph 11 warns against prolixity, lack of clarity due to of a careless or confused presentation of events, implausibility, and the omission of the specific circumstances of time and place. In paragraph 73 of the *Summa,* the narration is briefly described in Ciceronian language [Narratio, ut a Tullio diffinitur, est rerum gestarum vel proinde ut gestarum expositio. . . . Et nota quod narratio debet esse brevis, dilucida et probabilis]. Guido then expands the gloss on *probabilis* with the notion of interpretation and opinion. "Probabilis est si morem sectetur, opinionem referat, et sicut natura postulat exponatur" [It is plausible if it follows common usage, conveys an opinion, and is expressed "naturally," as nature postulates, or with verisimilitude]. Apparently following Bene of Florence, who had articulated in the *Candelabrum* the importance of opinions and of examining causes [4.23.8; 8.52-3], Guido illustrates the concept of "like the facts" with a text that expresses both motive and moral judgment.

> Verbi gratia rerum gestarum cum dicitur: "Scias quod Petrus dedit B. archipresbitero X lib. et factus est canonicus Ymolensis" vel proinde ut gestarum, ut si dicam: "Petrus factus est canonicus talis loci simoniaca pravitate." [73]

An example of an account of the facts is when it is said: "Know that
Peter gave the Archbishop B. ten pounds and was made canon of
Imoli," or like the facts if I were to say, "Peter was made canon of
such a place because of depraved simony."

In fact, this particular example closely resembles some found in the
eleventh- and twelfth-century French commentaries on the *De
Inventione* that were inspired by the reform agenda of the late eleventh
century,[44] but in theory, Guido is expressing a more complex notion of
plausibility and its dynamic integration into the epistolary appeal.

After illustrating the parts of the letter, Guido broadens his
discussion to the entire process of epistolary composition, with a lucid
explanation of *inventio, dispositio,* and *ornamentatio.* Most of the
remainder of the *Summa* is taken up by stylistic concerns, including the
cursus; the use of rhetorical colors, proverbs, and sentences; drills on
grammatical conversions to develop an agile exercise of the *cursus,* and
a brief discussion of privileges.[45] In the final analysis, Guido's manual
is a culminating work of the tradition, and its practical, minimally
theoretical exposition of the ascendant mode of epistolography,
premised on harmony and the expectation of willing acquiescence,
probably accounts for its success.

One of the texts on which Guido Faba relied extensively is Bene of
Florence's *Candelabrum.* Throughout the *Candelabrum* Bene operates
on several planes; on the one hand, he is writing an epistolary manual
that draws on early Bolognese and the French traditions, and on the
other he is absorbing into his teachings the traditions of Cicero,
Boethius, the *artes poeticae,* and later medieval writers. He also
comments on current controversies like the question of whether the use
of a proverb in the exordium serves to persuade, or to obscure an
argument as Boncompagno had maintained [4.18]. There is not the
same degree of assimilation of the materials as in Geoffrey's *Summa,*
but a zeal to include and arrange all known doctrine in an encyclopedic
volume.

Like his predecessors of the previous century, Bene is ambitious on
the subject of the training of a *dictator:* "Quicumque vult ergo perfecte
dictandi lauream adipisci legat dilgenter philosophos et autores, legat et
quoscumque potest nobiliores libros ex quibus facundiam et sapientiam
consequatur" [Whoever wishes, therefore, to acquire expertise in
composition, must apply himself to the philosophers and the classics,

and read whichever he can of the greater books from which proceed eloquence and wisdom] [1.5.4]. For Bene, rhetoric is not merely elegance and excellence in composition, but mastery of the persuasive function of language. He defines it in terms of its ancient disciplines: *inventio, dispositio, memoria, pronuntiatio,* and *elocutio.* The *ars dictaminis* teaches correct and appropriate style, only one part of the technically inseparable skills of rhetoric: "Unde ars ista, que dictatoria nuncupatur, non est ipsa rethorica sed pars eius elocutio nominata" [Whence this art, which is called composition, is not rhetoric itself but a part of it called style] [1.4.16].

The *Candelabrum* portrays the relationship between exordium and narration not as a major and minor premise but in terms of complementarity and difference. For example, Book 3, paragraph 5, thought to be original to Bene, explains the requisite verbal modes for the exordium and narration in terms of the function of the two parts of the letter.[46] The infinitive is appropriate to the exordium, "quia sicut infinitivum est vagum nec per se firmiter stare potest, ita exordium, nisi causa cognita, est incertum . . ." (because just as the infinitive is vague and cannot be firmly fixed, thus the exordium, unless the case has been examined, is uncertain . . .). The narration is written in the indicative "quia in ipsa totius negotii seriem plenius indicamus" (because in it we tell fully the sequence of all that has happened). The paragraph implies that Bene did not view the letter as a passive instrument that merely recorded the facts, but as an instrument to investigate and to establish them. Contrary to the early *dictatores,* he suggests that the letter itself acquires meaning from the discovery of the specific details of a situation. In Book 4, which moves from the limited topic of the letter back to a more general discussion of effective rhetoric, an exordium is actually described as the preamble to the narration (Exordium est preambulus narrationi) [4.1.2]. The reduction of the exordium to the role of "preamble" is without known precedent, although obviously the second part of the sentence (affatus ad audiendum preparans animum auditoris [spoken to prepare the spirit of the listeners]) may be traced to the ancient oratorical handbooks. In paragraph 31 of the same book, Bene compares the relationship of the exordium and narration to a logical structure.[47] Bene's description of the narration in Book 4, taken from the *Ad Herennium.* (Narratio est rerum gestarum aut proinde ut gestarum expositio) [4.19.2], is specified as a forensic narration. The narration of a letter, on the other hand, is not specific to epistolography

[4.22.5]. It should be brief and uncluttered, clear and stylistically appropriate to the intended public's culture and size, and plausible.[48] In Book 5, Bene adds that the appearance of falsehood will immediately fill the mind of the listener with indignation and subvert the entire enterprise. "Nam si narratio videbitur falsitatis interpres, subito quidem et auditoris animum indignatione obruet et totius negotii fundamenta subvertet" [5.26.4].

Book 8 of the *Candelabrum* examines argumentation, be it epistolary or oratorical. Bene opens Book 8 with the relationship between rhetoric and dialectic, the only two disciplines that teach the art of argumentation. Both types of argument are used whether one is discussing grammar, law, theology, or any other field [8.16.5]. Rhetorical argument is differentiated from logical argument according to the standard formula: the former admits circumstantial and contingent evidence; the arguments of logic are instead based on universally accepted propositions [8.16.6]. Bene describes the sources of rhetorical argument in the subsequent thirty-four paragraphs. He returns directly to Cicero and lists and illustrates the attributes of persons and circumstances of events ("Quis, quid, ubi, quibus auxiliis, cur, quomodo, quando" [8.49.2]), to guide the writer to the sources of argument.

> Consulimus ergo dictatoribus, decretistis, theologis et legistis quod predictorum cognitionem locorum non vilipendant nec ullatenus pretermittant, quia predicte circumstantie valent in themate[49] bene dando, in causarum examine cognoscendo, in vitiis et virtutibus secundum propria merita perpendendis. Hinc etiam salutationum, exordiorum et aliarum partium epistole sive alterius compositionis tota vis et natura dependet. [8.53.2-3]

> So, we advise professional writers, decretalists, theologians, and lawyers not to disdain in any way or hold in contempt the knowledge of the above-mentioned topics, because the aforesaid circumstances serve to correctly formulate a theme, to judge legal cases, and to evaluate vices and virtues appropriately. The efficacy and essence of the greetings, exordia, and other parts of the epistle or of other compositions depend on them.

The juxtaposition of Bene's instruction and Hugh's, written a century earlier, shows that the presentation of the issue that provoked the letter has changed in fundamental ways. The discovery of effective strategies of persuasion has been refocused from the abstract and universal to a balance between the general principle and the specific circumstances of the issue that requires action or resolution. The particulars of a situation become essential to the message of the letter that will effectively persuade the addressee to accept one's proposition or act according to one's wishes. Bene advocates the investigation of the contingencies whether one is writing a petitionary epistle, a public document, a theological treaty, a legal brief, or a commentary on the canons.

Bene specifically evokes both of the milieus that will be the focus of the remainder of this book. At the outset he writes that his model is the papal chancery. "Autoritatem igitur Romane curie, que caput est omnium et magistra, principaliter imitantes. . . ." (principally imitating the authority of the Roman curia, which is the head and master of all) [1.1.7]. We also learn that the imperial chancery solicited the services of Bene [3.54.6], but that he preferred to remain in "nobilissima Bononia," his alma mater, for "quidquid habemus scientiae vel honoris ab ipsa post Deum credimus nos habere" (whatever we have of science or honor we believe we have from that place after God).

In the course of just over a century the *ars dictaminis*, driven by the demands of rapidly expanding secular and ecclesiastical executive and judicial establishments, became an autonomous discipline, separate from the traditional *ars grammatica* and *ars rhetorica* of the trivium. Intrinsic to the letter is a tension between the universal and timeless and the temporal and urgent, which is expressed in the dialectic between the exordium and the narration. In the early twelfth century, the narration is minor and accidental; the entire persuasive impetus of the letter is posited in the general principle stated in the exordium, as well as the tone and appropriateness of the greeting and the other parts of the letter. But the theory of letter-writing evolves and a new balance is struck between the exordium and the narration, between the timeless and the temporal, the general and the specific. That the narration need not be truthful is explicitly stated toward the end of the twelfth century, and while this may represent no more than the recuperation of ancient doctrine that had always been implicit in the instruction of rhetoric and the *ars dictandi,* it authorizes the writer to control the events that prompted the act of writing, as well as the reaction of the addressee.

Contemporaneously, the instruction of the narration moves toward greater specificity and probing of attendant circumstances. The same redress of the balance between the eternal and the temporal, the general and the specific, will occur in letters exchanged between the papal and imperial chanceries, where an epistolary rhetoric based on spiritual harmony and a celebration of the status quo that resolves all disquiet is replaced by one that grapples with serious differences and explores the conflict that prevents the two parties from enjoying desired harmony.

NOTES

1. Ronald Witt, "Medieval *Ars Dictaminis* and the Beginnings of Humanism: A New Construction of the Problem," *Renaissance Quarterly* 35.1 (1982): 14-5. Ronald Witt calls our attention to the contrast between the dominant epistolary rhetorical mode of the twelfth and thirteenth centuries, which posits persuasion in the communication of harmony and good will between writer and addressee, and the style of the papal-imperial exchange, the subject of this book. The latter is not consistently predicated on harmony and good will; on the contrary, it "acknowledges conflict where it exists, and persuasion takes the form of debate." Witt speculates that the new paradigm or *stilus rhetoricus* may have been influenced by crusade predication in the twelfth century.

2. Martin Camargo, *Ars Dictaminis, Ars Dictandi,* Typologie des sources du moyen âge occidental 60 (Turnhout: Brepols, 1991) 18.

3. The widely diffused thirteenth-century papal manual, by Thomas of Capua, explains the definition, etymology, persuasive intention, and importance of *epistola* in paragraph 3: "HIC DISTINGUIT, QUID SIT EPISTOLA ET UNDE DENOMINETUR ET DICATUR. Est ergo epistola litteralis legatio diversarum personarum capax, sumens principium cum effectu salutis. Denominata est autem epistola ab 'epi,' quod est supra, et 'stolen,' quod et missio; inde dicitur epistola quasi supramissio, quia supra intentionem mittentis gerere videtur ministerium nuntiantis, id est elegantius et locupletius in ea mentis explicatur affectus, quemadmodum faceret aliquotiens ipse nuntians vel delegans." Emmy Heller, "Die *Ars Dictandi* des Thomas von Capua," *Sitzungsberichte der Heidelberger Akademie der Wissenschaften* 4 (Heidelberg: Carl Winters, 1929) 15-6.

4. Janet Martin, "Classicism and Style in Latin Literature," *Renaissance and Renewal in the Twelfth Century,* Eds. Robert L. Benson, Giles Constable, and Carol D. Lanham (Cambridge, MA: Harvard University Press, 1982) 539.

5. Camargo, *Ars Dictaminis* 47.

6. Some definitions of the technical terminology are required at this point. The most general term that we find is *dictamen,* from the verb *dictare* (to compose), and it meant "composition." The *ars dictaminis* referred to prose composition, and to "a composition that followed the rules of the *ars dictaminis*." The professor who taught the *ars dictaminis* was a *dictator.* The composition of correct and effective letters was instructed in manuals known as *artes dictandi.* The above quotations are from Camargo, *Ars Dictaminis* 17, where a more extensive discussion of technical terminology is to be found.

7. A number of recent surveys and editions have greatly enhanced our understanding of the technical manuals or *artes dictandi,* their evolution and diffusion. Of fundamental importance is Martin Camargo, *Ars Dictaminis.* Also useful are Gian Carlo Alessio, "Brunetto Latini's *Rettorica* and the Rhetorical Trends in Thirteenth-Century Italy," Div. on *La Rettorica* of Brunetto Latini, International Congress of Medieval Studies, Kalamazoo, Michigan, May 4-7, 1989; Martin Camargo, "The *Libellus de Arte Dictandi Rhetorice* Attributed to Peter of Blois," *Speculum* 59.1 (1984):16-41, and James Jerome Murphy, *Rhetoric in the Middle Ages: A History of Rhetorical Theory from St. Augustine to the Renaissance* (Berkeley: University of California Press, 1974), especially Chapter 5, "*Ars Dictaminis:* The Art of Letter-Writing." Other important studies include Noel Denholm-Young, "The Cursus in England," *The Collected Papers of N. Denholm-Young* (Cardiff: University of Wales Press, 1969) 42-73; Charles Homer Haskins, "The Early *Artes Dictandi* in Italy," *Studies in Medieval Culture* (New York: Frederick Ungar Publishing Co., 1958) 170-92; Charles Homer Haskins, "An Italian Master Bernard," *Essays on History Presented to Reginald Lane Poole,* Ed. Henry W. C. Davis (1927; Freeport: Books for Libraries, 1967) 211-26; Ernst Kantorowicz, "Anonymi *Aurea Gemma,*" *Medievalia et Humanistica* 1 (1943): 41-57; Carol Dana Lanham, *"Salutatio" Formulas in Latin Letters to 1200: Syntax, Style, and Theory* (Munich: Arbeo-Gesellschaft, 1975); Michael C. Leff, "Boethius' *De Differentiis Topicis,* Book IV," *Medieval Eloquence: Studies in the Theory and Practice of Medieval Rhetoric,* Ed. James Jerome Murphy (Berkeley: University of California Press, 1978) 3-24; Franz-Josef Schmale, "Die Bolognese Schule der *Ars dictandi,*" *Deutsches Archiv für die Erforschung des Mittelalters* 13.1 (1957): 16-34; Giuseppe Vecchi, "Il Magistero delle *Artes* latine a Bologna nel Medioevo," *Pubblicazioni della Facoltà di Magistero* 2 (1958): 7-27, and John O. Ward, "From Antiquity to the Renaissance: Glosses and Commentaries on Cicero's *Rhetorica,*" *Medieval Eloquence,* Ed. Murphy 25-67. The many editions that I have consulted are listed as they are discussed.

The most useful to my understanding of the development of the genre in the course of the twelfth and thirteenth centuries, because of its meticulous and copious notes, is Gian Carlo Alessio, Ed. *Bene Florentini Candelabrum* (Padova: Antenore, 1983).

Camargo points out the inadequacies of the tripartite schema as a description of the early development of the *artes dictandi*. First, although the oldest *artes* date from Bologna in the early twelfth century, "the practices they describe had long been observed not only in Italy, but also in France and Germany." Second, many of the texts associated with the French period are "reworkings" of manuals written in Italy in the previous period ("Rhetoric," *The Seven Liberal Arts in the Middle Ages,* Ed. David L. Wagner [Bloomington: Indiana University Press, 1983] 109).

8. Camargo, *"Libellus"* 38.

9. For discussions of the *cursus* see Charles Sears Baldwin, *Medieval Rhetoric and Poetics* (1928; Gloucester: Peter Smith, 1959); Camargo, "The *Libellus*"; Francesco di Capua, *Scritti minori,* 2 vols. (New York: Desclée and Co., 1958), particularly the following essays: "Appunti sul *cursus* o ritmo prosaico, nelle opere latine di Dante Alighieri," 2 (564-85); "Lo stile della Curia Romana e il *cursus* nelle epistole di Pier della Vigna e nei documenti della cancelleria sveva," 2 (500-23); "Per la storia del latino letterario medievale e del *cursus*," 2 (524-63); Ann Dalzell, "The *Forma Dictandi* Attributed to Albert of Morra and Related Texts," *Mediaeval Studies* 39 (1977): 440-65; Tore Janson, *Prose Rhythm in Medieval Latin,* Studia Latina Stockholmiensis 20 (Stockholm: Almquist and Wiksell Int., 1975), and Marian Plezia, "L' Origine de la théorie du *cursus* rythmique au XIIe siècle," *Archivum Latinitatis Medii Aevi* 39 (1974): 5-22. The oldest extant discussion of the *cursus* is found in the *Forma Dictandi* and preserved in a late twelfth-century manuscript. This treatment of the *cursus* is based on French, not Roman practice and terminology, although the title (*Forma Dictandi Qui Romae Notarios Instituit Magister Albertus Qui et Gregorius Octauus*) suggests that an attempt was made to associate the treatise with the papal chancery and Albert of Morra, papal chancellor there from 1178 until he became pope in 1187. See Camargo, *"Libellus"* 19-20.

10. A debate originating with Rockinger's mistaken attribution of the 1135 *Rationes Dictandi* to Alberic has focused on the monk's role in the development of the new genre. Franz-Josef Schmale ("Die Bolognese") and Vicenzo Licitra ("Il mito di Alberico di Montecassino, iniziatore dell'*Ars dictaminis*," *A Gustavo Vinay* [Spoleto: Centro Italiano di Studi sull' Alto Medioevo, 1977] 607-27) argue against Alberic's reputation as founder of the

ars dictandi as an autonomous genre on the grounds that Alberic treats it as an integral part of the discipline of rhetoric. On the other hand, Haskins, Murphy, and others read the *ars dictandi* as a specialized development within the rhetorical tradition and not as an absolute pedagogical and ideological break from the past, and view Alberic as the founding father. See James Jerome Murphy, "Alberic of Monte Cassino: Father of the Medieval *Ars Dictaminis,*" *American Benedictine Review* 22 (1971): 129-46, and Charles Homer Haskins, "The Early *Artes,*" and "Albericus Casinensis," *Casinensia* 1 (1929): 115-24. Obviously the issue of Alberic's role as originator of the *ars dictandi* is less important than the relationship between the new pragmatic genre and the traditional theoretical instruction of rhetoric (Lanham 97). A part of Alberic's *Breviarium de Dictamine* was published by Ludwig Rockinger, Ed., *Briefsteller und Formelbücher des eilften bis vierzehnten Jahrhunderts,* 2 vols. (1863-1864. New York: Burt Franklin, 1961) 28-46. The *Flores Rhetorici,* also known as the *Dictaminum Radii,* was published by D. M. Inguanez and H. M. Willard, "Alberici casinensis *Flores Rhetorici,*" *Miscellanea Cassinese* 14 (1938).

11. This we know from Hugh's *Rationes Dictandi:* "Sic enim Alberici monachi viri eloquentissimi librum viciant, qui, et si plene per singula dictaminis documenta non scriberet, in epistolis tamen scribendis et dictandis privilegiis non iniuria ceteris creditur excellere" (54). Hugh's text is found in Rockinger 53-94.

12. Franz-Josef Schmale, Ed. *Adalbertus Samaritanus "Praecepta Dictaminum."* Monumenta Germaniae Historica. Quellen zur Geistesgeschichte des Mittelalters 3 (Weimar: Hermann Böhlaus Nachfolger, 1961). "Inter breve enim temporis spatium, si meis ammonitionibus obsecundare volueritis, huius artis scientiam adipisci valebitis ac per nostrarum regularum compendiosam traditionem prosaicarum epistolarum poteritis comprehendere rationem, quam specialiter vestre utilitati enucleandam suscepi, generaliter tamen omnibus profuturam nullius spernat invidia" (31).

13. Quintilian, *Institutiones Oratoriae Libri Duodecim,* Ed. M. Winterbottom (Oxford: Clarendon Press, 1970) 4.2.31: "Eam plerique scriptores maximeque qui sunt ab Isocrate volunt esse lucidam, brevem, veri similem."

14. Charles B. Faulhaber, "The *Summa Dictaminis* of Guido Faba," *Medieval Eloquence,* Ed. Murphy 97.

15. See note 11 above.

16. Faulhaber, "*Summa*" 96.

17. Murphy, *Rhetoric in the Middle Ages* 218. The use of formularies with models to assist in the drafting of documents and letters dates back to the early

Middle Ages when textbooks like the *Formulae Marculfi* supplied standardized statements, with blanks to be filled in with the appropriate particulars.

18. The anonymous *Rationes Dictandi* is in Rockinger 9-28. The translation, with some minor modifications, is from James Jerome Murphy Ed., *Three Medieval Rhetorical Arts* (Berkeley: University of California Press, 1971) 5-25.

19. Martin Camargo elaborates the importance of the distinction in "Toward a Comprehensive Art of Written Discourse: Geoffrey of Vinsauf and the *Ars Dictaminis,*" *Rhetorica* 6.2 (1988): 167-94. "If the *dictatores* were perceptive enough to recognize and articulate a distinction between two major types of written composition, the motive (and the reason for their indifference to the type that was not their specific concern) may have been their effort to legitimize the new discipline of the *ars dictaminis.* For if the study of the *dictamen metricum* characterized the *ars grammatica,* as it clearly did, than it stood to reason that *dictamen prosaicum* stood in a similar relationship to the second art of discourse, the *ars rhetorica"* (172).

20. Witt makes this point in reference to the letter as a whole: "The letter has a ritualistic quality derived from strict adherence to a number of limited rules" (13).

21. Vincenzo Licitra, "La *Summa de Arte Dictandi* di Maestro Goffredo," *Studi Medievali,* 3rd ser. 7 (1966): 868-69.

22. This section is omitted in Murphy, *Three,* but included as a note on pages 19-21 of Rockinger.

23. Camargo, *"Libellus"* 25. There exists, in addition, "a much later, heavily interpolated version of this northern (French) redaction." Because of the pivotal role his work played in the evolution of the *ars dictandi,* the identity of the author and the interdependence of the various redactions of his *Summa Dictaminum* have been the subject of a fair amount of scholarly speculation and research. See Camargo, *"Libellus"* 18-27.

24. Camargo, *"Libellus"* 33, n. 59, edits the passage from B. L. Add. 18382, fol. 69r. The translation of the last two sentences is taken from Murphy, *Three* 18.

25. The dependence of the *Libellus de Arte Dictandi Rhetorice* on both the Italian Bernard and the French *Floribus Rhetoricis* is discussed in Camargo, *"Libellus"* 26-33. The prolix and repetitive description of the narration in the *Floribus Rhetoricis* is transcribed in Camargo, *"Libellus"* 38: "Succincta enim breuitate gaudet narratio; totam etenim orationem dilucidat si breuis sit et serena. Sed si uice corripitur, eadem nebulosa est: 'dum breuis esse laboro, obscuro fio.' Iterum prolixitate uerborum non debet onerari narratio, immo oportet eam dilucidam et succintam esse si breuis sit et serena. Dilucida

narratio dicitur quando res eodem modo quo agitur perspicue et uerbis dilucidis enarratur. Succinta ideo debet esse narratio, ne sacietatem pariat auditorj uerborum superflua multitudo. Cauendum est item in omnj narratione ne eam inpinget turgidum uel inflatum, ne decetero macilentet aridum et exangue. Quid plura? Semper narratio quelibet debet esse breuis dilucida et aperta. Et hec ad presens de narratione sufficiant" (Camargo, *"Libellus"* 32. Camargo notes that the compiler of the *Libellus de Arte Dictandi Rhetorice,* either Peter of Blois or a contemporary working in the first half of the 1180s "sought . . . to harmonize the two traditions. He mixes in almost equal proportions precepts developed in the northern Italian schools and disseminated in the *Summa dictaminum magistri bernardi* with material from French centers like Tours, Orléans, Meung and Blois. . . . The *Libellus* . . . is an exceptionally rich compendium of the material bearing on prose composition available to a late twelfth-century French teacher" (Camargo, *"Libellus"* 38).

26. The *Ad Herennium* advocates cautious deceit in the interest of plausibility in the following passage concerning the narration: "Si vera res erit, nihilominus haec omnia narrando conservanda sunt, nam saepae veritas, nisi haec servata sint, fidem non potest facere; sin erunt ficta, eo magis erunt conservanda. De iis rebus caute confingendum est quibus in rebus tabulae aut alicuius firma auctoritas videbitur interfuisse" (1.9.16). For the study of Ciceronian forensic texts in France see Mary Dickey, "Some Commentaries on the *De Inventione* and *Ad Herennium* of the Eleventh and Early Twelfth Centuries," *Mediaeval and Renaissance Studies* 6 (1968): 1-41; Karin Margareta Fredborg, "The Commentaries on Cicero's *De Inventione* and *Rhetorica ad Herennium* by William of Champeaux," *Cahiers de l'Institut du Moyen-Age Grec et Latin* 17 (1976): 1-39; *The Latin Rhetorical Commentaries by Thierry of Chartres*, Toronto: Pontifical Institute of Medieval Studies, 1988, especially pp. 118-23 and 234-36, and Ward, "From Antiquity," *Medieval Eloquence,* Ed. Murphy 25-67.

27. The *Ars Dictandi Aurelianensis* is published in Rockinger 103-14.

28. M. Brini Savorelli, "Il *Dictamen* di Bernardo Silvestre," *Rivista critica di storia della filosofia* 20.2 (1965): 182-230.

29. *De Doctrina Christiana* 4.2.3 reads, " Nam cum per artem rhetoricam et vera suadeantur et falsa, quis audeat dicere, adversus mendacium in defensoribus suis inermem debere consistere veritatem, ut videlicet illi, qui res falsas persuadere conantur, noverint auditorem vel benevolum vel intentum vel docilem prooemio facere, isti autem non noverint? illi falsa breviter aperte verisimiliter et isti vera sic narrent, ut audire taedeat, intellegere non pateat, credere postremo non libeat? illi fallacibus argumentis veritatem oppugnent,

adserant falsitatem, isti nec vera defendere nec falsa valeant refutare? illi animos audientium in errorem moventes impellentesque dicendo terreant, contristent, exhilarent, exhortentur ardenter, isti pro veritate lenti frigidique dormitent? Quis ita desipiat, ut hoc sapiat? Cum ergo sit in medio posita facultas eloquii, quae ad persuadenda seu prava seu recta valet plurimum, cur non bonorum studio comparatur, ut militet veritati, si eam mali ad obtinendas perversas vanasque causas in usus iniquitatis et erroris usurpant?" Augustine, *De Doctrina Christina; De Vera Religone,* Corpus Christianorum, Seria Latina 32, Aurelli Augustini Opera Pt. 4.1, Ed. Joseph Martin (Turnhout: Brepols, 1962) 117.

30. See also note 12 above.

31. My understanding of Augustine's *De Mendacio* was greatly enhanced by a lecture entitled "Notes for Medieval Defense of Lying," presented by Professor Calvin G. Normore at the Boston Colloquium in Medieval Philosophy on November 6, 1995. *De Mendacio* is in J.-P. Migne Ed., *Patrologie cursus completus,* Series Latina 40 (Paris: Garnier, 1890) Cols. 517-47.

32. See Charles Halm, *Rhetores Latini Minores.* (1863. Dubois: Wm. C. Brown, n.d).

33. *Etymologiae* [2.7.1]. Isidore of Seville, *Etymologies.* Ed. Jacques André (Paris: Les Belles Lettres, 1981). For Isidore's conception of rhetoric, see Jacques Fontaines, *Isidore de Seville et la culture classique dans l'Espagne wisigothique* (Paris: Etudes augustiniennes, 1959), especially Part 2, "La rhétorique isidorienne."

34. This is pointed out by C. R. Cheney, "The Letters of Pope Innocent III," *Bulletin of the John Rylands Library* 35 (1952-53): 32. Other formulas indicating the papal chancery's concern about reporting or issuing judgments based on false testimony include *si res ita se habet* or *si ita est.* See C. R. Cheney and Mary G. Cheney, Eds., *The Letters of Pope Innocent III (1198-1216) Concerning England and Wales. A Calendar with an Appendix of Texts* (Oxford: Clarendon Press, 1967) ix.

35. Heller, "Die *Ars Dictandi,"* 32.

36. Under the heading "PROOEMIUM CONTRA MALE CONIECTURANTES," Thomas writes: "Romana curia non patitur coniecturas, que verbis exponi minime patiuntur, quia multa possunt in mente concipi, que non valent narrationibus explicari, eo quod nec omnium, que scripta sunt, ratio reddi potest" (41).

37. The text is edited by Vincenzo Licitra, "La *Summa."*

38. The *Candelabrum* has been edited by Gian Carlo Alessio, *Bene*. Important preliminary and related studies by Alessio include "La tradizione manoscritta del *Candelabrum*," *Italia medioevale e umanistica* 15 (1972): 99-148 and "Brunetto Latini e Cicerone (e i dettatori)," *Italia medioevale e umanistica* 22 (1979): 127-29; 160-69. Bene is also discussed in Murphy, *Rhetoric in the Middle Ages* 255-56; Aldo Scaglione, *The Classical Theory of Composition from Its Origins to the Present: An Historical Survey* (Chapel Hill: University of North Carolina Press, 1972) 102-04; 116; Giuseppe Vecchi, "Il magistero," and "Giovanni del Virgilio e Dante: La polemica tra latino e volgare nella corrispondenza poetica," *Dante e Bologna nei tempi di Dante* (Bologna: Patron, 1967) 67-76, and Hélène Wieruszowski, "Rhetoric and the Classics in Italian Education of the Thirteenth Century," *Politics and Culture in Medieval Spain and Italy* 121 (Rome: Edizioni di Storia e di Letteratura, 1971) 589-627.

39. Augusto Gaudenzi published the *Summa Dictaminis* in "Guido Fabe Summa Dictaminis," *Il Propugnatore* 3 (1890): 287-338; 345-93. That the text may be based on a series of notes is suggested by Faulhaber, "*Summa*" 94, n. 34. The Guido Faba bibliography includes Arrigo Castellani, "Le formule volgari di Guido Faba," *Studi di filologia italiana* 12 (1955): 5-78; Augusto Gaudenzi, "Magistri Guidonis *Epistole*," *Il Propugnatore* 6 (1893): 359-90; 373-89, and "Guidonis Fabe *Dictamina Rhetorica*," *Il Propugnatore* 5 (1892): 86-129, as well as "Sulla cronologia delle opere dei dettatori bolognesi da Boncompagno a Bene di Lucca," *Bollettino dell'Istituto Storico Italiano* 14 (1895): 85-161, and *I suoni, le forme e le parole dell'odierno dialetto della città di Bologna* (Turin: Loescher, 1889); Denholm-Young, "The *Cursus*"; Faulhaber, "*Summa*", Ernst Kantorowicz, "An 'Autobiography' of Guido Faba," *Mediaeval and Renaissance Studies* 1 (1941): 253-380; Angelo Monteverdi, "Le formule epistolari volgari di Guido Fava," *Saggi neolatini* 9 (Rome: Edizioni di Storia e Letteratura, 1945) 75-109; Murphy, *Rhetoric in the Middle Ages* 256-58; Virgilio Pini, "Summa de Vitiis et Virtutibus," *Quadrivium* 1 (1956): 41-152; Cesare Segre and Mario Marti, "Guido Faba," *La Prosa del Duecento* (Milan: Ricciardi, 1959) 3-18, and Wieruszowski, "*Ars Dictaminis* in the Time of Dante," *Medievalia et Humanistica* 1 (1943): 95-108. Faulhaber lists 41 manuscripts of the work (Faulhaber, "*Summa*" 86), and Camargo estimates that there are at least fifty extant copies of the *Summa Dictaminis* (Camargo, *Ars Dictaminis* 48-9). The *Candelabrum* survives in thirteen fairly complete manuscript copies and five fragments, an indication of a mediocre diffusion when compared to that of the *Summa* of Guido Faba (Alessio, *Candelabrum* 28).

40. Aldo Scaglione, *Classical Theory* 102.

41. Camargo, *Ars Dictaminis* 48-9.

42. J. K. Hyde, *Society and Politics in Medieval Italy* (London: Macmillan, 1973) 111.

43. Augusto Gaudenzi, "Boncompagni *Rhetorica Novissima,*" *Bibliotheca Iuridica Medii Aevi,* Scripta Anecdota Glossatorum 2 (Bologna: Petri Virano, 1892) 297.

44. Dickey 15-8.

45. A concise and accurate description and interpretation of the *Summa* is provided by Faulhaber, "*Summa.*" Faulhaber insists on the fact that Guido keeps the theoretical expositions of his *Summa* minimal and teaches by example (108).

46. Thus Bene moves beyond the 1135 *Rationes Dictandi* which prescribes tense but not mode. Book 3 is almost entirely devoted to the instruction of the epistle.

47. The rubric of paragraph 4.31 reads "SIMILITUDO EXORDIUM ET NARRATIONIS CUM LOGICA. Si vero exordium non precedat, horum signorum nullum erit narrationis principio necessarium sed sicut exordium liberum est a salutationis clausula que precessit, ita narratio tunc est libera, nulli signo illationis obnoxia. Habent enim se narratio et exordium ad similitudinem antecedentis et consequentis, quia illa duo quandoque divisim accipiuntur, ut: 'Sor. est homo. Ergo Sor. est animal', quandoque coniunctim, precedente coniunctione, ut: 'Si Sor. est homo, Sor. est animal'. Idem in exordio et narratione contingit."

48. "QUOT ET QUE AD BENE NARRANDUM EXPEDIANT. Debet autem narratio esse brevis, dilucida et verisimilis. Brevis est que non nisi necessaria comprehendit, habito respectu ad materie quantitatem. Dilucida esse debet, id est intelligibilis et aperta, secundum capacitatem et suficentiam ingenii auditorum. Narrabimus ergo dilucide si nil dixerimus perturbate, nil contorte, nil noviter, nil ambigue, si transitum in rem aliam non fecerimus, si nimis a remoto principio non inceperimus, si nec longe materiam fuerimus prosecuti, si nichil de his que ad negotium pertinent principaliter ommittemus et si brevitati que convenit insistemus. Verisimilis est narratio si de rebus et personis debitas circumstantias assignemus, narrantes ut mos, ut opinio et ut natura videbitur postulare" (4.23.1-8).

49. The same terminology, *thema,* is used by Guido Faba, several years later. The *thema* is the "subject matter" of the letter (Faulhaber, "*Summa*" 98-9).

CHAPTER 2

Persuasion and Reception

The letters composed at the papal and imperial chanceries, discussed in this chapter and the remainder of the book, frequently refer to specific political situations, and the reader who is not familiar with the history of the period might benefit from reading the schematic political history presented in Chapter 3 before pursuing the following discussion.

In a practice dating back to the Roman imperial period, the medieval papacy communicated much of its business in epistolary form. "Decretals, encyclical letters, bulls defining the Pope's authority or denouncing alleged invasions of it, equally with commissions, licenses, and other documents of every-day business, all belong to the form of Letters."[1] The medieval papacy was an extremely complex, rapidly evolving organization, but this book focuses on its epistolary production, not on the organization itself. I will follow Poole's usage of the term *chancery* to denote "the machinery by means of which the Pope conducted his business, his secretarial office."[2] The two principal functions of chancery employees were the drafting of letters and the recording of vital information in official registers.[3] From the eleventh century on, the pope named a "chancellor" to be in charge of his correspondence, and in the course of the twelfth century the position was considered important enough to be assigned to cardinals, of whom five acceded to the papal throne. In the early thirteenth century a change occurred: a vice-chancellor who was not a cardinal, but a master of the art of letter-writing, directed the chancery.[4] Despite the apparent move toward administrative specialization, Cheney insists that medieval papal chancery was not a modern, professional bureaucracy with clearly delineated divisions of labor.[5]

The papal and imperial chanceries were in constant communication: numerous conflicts were resolved by a solemn reiteration of common goals, and periods of hostility concluded with statements of joyful reconciliation and concord. Even in times of crisis the chancellors continued to circulate missives in the opposing camp, often intended as material for potential sympathizers there. Although chancellors in both camps criticized the other's approaches, they quickly appropriated whatever appeared to be effective. Evidence of the preoccupation with rhetorical persuasion and the chancellors' belief in the effectiveness of rhetoric in swaying public opinion is provided by the number of complete documents that were copied and preserved (in the case of Pope Innocent's chancery over 5,000 letters are extant,[6] and from the chancery of Frederick II 600 to 700 epistles have been preserved[7]), the elaborate style of the letters, the varied strategies of persuasion that characterize the papal-imperial correspondence, as well as the frequent warnings about the opposition's deceptive words.

When it came to determining which persuasive strategy was appropriate for a letter, the subject matter and perception of the public's mentality were critical factors. Thought was devoted to the appropriate stylistic level, given the linguistic competence of the addressee and the subject of the letter, to the fitting recognition of the addressee's relative social standing, and to the intellectual milieu of the intended public. The imperial chancery sent its clients, allies, and adversaries letters that employ different styles, and arguments based on divergent interpretations of events. Some are richly ornamented and focused on abstract principles, others give more weight to a straightforward and detailed narration of events. Although the papal chancery tended to be more consistent in tone and persuasive strategy, it also treated events differently, adding or excluding information in encyclicals dispatched to its various publics.[8]

The church quite obviously possessed the means to coerce a wayward prince or bishop to obey its orders. Nevertheless, the coincidence of Rome's campaign to assert its authority in Latin Christendom and the flowering of papal persuasion expressed in a highly ornamental language known as the *stilus supremus* or elevated prose style, a practice that was institutionalized by the decision to assign the direction of the chancery to a *magister* trained in the *ars dictaminis,* suggests that persuasion had a role to play that was more than ornamental in the minds of ecclesiastical reformers like Innocent

III. The elevated prose style is generally characterized by lexical, phonic, and rhythmic patterns or figures, clauses arranged in parallel structures or ordered into a crescendo or climax, interspersed Biblical or literary citations, and the use of the *cursus*. The musicality of the phrases gives pleasure, as do the attendant expressions of esteem and interlaced quotations.[9] This kind of esthetic and symbolic language may be persuasive in a situation where a vision of human society is shared by both the writer and the intended public, where there is no need for rigorous argument over what is new, different, and antagonistic.[10] It is illustrated in the letters of the Innocentian and Honorian chanceries, discussed in Chapters 4 and 5 of this book, and in the production of the imperial chancery immediately after the Roman coronation, discussed in Chapter 7. The ornament, tone, and standardized formulas associated with papal protocol assumed a symbolic quality, in some ways analogous to the poses and gestures of investiture or coronation ceremonies, and each letter reenacted the relationship between writer and addressee. The *cursus* or rhythmic prose cadence became standard in the thirteenth century, although its function was definitely not merely ornamental; the characteristic patterns of clause endings at the pontifical chancery also served with some success to guarantee the authenticity of important documents.[11]

But what do we know of the public's response to the florid (and sometimes obscurely worded) letters issuing from the papal and the imperial chanceries?[12] In this chapter I shall attempt to gauge the reaction to papal and imperial polemics. Besides the quantitative and qualitative evidence of the documents themselves, some direct testimony of the influence of the letters on public opinion exists. The effectiveness of rhetorical persuasion in instigating or delaying action is another, more elusive measure of its success or failure. There is, finally, a technical response to the question of efficacy: the chancellors themselves criticize the persuasive strategies employed by the other camp, and in the process reveal their understanding of epistolary rhetoric, its symbolic qualities, its limits, and its potential to influence minds.

Matthew Paris, a monk and keeper of the chronicle at the politically well-connected monastery of St. Albans from 1236 to 1259, provides the most extensive evidence of the reaction of the public to papal and imperial missives that I have been able to find.[13] The importance of St. Albans is signaled by the nine royal visits there between 1220 and 1259. Matthew's chronicle of contemporary events is rich in detail, and his sources are impressive: besides King Henry III and his brother, Richard, Earl of Cornwall, Matthew obtained information from various nobles, royal official and eminent prelates. There are hundreds of documents in Matthew's *Chronica Majora,* including letters from the papal and Frederican chanceries.

Matthew is interested in the politics of church and state to the extent that they threaten or enhance his monastery's financial situation. He chastises the king for imposing taxes, which he tends to refer to as extortion, regardless of the circumstances, and his attitude toward the papacy is colored by a sense of indignation at England's status as a papal fief.[14] He is not an impartial chronicler—Matthew is more sympathetic to the emperor, whom he "thought of . . . as, like himself, a victim of, or at least a sufferer from, the activities of the papacy."[15]

Only in 1238, at the pitch of the battle between the papacy and the empire, do we note a vacillation in Matthew's attitudes towards the emperor, which the monk attributes to the persuasiveness of slander. The *Chronica Majora* reads:

> In the course of the same year, the fame of the emperor Frederick was clouded and stained by his envious enemies and rivals; for it was imputed to him that he was wavering in the Catholic faith, or wandering from the right way, and had given utterance to some speeches, from which it could be deduced and suspected that he was not only weak in the Catholic faith, but what was a much greater and more serious crime, that there was in him an enormity of heresy, and the most dreadful blasphemy, to be detested and execrated by all Christians. For it was reported that the emperor Frederick had said (although it may not be proper to mention it), that three conjurers had so craftily led away their contemporaries as to gain for themselves the mastery of the world: these were, Moses, Jesus, and Mohammed; and that he had impiously put forward some wicked and incredible ravings and blasphemies respecting the most holy Eucharist. Far be it, far be it, from any discreet man, much less a Christian, to unlock his mouth and tongue in such raving blasphemy. It was also said by his rivals that the emperor agreed and believed in the law of Mohammed more than that of Jesus Christ, and that he had made some Saracen harlots his concubines. A whisper also crept amongst the people (which God forbid to be true of such a great prince), that he had been

for a long time past in confederacy with the Saracens, and was more a friend to them than to the Christians; and his rivals, who were endeavoring to blacken his fame, attempted to establish this by many proofs. Whether they sinned or not, He alone knows who is ignorant of nothing.[16]

Modern historians tend to dismiss such accusations as outright lies, "the facile weapons of character assassination in all ages."[17] But Matthew, an educated contemporary and—before 1245 at least—more sympathetic to the emperor than the pope, is shaken.

Pope Gregory (1227-1241) used these rumors to secure public support for the excommunication of Frederick in the 1239 encyclical, *Ascendit*.[18] After copying the encyclical into his *Chronica*, Matthew suggests that Gregory has gone too far. Apparently the monk of St. Albans considers the rumors in a different light because of an imperial letter, *Levate*, recently registered in his *Chronica*, in which imperial and papal responses to the conflicts that divide the two parties are explained in political terms. Matthew admits the plausibility of the emperor's recent arguments in defense of his actions in editorial remarks that follow the transcription of *Ascendit*. At another level, Matthew's comments reflect the complex self-interest with which European princes and prelates responded to the struggle between pope and emperor. Pope Gregory's rhetoric is forceful, and were it not for the common and widespread experience of papal avidity, the public's rejection of the emperor would have been universal. Matthew's editorial on *Ascendit* reads:

> The letter [*Ascendit*], having been published and sent to a great many kings, princes and nobles throughout the world, with only the titles changed, struck fear and dread as well as astonishment to the hearts of those of the true faith, and rendered the emperor's letter [*Levate*] suspect although it contained probable statements [probabilia], and re-established the minds of many which had formerly been in a wavering state. And, had it not been that the Roman avarice had alienated the devotion of people from the pope more than was expedient and proper, the whole world would have been exasperated by this letter [totus mundus hac epistola exasperatus], and would have risen unanimously against the emperor as an open enemy of Christ and the Church. . . . The pope unjustly stated [injuste improperat] that

he loved the said Frederick, and advanced his interests at the beginning of his promotion; yet all this was done out of hatred to Otho, whom the Church, with Frederick's assistance, persecuted to death, because . . . he endeavored by force to assemble together the scattered portions of the empire, as the present emperor Frederick also is endeavoring to do; wherefore, by doing this, Frederick fought for the Church, and the church of Rome was more bound by obligations to him than the emperor was to the Roman church. The church in the West, especially the orders of religious men, and the church of England, which was of all others most devoted to God, felt the daily oppressions of the Romans, but it has never as yet felt any from the emperor. The people, too, added, "What is the meaning of this? In times past, the pope accused the emperor of believing in Mohammed and the Saracenic law, more than in Christ and the Christian faith but now, in his abusive letter, he accuses him of (what is horrible to mention) calling Mohammed, as well as Jesus or Moses, Baratazem (an impostor?). In his letters, the emperor writes humbly and in a Catholic manner of God except that in this last one he derogates from the person of the pope, not from the office; nor does he utter or support anything heretical or profane, as we know of as yet, and he has not sent usurers or plunderers of our revenues amongst us."[19]

Matthew's editorial reveals his understanding of rhetorical persuasion: the defense presented in the imperial letter is qualified as plausible, and the papal letter is also effective (unde corda multorum qui prius cum alterutro steterant fluctuantia reddiderunt). Nevertheless, Matthew harbors reservations because he knows that Gregory's account of pontifical support for the future emperor during Frederick's minority is inaccurate. The monk's response calls to mind Bene's warning that the appearance of falsehood will immediately fill the mind of the listener with doubt, potentially subverting the entire appeal (*Candelabrum* [5.26.4]). Matthew's grievance at England's status as a papal fief also appears to govern his reaction to *Ascendit*. In contrast to his derogatory reference to Rome's corps of "usurers and plunderers," a neutral tone is used to describe the efforts by both Otto and Frederick to restore the empire by whatever means necessary. Nevertheless, the pope's letter has apparently exasperated everyone against the emperor (totus mundus hac epistola exasperatus in imperium). Nothing is proven, but papal rhetoric has struck a chord.

In *Ascendit,* Gregory attacks Frederick as the beast from the sea, a precursor to the Antichrist. According to Abulafia, neither the kings of France and England nor the governors of the Italian states paid attention to such apocalyptic prophecies. Italian chroniclers record papal and imperial letters but express very little concern on this point.[20] Inflammatory language did not persuade rulers who were more concerned with issues that affected their own vital interests, and Matthew makes this point when he ignores the more dire predictions contained in *Ascendit* and notes that, in contrast to the oppressive intervention in the affairs of "the Church in the West" by the Roman pontiff, no one has ever "felt any from the emperor." One literature that does reflect radical imperial propaganda is the vernacular political poetry associated with the counts of Toulouse. Peire Cardenal, a thirteenth-century troubadour and secretary at the court, criticizes the political ambition and the corruption of Rome in many of his political lyrics or *sirventes.* As court secretary, Peire probably had firsthand knowledge of the polemic being carried out by Rome and the emperor. His *sirventes* "Clergue si fan pastor" lambastes Rome for usurping secular power, an argument that calls to mind imperial letters of the second half of the 1220s like the one in which King Henry of England is reminded of the disastrous consequences of Pope Innocent's intervention in the affairs of Henry's father, King John.[21] Differences in language, genre, mode of diffusion, and intended public move Peire to simplify the chancellors' elaborate language; the poet communicates effectively by repeating his salient points and embedding them in rhyme. Guilhem Figueira, one of the few troubadours to find patronage at the Frederican court at Palermo, also broadcasts imperial themes— and even the apocalyptic language of the late 1230s—in *D'un sirventes far en est son que m'agenssa.* Both Peire's and Guilhem's *sirventes* were considered dangerous and evidence of heretical ideas, and the recitation of either is cited in inquisition records of the thirteenth and fourteenth centuries.[22]

An examination of the efficacy of imperial and papal rhetoric measured in terms of the action or inaction that it inspired is informative. The kings and princes of Christendom quite obviously consulted their own designs before complying with the will of others, and they were not eager to become directly involved in the conflict between the pope and the emperor, despite the fervent appeals for them to take a stand. Furthermore, a certain level of hostility between the papacy and the empire was probably perceived as useful because it kept Rome's attention focused on the Italian peninsula. But on the Lombard question (discussed in Chapter 3), imperial rhetoric seems to have been somewhat successful, especially when Frederick suggests that his rebellious Lombard "subjects" had discreet backing from the pope. The imperial chancery notes that Frederick's plight is no different than that of other secular rulers, and if the emperor were to be diminished by papal interference, lesser princes might very well suffer the same fate. The argument appears in *Inviti loquimur,* a 1236 missive addressed to the French king Louis, by the imperial chancery,[23] and again in the 1239 encyclical of self-defense, *Levate.*[24] In any case, the emperor's armies in Lombardy were increased by royal and mercenary soldiers from France, Spain, England, Hungary, and Greece,[25] and, according to Kantorowicz, the King of England wrote that he would like to "gird his sword and come himself."[26]

The essential argument, that the emperor stands as a bulwark for secular princes against the dangers of papal interference, shows up in Matthew's account of the French King Louis's response to Gregory when the latter appealed to him to support the "deposition" of Frederick in 1239. Apparently Gregory hoped that advisors would persuade Louis in case the letter failed to do so, because it carried instructions that it be "solemnly and thoughtfully read in the presence of him (the king) and the whole of the barons of France." While there is no reason to assume that Matthew was present, Vaughn affirms that many of the accounts in the *Chronica Majora* were "written down more or less directly from oral reports."[27] Matthew Paris records the scene of Louis's staunch refusal to condemn the emperor. The letter announces,

> We, [the Papal chancery] after careful discussion and deliberation with our brethren, have condemned and cut off the so-called emperor Frederick from the imperial dignity, and have elected Count Robert, brother of the French king, in his stead, whom not only the Church of Rome, but the Church universal, has thought fit with its utmost endeavors to assist and promote to that dignity. Be not, therefore, on any account slow to receive with open arms such a great dignity, which is voluntarily offered. . . . For the manifold crimes of the

aforesaid Frederick, of which the world is well aware, have irrevocably condemned him.

According to Matthew's account, Louis responded,

> In what spirit, or by what rash presumption has the pope disinherited
> and hurled from the imperial dignity such a great prince, than whom
> there is no greater, yea, whose equal is not to be found among
> Christians, when he has not been convicted of, nor confessed, the
> charges brought against him, who even, if he merited to be deposed,
> owing to his urgent sins, could not be deprived of his crown, unless
> by a decision of a general council.[28]

The French king goes on to defend Frederick and to argue a line that is often used by the imperial chancery. Louis's version, according to Matthew, is the following: "If the pope should conquer him by our means, or the help of others, he would trample on all the princes of the world, assuming the horns of boasting and pride, since he had conquered the great emperor Frederick." There is no reason to believe that Matthew did not doctor the scene, except that Louis is known by historians to have been hostile to Gregory's ambitions for his brother, Robert. On the other hand, a case may be made that the barrage of missives in defense of imperial policy sent to the courts of France and England in the latter part of the 1230s forestalled action against Frederick.

Persuasion and the limits of rhetoric to establish truth are issues of concern in many papal and imperial epistles. Matthew expresses his concerns at the conclusion of the first passage of the *Chronica Majora* cited above, "Whether they (Frederick's accusers) sinned or not, He alone knows who is ignorant of nothing." The fact that both the papal and imperial chanceries wrote letters in their own defense indicates the extent of the damage that they believed possible from the other's rhetoric. As Gregory writes in *Ascendit,* "sometimes a concealed lie takes possession of the seat of truth in the ear of sincerity, where truth finds no advocate for itself therein."[29] And in *Si memoriam* Gregory rails at the inflamed rhetoric directed against the church that the imperial chancery has sent to kings and princes to spread dissension (in eo rhetorico fulcata colore quod apud reges terrarum et principes de Ecclesia . . . comminaris).[30] The chancellors themselves were the first, most interested public whose reactions have been preserved, and the discussions of rhetorical persuasion that occur in papal and imperial letters attest to the chancellors' anxiety about its potential to deceive and compromise the truth in men's minds. Both chanceries delighted in pointing out logical flaws in the other's missives. Tone was of paramount importance and the papacy took issue with imperial letters that did not express obedience and gratitude, and read them as the sign of a mind that was not illuminated by God's Word.

Miranda tuis, issued from the papal chancery in 1226, signals an end to the apparently cordial correspondence between pope and emperor of the early 1220s.[31] Significant to the present discussion is the papal attack against an imperial letter that is no longer extant. Honorius specifically condemns the imperial chancery for substituting arguments premised on opinion for arguments from the facts, or rather, from documentary evidence kept in the papal archives.[32]

Miranda tuis sensibus nostra venit epistola ut scripsisti, sed mirabilior tua nostris. . . . Tue quidem tenor epistole continebat, quod preter omnium opinionem et consilia principum, ut tuis verbis utamur, te invenerimus ad nostra beneplacita paratum, ita ut nullus predecessorum tuorum nullis retroactis temporibus recolatur adeo Ecclesie fuisse devotus ut tu. Sed de principibus tuis non aliter ex hiis verbis informabimus animum, qua probabilis credulitas habeat facti experimento probata. De quibus Apostolice Sedis constantia recte opinionis judicium sinistre suggestionis instancia non mutabit, cum facta preferenda sint dictis et certa prejudicent positivis. Ecce de archivio ecclesie publica monimenta prodeunt, que singulorum pene omnium principum munita sigillis opinionem repudiant quam forte videris ingerere contra illos, eo quod verisimilitudo non tales et tantos viros patitur excellentie tue dedisse consilium contrarium scripto tui et ipsorum signato signaculis.

As you wrote that our letter is astounding to you, we read yours with even greater astonishment. . . . Indeed the gist of your letter holds that, contrary to common opinion and the advice of princes—using your words—we would find you prepared to do our pleasure, so much so that not one of your predecessors at any previous time could be recalled who was as devoted to the church as you. But as to your princes, we will not change our mind on the basis of those words

because credibility lies in deeds. The Apostolic See's constancy will
not alter a correct judgment because of the vehemence of a wayward
idea since deeds must be preferred to words and sure things reckoned
better than conjectures. Behold the public records that come forth
from the archives of the church, furnished with the seal of almost all
those princes: they repudiate the opinion that you seem so casually to
tender against them. That so many and such men would have given
your excellency advice that was contrary to their signed and sealed
writings does not seem likely.

Honorius insists on the superior authority of the papal archives, and
derides mere opinion. Furthermore, experience teaches that imperial
statements asserting that "such great men offered advice to your
imperial highness that is the opposite of their officially designated
opinion" smack of falsehood. Frederick's casual attitude toward the
truth is not merely impudent; it is also impious. Honorius's reaction
calls to mind the warning of his chief chancellor Thomas when he
denounces the substitution of conjecture for fact in the narration.[33]
　　The attacks against the emperor's impiety become more explicit in
the letters of Honorius's successor. Gregory IX specifically denounces
the emperor's tone or verbal posture as insufficiently humble.
Frederick's hostile rhetoric, the pope insists, is not rational.

Sane ex pluribus litteris ad nos et fratres nostros nuper ab imperiali
excellentia destinatis plura collegimus que si stilus mitigasset
humilior et amaritudinem pagine dulcorasset affectus reverentie
filialis, virtus discretionis sub manna dulcedinis irascibilem spiritum
temperasset, et imago Dei que resultat in speculo rationis ac
similitudo eius que per affectum bonum et zelum rectitudinis in
potentiis anime naturalibus invenitur, non fuissent sic scribendo
forsitan deformate.[34]

Clearly, in the case of the many letters we have collected, sent to us
and our brothers from the imperial excellency, if a more humble style
had mitigated and a sentiment of filial piety had sweetened the
bitterness of the page, if the virtue of discrimination had been
tempered by the manna of reason, the anger of the spirit by
sweetness, then the image of God that reflects in the mirror of the
intellect, and his likeness that is found in the natural powers of the

soul through good feeling and the zeal for righteousness would
perhaps not have been so deformed as by writing in this way.

This accusation of an improperly arrogant and angry tone in the
imperial letters underlines the fact that tone was not a superficial
concern. The thirteenth-century church defined the emperor as the
defensor ecclesiae, subordinate to and dependent upon the pope, and in
return for his exalted office, the Holy Roman Emperor owed gratitude,
humility, and obedience to the pontiff. Expressing humble gratitude
signaled spiritual well-being, and in the case of the recent imperial
letters, the lack of humility is interpreted as a symptom of the
corruption of Frederick's soul. Frederick's failure to show proper
submission to the pope, whether in act, or in mode of expression, is
disruptive to the order of Christendom and requires correction.

Si memoriam, the letter quoted above, is written in response to an
imperial letter in which the circumstances of the imperial treatment of
churches in Sicily are elaborated at some length. Although this letter is
not extant, we know this from another paragraph of *Si memoriam,*
where Gregory complains that the imperial chancery has answered
inappropriately, offering specific information in response to charges
made in a general or abstract way. Gregory disputes the imperial
chancery's act of defending its sins against the church, and condemns
its failure to acquiesce to Rome on this and a host of other issues.

> Sed ecce super facto ecclesiarum regni quod tibi in litteris nostris
> primo directis sub genere indefinite proponitur, quod ad hoc non
> tenearis quasi dubia respondere, a te reali responsione preterita vocali
> commentario incongrue respondetur, tum quia frustra requiritur ut
> singularia speciei vel specialia fidem faciant generi, cum genus et
> species manifestam ex se prebent notitiam veritati, et cum
> individuorum scientia quasi ex infinitate confunditur, ad doctrinam
> universalium supervacue singularia colliguntur.

> But look, as for what is proposed to you generally and indefinitely in
> our initial letter, about what was done to the churches in the kingdom,
> although you are not bound to make, as it were, dubious responses, it
> is inconsistent of you to reply with a word by word commentary, and
> not with a response to our point: both because it is futile to demand
> that singulars or specifics should confirm something generic

inasmuch as genus and species of themselves provide public knowledge of the truth, and since the knowledge of individual things is almost infinitely confused, it is useless to collect single facts in order to confirm a universal proposition.

In fact the papal chancery had previously made pointed accusations on specific issues, as Gregory's letter goes on to say, and the imperial response has been too little and too late. The strategy that the papal chancery is protesting, in which universal principles and laws are countered by detailed and nuanced accounts of the specific contingencies of a situation in the narration, is characteristic of the challenge to established epistolary persuasion developed at the imperial chancery. Gregory was not impressed, according to Matthew. Given the emperor's record on the churches in Sicily, Pope Gregory "held all the . . . arguments as frivolous and useless quibbles, and despised them as fictions."[35]

Some evidence suggests that Matthew Paris was cognizant of the different approaches to persuasion. In a comment on the imperial "usurpation" of Sardinia in 1239, on the eve of the second excommunication of the emperor, Matthew writes that the emperor has sinned, but that he "pleaded excuse for his sins" (et dicta sua peccatum suum excusantia) in his letters to Christendom, and "excused his deeds with certain evident motives, supported by reason" (et sua facta quibusdam causis apparentibus ratione fultis excusasset). The monk contrasts the imperial chancery's defense of its claims to Sardinia based on recent events to the pope's assertion of church sovereignty founded on ancient rights and guaranteed by canon law.

> In Lent, of the same year, the pope, seeing the rash proceedings of the emperor, and that his words pleaded excuse for his sins namely, that by the favouring assistance of some of the nobles and judges of Sardinia, he had taken into his own possession, and still held, the land and castles of the bishop of Sardinia, and constantly declared that they were a portion of the empire, that he by his first and chief oath would preserve the rights of the empire to the utmost of his power, and would also collect the scattered potions of it, he [the pope] was excited to the most violent anger against him, setting forth some very heavy complaints and claims against him [the emperor], and writing often boldly and carefully to him, he advised him often by special

messengers, whose authority ought to have obtained from him the greatest attention, to restore the possessions he had seized on, and to desist from depriving the church of her possessions, of which she was endowed by long prescription [ira vehementissima commotus (est) contra imperatorem, gravissima contra eum proponens quaestiones et reponens querimonias, scribens et scribenter constanter et diligenter persuadens per plures et pluries nuntios solempnes, quorum auctoritas meruit exaudiri ut ablata restitueret et desineret ecclesiam suis possessionibus viduare, quam constat diuturna temporis praescriptione praedotari], and like a skilled physician, who at one time makes use of fomentations, at another of instruments of incision, and at another of the cauterizing instrument, he mixed threats with blandishments, friendly messages with dreadful denunciations. As the emperor, however, impudently refused his request [procaciter renuisset], and excused his actions by arguments founded on reason, his holiness the pope, on Palm Sunday, in the presence of a great many of the cardinals, in the spirit of growing anger, solemnly excommunicated the said emperor Frederick, as though he would at once have hurled him from his imperial dignity.[36]

That the conflict is a matter of sin that endangers the emperor's soul is not emphasized in Matthew's comment. Nevertheless, his account of Frederick's obstinate refusal to heed repeated papal warnings, careful instructions, and prominent messengers describes a situation in which the emperor is guilty of contumacy, punishable by excommunication.

The imperial chancery also protested papal argument. For example, *Evidentium clara,* the imperial response to *Si memoriam,* accuses Gregory of mocking common logic when he insists on the purity of the motives of James of Palestrina, his supposedly impartial legate in Lombardy, notwithstanding James's active and effective resistance to every imperial undertaking in the region.

Evidentium clara cognitio certum plerumque facit hominibus quadam ratione probabili judicium de occultis nec casus eventibus ascribi patitur quod procuratum consiliis hominum et curiosa subtilitas intrinseca colligens manifeste convincit. Illud tamen inficiari nolumus quin absit rerum veritas a conjectis, quin a factis interdum intentio sit remota. . . . In verbo verumtamen patris justissime miratus est filius dum id quod per industriam hominis, si tamen cardinalis est homo, in detrimentum imperii provenisse non conjectura, sed veritas manifeste testatus, serenitatem nostram impinxisse descripsit Ecclesie puritati.[37]

For men who have some faculty of reasoning, certain knowledge of the evidence results in a sound judgment regarding the plausibility of hidden motives; nor does chance allow to be ascribed to unforeseen occurrences whatever intrinsic, inquisitive, ordering intelligence clearly proves [to be] brought about by the deliberations of men. We do not wish to infer on the basis of conjecture, since sometimes intention is remote from the facts. . . . But the son rightly marvels at the word of the father who ascribes to the purity of the church what is brought about by the effort of a man—if indeed the cardinal is a man—to the detriment of the empire, attested by truth and not by conjecture.

The imperial chancery rejects the pope's "spiritual" defense of the actions of the papal legate. Gregory has shifted the argument from the consequences of James's actions (the alienation of Piacenza from the imperial camp) to his intentions, which he attributes to the purity of the church. The tone of Frederick's response is scornful—yet in other letters the imperial chancery uses the same argument and defends imperial actions on the basis of the purity of intentions.[38]

In exordio, written in 1239, makes a more direct attack on papal arguments: the emperor, eager to portray Gregory as an unworthy judge, accuses the pontifical chancery of spreading and defending lies with deceptive arguments that substitute foregone conclusions for proofs.

Nostre majestatis jubar intendit ducere in eclipsim, dum veritate in fabulam commutata, plene mendaciis ad diversas mundi partes papales mittuntur epistole, de complexione, non de ratione, accusantes nostre fidei puritatem.[39]

He attempts to eclipse the splendor of our majesty when, the truth transformed into tales, papal letters are sent out to different parts of the world attacking the purity of our faith, not with proofs but with foregone conclusions.

The terms *complexio* and *ratio* are used in classical manuals like the *Ad Herennium* and by Bene of Florence to describe the parts of an argument. The *rationes* are the reasons that prove the original proposition. *Complexio* refers to the conclusion of the argument. The chancery is protesting the Rome's use of arguments in which the original proposition is not proven, but merely repeated, ornamented, and accepted as a foregone conclusion. In other words, the papacy is accused of begging the question in its accusations. Of course the ascendant mode of epistolary persuasion in the Middle Ages, as described in the manuals of epistolography from Hugh to Guido Faba, is founded on this very principle; the premise on which a petition is based, together with an ingratiating tone, will insure the petitioner's success.[40]

Celebratory language and persuasive modes, often remote from the reality of a situation, promoted common goals. On the other hand, the ferocity of the polemic, in periods of crisis like the final years of the 1230s, shows that rhetoric was a fundamental political reflex in the period. Papal and imperial letters clearly betray cognizance of the potential danger that each camp attributed to the persuasive language of the opponent. Even the letters characterized as a tissue of lies were perceived as hazardous because those lies were plausible and pertained to well-known circumstances and events. Political rhetoric occupies a middle ground between fiction and truth; the "opinions" are persuasive because common experience makes them plausible. The papal chancery is forced to respond to imperial transgressions, and it does so with threats and flattery as well as arguments that include detailed accounts of papal and imperial actions. Matthew compares papal appeals to a physician's fomentations, to cauterizing and soothing a wound to make it heal; a good physician should produce some salutary effect on the invalid. Matthew's simile captures the power and the limits of persuasion: like the physician's invalid, the mind of the addressee may or may not respond as the writer desires; it will not be forced, but merely courted.

NOTES

1. Reginald L. Poole, *Lectures on the History of the Papal Chancery Down to the Time of Innocent III* (Cambridge: University Press, 1915) 101. Traditionally, the form of *littere* is distinct from the more unvarying

privilegium, the "instrument of the grant or confirmation of rights of property and jurisdiction to churches and religious houses" (100). The form of the privilege tended to change little over time, although by the twelfth century, property and jurisdictional rights were also communicated in the form of letters. This book is concerned almost exclusively with *"Littere de Justitia,* Letters of Justice or mandates which convey the Pope's administrative orders," which represented the "mass of his official correspondence on all matters of all sorts both political (*littere secrete*) and administrative (*littere de curia*)" (116-17). For a brief taxonomy of the production of the papal chancery see also C. R. Cheney and Mary G. Cheney, Eds., *The Letters of Pope Innocent III (1198-1216) Concerning England and Wales. A Calendar with an Appendix of Texts* (Oxford: Clarendon Press, 1967) xiii.

2. Poole 2. See C. R. Cheney, *The Study of the Medieval Papal Chancery,* The Second Edwards Lecture Delivered within the University of Glasgow on December 7, 1964 (Glasgow: Jackson, 1966) for a discussion of the organization of the papal chancery in the thirteenth century. The chief personnel of the papal chancery are listed in Harry Bresslau, *Handbuch der Urkundenlehre für Deutschland und Italien* 1 (Berlin: Walter De Gruyter, 1958) 248-50. For the imperial chancery, see Hans Martin Schaller, "Die Kanzlei Kaiser Friedrichs II. Ihr Personal und ihr Sprachstil 1," *Archiv für Diplomatik* 3 (1957): 207-85, and Hans Martin Schaller, "Die Kanzlei Kaiser Friedrichs II. Ihr Personal und ihr Sprachstil 2," *Archiv für Diplomatik* 4 (1958): 264-325. The notaries employed by the imperial chancery between 1220 and 1250 are listed by Schaller in "Die Kanzlei 1," 258-85. See Chapter 7 in this book for an overview of the imperial chancery.

3. Like so many other aspects of the medieval papacy, the registering of documents is problematic. "What part of the pope's correspondence do these registers contain? The question is answered by the canonist, Stephen of Tournai, late in the twelfth century: 'It is the custom of the Roman church,' he says, 'that these copies were put into one book called a register.' This is palpably untrue as regards the registers of the thirteenth century. Many important letters were not enregistered, and we cannot in all instances tell why. The registers are incomplete records, and no registrar can even have aimed at including copies of all letters dispatched. . . . Foremost in this selection of letters chosen for registration come those required for the use of the Curia: the most notable diplomatic correspondence, and letters which provided formulas to be used again. But even in this category there are occasional startling omissions. . . . We must not expect to find in the registers exact reproductions of original letters. To begin with, the protocol is always abridged. This consists

of the pope's name and title, the addressee's and a form of greeting. . . . Sometimes their practice suggests that they have copied from a draft of an incomplete engrossment; at other times their exemplar must have been the finished letter. . . . But all these vagaries do not usually affect the trustworthiness of the *text,* that is the central part of the letter. That is generally copied conscientiously, the handwriting is regular and clear, and inaccurate transcription is rare" (Cheney and Cheney xx-xxi).

4. Poole 140-41.

5. Cheney, *The Study* 33.

6. C. R. Cheney, "The Letters of Pope Innocent III," *Bulletin of the John Rylands Library,* 35 (1952-53): 23.

7. The best discussion of the history of the Frederican documents, a body of literature that was not protected by the institutional stability of the Vatican, is provided in an article by Hans Martin Schaller, "Zur Entstehung der sogenannten Briefsammlung des Petrus de Vinea," *Deutches Archiv für die Erforschung des Mittelalters* 12 (1956): 114-59. I include a brief discussion of the transmission of the imperial documents, based on Schaller's research, to illustrate the importance accorded to them in different milieus.

Between 600 and 700 different documents attributed to the Frederican chancery were copied and preserved in manuscripts entitled *Epistole, Dictamina,* or *Summa* of Pier della Vigna. Other documents are found in chronicles of the first half of the thirteenth century and miscellaneous epistolaries. Schaller proposes that the chancery kept a collection of rough drafts alongside the chronologically ordered official registers that contained material in an abbreviated form, all non-essential text being omitted. The rough drafts were arranged by subject matter for the convenience of the chancellors. Following the defeat of Frederick's grandson Corradin, in 1268 at Tagliacozzo. Charles I of Anjou appropriated the Frederican chancery material for use in his own administration, and some of the chancery material found its way to the court at Paris, and almost immediately after that, to the scriptorium of the University of Paris. In 1268 Jean de Caux, archivist for Louis IX and Philip II, composed a large documentary collection pertaining to the conflict between the university and mendicant orders. He included twenty Frederican letters and a number of papal responses. These documents could not have come from the archives of the French court, and must have been copied directly from the imperial chancery material. Roman interference was at the heart of the struggle between the secular and regular clergy that plagued the University of Paris for over half a century and reached a pitch in 1281, and this may explain the interest of the imperial documents there. An indication that the documents were actually studied at the university is provided by several extant manuscripts that are composed of *pecia* or individual pages, mass-produced to provide students with inexpensive and convenient texts. The marginal notes in these manuscripts are in French. We know that at the outbreak of strife between King Philip IV the Fair and Pope Boniface VIII, in 1296, the letters were studied by the royal chancellors.

A manuscript at the Bibliothèque Nationale, the B. N. lat. 4042, was copied by the cleric Antonius Sici or Cici in the year 1294, *regnante domino Celestino V, primo anno,* probably at the papal chancery. It is the earliest extant dated manuscript. According to Schaller, the letters of Pier della Vigna and an account of the life of the emperor might have arrived at the Roman chancery in a single volume composed by Guido Ebroicensis, a Dominican friar at the University of Paris around 1230, who wrote a life of Frederick II entitled *De Gestis Frederici Imperatoris et Eius Quaerimonia.* Numerous Frederican documents were copied and disseminated from the papal chancery under Boniface VIII. There is also evidence that a collection of Frederican letters existed both in Paris and at the pontifical chancery at a much earlier date, as a part of the *Summa* of Thomas of Capua.

The quantity and quality of the manuscripts containing significant collections of Frederican documents attests to the importance attached to them by contemporaries and successive generations. The considerable variation that occurs in the texts prompts yet unanswered questions about the manner in which the Frederican documents were received and utilized in the courts and chanceries of Europe. On this question see also Hélène Wieruszowski, *Vom Imperium zum nationalen Königtum,* Beiheft der Historischen Zeitschrift 30 (Munich: R. Oldenbourg, 1933).

For my research, I have mostly relied on the ten-volume edition of J.-L. A. Huillard-Bréholles, *Historia diplomatica Friderici Secundi,* 10 vols. (Paris: H. Plon, 1852-1861). Scholars have criticized Huillard-Bréholles's reordering of the material, even when the original order of the registered documents was known, and his expansion of abbreviations found in the registers. It is not a critical edition, but the advantage of Huillard-Bréholles is that it represents the only collection that can be considered complete. See David Abulafia, *Frederick II: A Medieval Emperor* (New York: Penguin, 1988) 321-27, and Wolfgang Hagemann, "La nuova edizione del registro di Federico II," *Atti del Convegno Internazionale di Studi Federiciani, 10-18 December, 1950. VII Centenario della morte di Federico II, Imperatore e re di Sicilia* (Palermo: A. Renna, 1952) 315-36. Hagemann includes a bibliography of works that treat the problems of Huillard-Bréholles.

8. The 1239 documents announcing Frederick's excommunication, *Cum nuper* and *Sedes apostolica,* are cases in point, discussed in John P. Lomax II, *"Ingratus" or "Indignus": Canonistic Argument in the Conflict between Pope Gregory IX and Emperor Frederick II,* diss., University of Kansas, 1987, 34-6. In Chapter 7 of this book the variation in the documents announcing the imperial victory at Cortenova sent to imperial clients, allies, and adversaries is examined.

9. The use of the elevated prose style at the papal chancery is discussed in chapters 4 through 6 in this book. For descriptions of the imperial elevated prose style see Emmy Heller, "Zur Frage des kurialen Stileinflusses in der sizilischen Kanzlei Friedrichs II.," *Deutches Archiv für die Erforschung des Mittelalters* 19.2 (1963): 434-50; Hans Niese, *Zur Geschichte des geistigen Lebens am Hofe Kaiser Friedrichs II* (1912 Darmstadt: Wissenschaftliche Buchgesellschaft, 1967) 48-9; Ettore Paratore, "Alcuni caratteri dello stile della cancelleria federiciana," *Atti del Convegno Internazionale di Studi Federiciani, 10-18 December, 1950. VII Centenario della morte di Federico II, Imperatore e re di Sicilia* (Palermo: A. Renna, 1952) 300-04; Aurelio Roncaglia, "Le corti medievali," *Il letterato e le istituzioni* (Rome: Einaudi, 1982) 139-40, and most important, Schaller, "Die Kanzlei 2".

10. Chaim Perelman and Lucie Olbrechts-Tyteca, *The New Rhetoric: A Treatise on Argumentation,* Trans. J. Wilkinson and P. Weaver (Notre Dame: University of Notre Dame Press, 1971).

11. The fear of forged or doctored documents was very real at the papal court. See Poole (152-62) for a discussion of the methods employed by Innocent to detect fraudulent documents, and the systems he endeavored to put into place to guarantee the integrity of papal documents. See also Cheney, "The Letters" 29-31, and James A. Brundage, *Medieval Canon Law* (New York: Longman, 1995) 133.

12. As the Bolognese jurist Odofredus notes, "Dictatores volentes obscure loqui et in supremo stilo ut facium summi doctores et sicut faciebat Petrus de Vinea." Hélène Wieruszowski, "Rhetoric and the Classics in Italian Education in the Thirteenth Century," *Politics and Culture in Medieval Spain and Italy,* Storia e Letteratura 121 (Rome: Edizioni di Storia e di Letteratura, 1971) 606.

13. A good introduction to Matthew Paris and the *Chronica Majora* is provided by Richard Vaughan, *Matthew Paris* (Cambridge: University Press, 1958).

14. Vaughan 140-41.

15. Vaughan 148.

16. The translation of this document is from J. A. Giles, *Matthew Paris's English History* 1 (London: Bohn, 1852) 157-58.

17. Thomas Curtis Van Cleve, *The Emperor Frederick II of Hohenstaufen, Immutator Mundi* (Oxford: Clarendon Press, 1972) 420.

18. Both *Ascendit* and *Levate,* mentioned below, are discussed in detail in Chapter 9 in this book.

19. Giles 229-39. The Latin text is from Henry Richards Luard, *Matthaei Pariensis, Monachi Sancti Albani, Chronica Majora* 3 (London: Longman, 1872-1883) 608-09.

20. Abulafia 319-20.

21. The imperial chancery had written to the English king in December 1227, "Habeat autem de premissis rex Anglorum ex se ipso exemplum cuius patrem, regem scilicet Johannem, tamdiu excommunicatum tenuit quousque ipsum et regna eius constituit sub tributo. Habeant etiam generaliter omnes idem exemplum de comite Tolosano et aliis principibus multis quorum terras et personas tamdiu sub interdicto concludere molitur, donec illos in consimilem redigat servitutem; simonias, exactiones diversas et a seculis inauditas quas in ecclesiasticas personas incessanter exercent, usuras manifestas et palliatas quibus hactenus incognitis totum mundum inficiunt, pretermittimus; sermones tamen super mel mellitos et super oleum mollitos . . . insatiabiles sanguisuge, dicentes curiam romanam esse Ecclesiam matrem nostra ac nutricem, cum sit curia pretaxata omnium malorum radix et origo, non maternos sed actus exercens novercalis, ex cognitis fructibus suis certum faciens argumentum. Revolvant hec inclyti barones Anglie quos papa Innocentius bullatis litteris communitos animavit ut in regem Johannem quasi Ecclesie inimicum insurgerent obstinatum, sed postquam enormiter memoratus rex est incurvatus, et se suumque regnum Ecclesie romane velut effeminatus mancipavit, predictus papa proceres quos prius sustinuit et excitaverat, postposito mundi pudore Dominique timore, conculcavit morti expositos et miserabiliter exheredandos ut more romano protervo hiatu quod pinguius erat, proh dolor! absorberet; et factum est quod incitante Romanorum avaritia princeps provinciarum facta est sub tributo." Huillard-Bréholles, 3, 48-50. Peire Cardenal's poetic corpus is edited by René Lavaud, *Poésies complètes du troubadour Peire Cardenal* (Toulouse: Privat, 1975).

22. Martin Aurell, *La vielle et l'épée: Troubadours et politique en Provence au XIIIe siècle* (Paris: Aubier, 1989) 226-27. Guilhem's *sirventes* is in Martin de Riquer, *Los Trovadores, Historia literaria y textos* 3 (Barcelona: Planeta, 1975) 1272-79.

23. *Inviti loquimur* reads: "Vos igitur cum ceteris regibus orbis terre interest plene perspicuas aures et oculos aperire et diligenter attendere quanta contradictionis fiducia omnibus a jugo dominii subtrahere se volentibus prebeatur, si Romanum imperium jacturam huiusmodi rebellionis pateretur. . . ." Huillard-Bréholles, 4.2, 873-80. The translation is a modified version of the text found in Giles, 1, 191-93.

24. The most cogent statement of the argument occurs in the end of *Levate,* an imperial encyclical of 1239, in which the imperial chancery accuses Pope Gregory IX of abusing his exalted office. "Ad domum vestram cum aqua currite, cum ignis accenditur in vicinis; causam motus pontificalis attendite, et cur hoc in favorem nostrorum rebellium procuratur: que causa licet ad presens expressa non fuerit, procul dubio tamen simila vobis et vestris imminere prima jacula sustinet, adversantium [conatibus] conteratur. . . . sed ut totus mundus agnoscat quod honor omnium tangitur, quicunque de corpore secularium principum offendatur." Huillard-Bréholles, 5.1, 295-306.

25. Abulafia 308. The imperial ranks were swelled, at least in part, by "young knights in search of a good war," according to the historian.

26. Ernst Kantorowicz, *Frederick the Second, 1194-1250,* Trans. E. O. Lorimer (NewYork: Frederick Ungar Publishing, 1957) 423.

27. Vaughan 135.

28. Giles 242-43.

29. "Licet autem hec figmenta publica notitia reprobat, quia tamen nonnunquam rectitudinis sedem velatum occupat in aure sincera mendacium, apud quam pro se veritas non invenit advocatum. . . ." *Ascendit* is in Huillard-Bréholles, 5.1, 327-39.

30. "Hoc in personis ecclesiasticis negari non potest quibus nos ex constitutione divina preficimur; imperialis vero potentia ex sola usurpatione in huiusmodi in injuriam divini nominis aliquoties dominatur, in eo rhetorico fulcata colore quod apud reges terrarum et principes de Ecclesia que usque modo non modificum imperiali pepercit honori, te depositurum querelas, quibusdam apud eos jam depositis, comminaris." *Si memoriam* is edited in Huillard-Bréholles, 4.2, 914-23.

31. *Miranda tuis* is in Huillard-Bréholles, 2.2, 589-99.

32. Cheney and Cheney observe that "the medieval papacy established and extended its authority on the basis of tradition, and the tradition of the Roman church was maintained by its care in preserving its archives. From early times registers were kept of some of the letters dispatched, though few remain from before 1198" (xix). There is some evidence that a special collection of documents pertaining to papal-imperial relations was maintained in the

pontifical chancery, which would have permitted Honorius easy access to the evidence he sought when composing his letter of reprimand to Frederick.

33. See in this book Chapter 1, note 36.

34. The text is from *Si memoriam,* which is in Huillard-Bréholles, 4.2, 914-23.

35. Giles 190.

36. Giles 166-67. The Latin text is from Luard, 3, 532-33. Giles translates Matthew's adverb describing Frederick's refusal to obey the pope with the legally charged word *contumaciously.* In fact Matthew describes imperial obstancy with the word *procaciter,* which might better be translated *audaciously* or *impertinently.*

37. *Evidentium clara* is in Huillard-Bréholles, 5.1, 33-34.

38. See the discussion of *In exordio* in Chapter 9 in this book.

39. *In exordio* is published in Huillard-Bréholles, 5.1, 348-51.

40. Walter Ullmann notes that "the *peitito principii* is perhaps the most striking feature of all medieval scholarship, and nowhere is it more glaringly marked than with the canonists in particular and the papalists in general." *Medieval Papalism* (London: Methuen, 1949) 77.

CHAPTER 3

Pope vs. Emperor:
The Issues of Contention

In the mid 1220s, Frederick published a letter proclaiming that the territorial and ecclesiastical prerogatives enjoyed by his ancestors were his by divine right, and that the church's bullying posture at the time of his mother's death and its neglect during his minority had diminished those prerogatives. Pope Honorius III took sharp exception to Frederick's statement, insisting that the imperial crown marked a man as the obedient servant of the papacy, there being no other justification for the high office.[1] This was particularly true in the case of Frederick, continued the pope, who had been nurtured from early childhood by the papal mother. Majestic mosaics of Christ serenely placing a crown on the head of a Norman ancestor dominated the interiors of several Sicilian churches, and may have dominated Frederick's imagination, but the church of Rome envisioned Frederick's sovereignty otherwise.

However modern historians judge the positions of emperor and pope in the period, both were quite reasonable given the ideological and historical contexts in which they developed. Early thirteenth-century politics were anything but serene, and a summary discussion of the complexities and contradictions of the period is useful to understand the political letters that are the subject of this book.[2] At the risk of oversimplifying extremely complex issues, this chapter offers a sketch of the relationship between Frederick II, Holy Roman Emperor from 1220 to 1250, and the four popes who occupied the Roman cathedra during his lifetime: Innocent III (1198-1216), Honorius III (1216-1227), and Gregory IX (1227-1241), and Innocent IV (1243-1254), and more generally of the historical events to which the letters refer either directly or indirectly.

The maturation of canon law in the late twelfth and thirteenth centuries had a profound influence on papal-imperial relations, so much so that historians have referred to the struggle between Frederick and the popes as a "conflict of laws."[3] At the pinnacle of a hierarchy of legal codes, divine and natural law expressed in the ancient *corpus iuris Romani* and the modern *corpus iuris canonici* were sacrosanct.[4] Canon law was studied throughout Europe and recognized in every court; it was received as universal, necessary, and inviolable.[5] A method of argument, criteria for the evaluation of data, and juridical procedure were established. Legal precedents were organized and made accessible to jurists.

Although the church succeeded in establishing legal dominance, the papacy was relatively weak in comparison to the empire in the second half of the twelfth century. Henry VI, father of Frederick II and emperor from 1190 to 1197, controlled Ancona, Spoleto, and territory in Tuscany, in addition to his German territories. In a union strongly opposed by the papacy, Henry married Constance of Hauteville, daughter of the ambitious King Roger II (1130-1154), who had ruled Sicily, Apulia, Capua, and the northern coast of Africa. In 1189 Roger's nephew, Tancred, claimed the Sicilian throne. In exchange for papal support, he conceded rights over the church in Sicily that had long been enjoyed by the Norman princes there.[6] When Tancred died, Henry overthrew his widow and child, took possession of the Kingdom of Sicily in the name of Constance, and aggressively rejected Tancred's ecclesiastical concessions. The blow to the papacy was stunning: not only was it deprived of recent gains in the Kingdom of Sicily, but even more damaging, finding itself encircled by imperial territories it lost the possibility of playing the power of the German emperor against that of the Norman princes of Sicily. As Robinson puts it, "The union of the kingdom of Sicily with the empire deprived the papacy of room for maneuver."[7] But Henry's rule over a fragile constellation of states was opposed in many quarters: German Welf princes objected to the ascendancy of the Hohenstaufen, and German barons in northern Italy and in Sicily sought to increase their own autonomy at the expense of the emperor's. The Norman-Sicilian nobles decried the rule of a German in the Kingdom of Sicily, and the pope was antagonistic both because of territorial disputes between the papacy and the empire in central Italy and because of Rome's long-standing opposition to an imperial state that surrounded papal lands. Even Constance was implicated in a plot to murder Henry, and when he died at the age of thirty-one, rumor had it that she poisoned him.

The memory of this former period and the shift in the balance of power that occurred when Lothario Conti di Segni became Pope Innocent III in 1198 explain, at least in part, the enduring conflict between pope and emperor in the early thirteenth century.[8] Lothario Conti di Segni ascended to the papacy three months after the death of Henry. He was, by all accounts, a highly intelligent, educated, ambitious, ascetic, and vigorous man in his late thirties. The task before the new pope was clear: to promote the recuperation of the Holy Land consecrated by Christ's blood and of church territory in central and southern Italy lost to Frederick Barbarossa, Holy Roman Emperor from 1152 to 1190, and his son Henry VI. The *recuperatio* remained paramount and inseparable from the goal of normalizing and centralizing ecclesiastical administrative procedures.

Frederick was born at Jesi in Ancona in 1194. He was a child of two when Henry died. Constance, shortly before her own death in 1198, detached the Kingdom of Sicily from the German Roman Empire and placed it in vassalage to the papacy. She also surrendered the ecclesiastical privileges held by her ancestors in Sicily.[9] Having achieved his goals of eliminating the hostile imperial state that encircled papal lands and normalizing the church in Sicily, Pope Innocent granted that Constance's three-year-old son Frederick be crowned King of Sicily. In her will Constance requested that Pope Innocent be Frederick's tutor and regent of the kingdom.

A power struggle ensued in Sicily and the child Frederick became the pawn of the warring factions. In one famous episode recounted to Innocent by his agent Rainald of Capua, and interpreted as a sign of Frederick's natural haughtiness, the seven-year-old Frederick, at the moment of capture by henchmen of the German prince Markwald of Anweiler, "angrily cast aside his robes, rent his clothing, and tore his own flesh with his nails."[10] Besides being a maelstrom of political intrigue, Palermo was a city of rich and varied cultural traditions. Although little is known of Frederick's early years in Palermo, his adult accomplishments attest to a systematic education, a vigorous intellect, and a breadth of intellectual pursuits that included agronomy, architecture, astronomy, biology, law, mathematics, philosophy, and poetry. Frederick knew Latin and Sicilian and some sources note that he spoke Arabic, Greek, and German as well. *De arte venandi cum avibus,* Frederick's book on falconry, reveals an unusually keen interest in scientific method for the period. His equestrian training and accomplishment served him throughout his life. During Frederick's minority, anarchy reigned and state finances deteriorated in the Kingdom of Sicily. Describing Frederick's papal protector, Innocent III, Van Cleve writes,

> The Pope, as regent, had been more zealous for the interests of the Church than the prosperity of the Kingdom. While stoutly denying the charge that he had encroached upon the domain of the King, Innocent III did not hesitate to claim as his own certain rights and privileges which, under the Norman kings of the twelfth century, had been a source of strength and unity to the Sicilian Kingdom.[11]

Frederick ascended to the Sicilian throne at the age of fourteen, and in the same year he married Constance, sister of King Peter II of Aragon.

Meanwhile, the struggle over Henry's successor continued in Germany. Frederick's uncle Philip's candidacy was fiercely contested by the Welf Otto of Brunswick. When Philip was murdered in 1208, Otto, promising absolute obedience to the pope, became emperor. He immediately reneged on his promises, granting followers privileges to lands claimed by the papacy in central Italy and raising an army to attack Frederick and the papal fief of Sicily. In 1211 Innocent excommunicated Otto and those who had sworn fealty to him. But there was no decisive victory in the standoff between the excommunicate emperor, backed by King John of England, and the pope, backed by the French King Philip Augustus.

Rivalry between France and England eventually broke the stalemate. In 1213 the excommunicate King John begged for absolution and submitted England and Ireland to Innocent as papal fiefs in return for remission of his sins. Although condemned by his countrymen, the move has been called a "diplomatic stroke of genius."[12] Threatened by the King of France as well as the barons and prelates of his own realm, John could now call on papal support against his enemies. King Philip had expended tremendous resources to mount a campaign against the excommunicate John, only to discover that he was prepared to wage a war against a papal vassal. Innocent, pursuing a policy of reform and normalization of ecclesiastical procedures, was the other beneficiary. Cheney writes,

> The "liberty of the Church" had been vindicated against an ancient English custom of royal control over ecclesiastical elections. . . . The prestige of pope Innocent III—and indeed his power in the world of secular politics—was greater for this display of spiritual authority. It would never be forgotten.[13]

At this point Philip resolved to Innocent's satisfaction the long-standing dispute over his marriage to Ingeborg of Denmark.

In 1214, John invaded France while Otto, his ally, marched south to meet him. At Bouvines John and Otto encountered Philip, who routed their armies. Otto never regained his ascendancy, and he died in May 1218. In the aftermath of Bouvines, King Philip presented Frederick the *opima spoglia:* the imperial golden eagle. Negotiations had been initiated several years earlier to name Frederick the King of the Romans. By transferring the enormous prestige of the papacy to Frederick, Innocent was once again able to envision the accomplishment of his goal of recovering central Italian lands lost by the church to Otto's armies. Furthermore, Frederick promised to renounce his right to the Kingdom of Sicily when crowned emperor, thus removing the threat that imperial territories would encircle the papal state. He swore to honor his feudatory obligations to Innocent and all his papal successors, to protect the pope and the papal *patrimonium,* and to recognize the ecclesiastical concessions that Constance had made at the time of her death. The one right that was not conceded, which would become a point of conflict between the emperor and Innocent's successors, was secular consent to ecclesiastical elections in Sicily. Lomax notes that "Frederick conceded free elections, confirmations, and consecrations, but he refused to relinquish consent or to allow elector chapters to bypass him or their metropolitan bishops by way of postulation."[14]

Frederick departed from Sicily at the age of seventeen to claim the German imperial crown. The journey extends the perilous tale of Frederick's childhood: according to chancery accounts, it was fraught with near-fatal encounters and fortuitous occurrences, sure signs that

Frederick's imperial coronation at Aachen in 1215 was predestined by God. In gratitude, the young emperor vowed to lead a crusade to the Holy Land, as his grandfather, Frederick Barbarossa, had done. The move was also calculated to enhance the youth's stature throughout Europe. It would take eight years for Frederick to solidify his position in Germany, although, like his father and grandfather, Frederick was willing to grant a large measure of autonomy to the German princes. Thirteen years would pass before he attempted to honor his crusade vow.

In spite of Innocent's continual intervention in the interest of peace, war raged in northern Italy, and between France and England, throughout his papacy. When Innocent died in 1217, the well-ordered Christendom that he envisioned had not come into being. Innocent's successor, Cardinal Cencius Sevelli, was elected Pope Honorius III on July 24, 1216. If he was not motivated by the reforming zeal of his predecessor, Honorius had achieved distinction as an able administrator. He served as papal chamberlain, and in 1192 issued the *Liber Censuum,* a catalog of institutions that depended on and owed taxes to the Holy See, which contributed substantially to the financial well-being of the church. He also circulated the volume known as the *Compilatio Quinta,* a canon law textbook.[15]

It was Honorius who crowned Frederick II emperor in Rome in December 1220. The coronation was carefully orchestrated, every participant and every gesture symbolic. Frederick was not anointed on the head with chrism, but on the arms and back with consecrated oil. He received his crown, scepter, imperial orb, and temporal sword from Honorius; he held the stirrup for Honorius while the pope mounted his horse, then led the papal horse, on foot, for a short distance.[16] In spite of Frederick's ritual submission, Honorius had some serious misgivings. Most worrisome was the fact that Frederick had crowned his son, previously named King of Sicily by Innocent, King of the Romans in Germany. The move was a transgression of the spirit of Frederick's 1213 promise to Innocent—a pledge that had been repeated in 1219 and again in 1220—to maintain the separation of the Kingdom of Sicily and the German Empire. Frederick himself, as emperor elect, persuaded Honorius to grant him the right to rule in Sicily during his son's lifetime, and to inherit Sicily should his son die without heirs. Thus the titles of Holy Roman Emperor and (Regent) King of Sicily were held by Frederick, King of the Romans and King of Sicily by his son Henry. Tillmann comments that

> the fight had become inevitable. The emperor who at the same time was king of Sicily could not but attempt to overcome the separation of his realms caused by the barrier of the Papal States; the Church for its part was forced to set out and to weaken and ultimately to destroy the power that encircled it.[17]

The willingness of Honorius to accede to the emperor's demands is generally described as indicative of his weakness, although Abulafia has suggested Honorius's ability to seek common ground with the emperor reveals his essential pragmatism.[18]

In 1220 Frederick returned to the Kingdom of Sicily and initiated an enduring and in large measure successful struggle to establish sovereignty over the various factions that had controlled the kingdom and devastated its finances since the death of the Empress Constance in 1198. A sign of the degree of control that Frederick was able to establish is Pope Gregory's comment to Frederick, in a letter of 1236, that in the Kingdom of Sicily, "no one moves hand or foot without your approval."[19]

Tension over Frederick's treatment of the Sicilian church began almost as soon as he was crowned in 1220. In the Edicts of Capua, claiming that the royal seal had fallen into inimical hands after his parents' deaths, Frederick initiated a policy of reviewing all charters that granted jurisdiction or property rights formerly belonging to the royal demesne. The pope objected because, as Lomax writes, "no matter how the Church acquired its possessions, it considered seizure of them to be a violation of ecclesiastical liberty. No statute could make such confiscations licit as far as the papacy was concerned."[20] Frederick also alienated the church by failing to fill the bishoprics of Aversa, Brindisi, Capua, Conza, and Salerno, by imposing a substantial tax burden on both clergy and laity, and by renewing the edict that clergy accused of murder or treason would be tried before secular rather than ecclesiastical authorities.

Suspicion generated by Frederick's failure to expeditiously fulfill his crusade vow further poisoned the relationship between pope and emperor. Although initially the pope had paid little attention to

Frederick's vow, as the situation in Damietta deteriorated in 1218, Honorius became more insistent that Frederick act. For his part, Frederick sought repeated postponements, claiming either the lack of vital support or more pressing issues requiring his attention. In the summer of 1225, Honorius renegotiated the terms of the crusade vow and the resulting Treaty of San Germano indicates the pope's deep distrust of the emperor's intentions. In fact, the most important goal of Honorius's papacy, the launching of the fifth crusade that had been announced by Innocent at the Lateran council in 1215, was never achieved.

In September 1225 the pope issued a sharp protest against Frederick's treatment of the Sicilian church and he filled the vacant bishoprics in Sicily without Frederick's consent.[21] It was at this point that Frederick marched an imperial army up the peninsula towards Cremona, with the stated intention of "the reformation of the political status of the Empire."[22] The imperial foray reinvigorated an alliance between the Lombard states and the papacy, and as Van Cleve observes, its dismal failure heightened Frederick's perception of papal opposition to what he regarded as his legitimate and divinely ordained territorial prerogatives. "This Lombard experience of 1226 is of the greatest consequence in that it marks a turning-point in the attitude of Frederick II towards the pope and Curia," from one of obedience and gratitude to one of challenge. "Henceforth, a progressive change in his attitude is apparent in which he comes more and more to regard the Pope, not as a bona-fide spiritual leader, but as a temporal rival demanding supervisory rights over all states and all temporal policies."[23]

At his Roman coronation in 1220, Frederick had renewed his crusade vow before the cardinal bishop of Ostia, Hugolinus Conti di Segni. In the following year, Frederick bestowed upon the cardinal bishop responsibility for the organization of the crusade. During the pontificate of Honorius, Hugolinus was active in church reform, especially concerned with the enforcement of ecclesiastical rights in the burgeoning cities of northern Italy. When Honorius died on March 18, 1227, Hugolinus, then in his late fifties, was immediately elected to succeed him. He chose to be called Gregory, a name that recalled the most determined reformers of the church and staunch opponents of the empire, and signaled, as Abulafia puts it, the end of a "golden era in papal-imperial collaboration."[24] Honorius had aptly described

Hugolinus as a man "forceful in word and deed."[25] The registers from his pontificate reveal a keen preoccupation with the mendicant orders that had both renewed and threatened to undermine the authority of the Roman church in the twelfth and early thirteenth centuries. Towards the emperor, Gregory behaved with the conviction of a universal monarch. The Roman nobles proved less tractable, and Gregory spent much of his pontificate in exile from Rome. Gregory was responsible for the compilation of the *Liber Extra,* a collection of decretals published in 1234 that invalidated all previous canon collections and remained the "basic corpus of canon law" until this century.[26]

Several months after Gregory's election to the papal cathedra, in the summer of 1227, Frederick finally attempted to fulfill his vow and launched a crusade from Brindisi. But the Christian army was devastated by disease before it could embark. The emperor, already ill, set sail for the Holy Land, then returned for treatment when his esteemed associate, the Landgrave of Thuringia, died at sea. Further arrangements were made to ensure Christian reinforcements in the Holy Land, and a commission was sent to Gregory to explain the turn of events. The pope refused to hear the commission, and immediately excommunicated Frederick on the grounds that he had failed to fulfill a voluntary vow.

In 1228, Frederick again set out for the Holy Land, an excommunicate leading a crusade bereft of papal blessing. A principal motive for Frederick's venture was to claim the territory of Jerusalem, since in 1225 he had married Isabella-Yolanda, daughter of John of Brienne and heiress to Jerusalem. He traveled to the Holy Land with an army that was not sufficiently large to meet the infidel in battle. Nevertheless, relying on his patience, diplomatic ties to the Sultan al-Kamil, and the influence of his friend, the Emir Fakhr ad-Din Ibn as-Shaikh, who had previously been sent as an envoy to Sicily by al-Kamil to seek imperial aid, Frederick negotiated a treaty that fixed the borders of the Kingdom of Jerusalem for ten years, gave Christians and Moslems access to the sacred shrines of Jerusalem, and guaranteed a corridor of safe passage to Christians from Jerusalem to the sea.[27] The pact was universally denounced by Christians and Moslems, but the emperor had accomplished his purpose. He entered Jerusalem in triumph, and on March 18, 1229, Frederick crowned himself. An imperial letter celebrates the achievement, joyfully proclaiming that

God had not forgotten His ancient mercy, and that He had shown His glory to the meek by granting to Frederick and an elite company of soldiers the success that had for so many years eluded other Christian princes and their armies.

In the meantime, on July 31, 1228, Gregory dissolved the oath of loyalty that bound imperial subjects to Frederick. The act may have triggered the invasion of papal lands in Ancona and Spoleto by Frederick's regent, Rainald of Spoleto. Gregory then sponsored an invasion of the Kingdom of Sicily, commanded by Frederick's alienated father-in-law, John of Brienne. (Frederick had insulted John by claiming the title of King of Jerusalem for himself on the eve of his marriage with Isabella-Yolanda.) The rebellion of Frederick's Sicilian subjects was encouraged and rumors circulated that the emperor was dead. Frederick cut short his Eastern tour, returned to Sicily, expelled papal troops, and restored authority. Rather than pressing his advantage beyond the borders of the kingdom, Frederick turned to Gregory as a humble suppliant. He offered significant concessions on episcopal elections in Sicily and reparations for ecclesiastical properties he had seized. Frederick was finally absolved in the summer of 1230 and embraced as a beloved son of the church in the treaty of San Germano and Ceprano. This, according to historians, was a sufficient victory for the emperor. But there can be little doubt that the events of the decade had taught Frederick the strength of papal opposition to his pretensions to sovereignty.

It was at this time that Frederick ordered the compilation of a major law code. Although the text always refers to Frederick as emperor, the Constitutions of Melfi are a royal legal code for the Kingdom of Sicily. The Constitutions open with an innovative articulation of the law as temporal and subject to emendation and extension by the prince in accordance with the circumstances of the kingdom.[28] Furthermore, "in direct affront to the claims of the contemporary church,"[29] the prince derives his authority from his covenant with God; there is no room for papal intervention in secular jurisdiction. In a letter to Jacob, Archbishop of Capua, Gregory protests the unjust laws (leges iniquas) being composed at the court.[30] Gregory wrote directly to the emperor in July 1231, but these issues are not raised. The pope instead pointed out that the promulgation of the Constitutions would imperil his role as the defender of the church, which alone ensured salvation.

It has reached our ears that you intend to promulgate new laws, either by your own impulse or led astray by the pernicious counsel of irresponsible men. From this it follows that men will call you a persecutor of the church, a destroyer of the freedom of the state. . . . If you, of your own volition, have contemplated this, then must we gravely fear that God has withdrawn his grace from you, since you so openly undermine your own good name and salvation. If you are instigated by others, then we marvel that you can tolerate such counselors who, inspired by the spirit of destruction, are bent on making you the enemy of God and Man.[31]

The *Constitutiones Regni Siciliae* were promulgated at Melfi in August, 1231.

In the 1230s, the emperor's ambition to establish a *Regnum Italicum* put him into conflict with the city-states of northern and central Italy, as well as the pope. The imperial chancery justified intervention as necessary in order to restore the rule of law in the region, and the rebellious Lombards were depicted as heretical. The restoration of peace and justice in Italy was also a prerequisite for the emperor to initiate preparations for a new crusade. Gregory, in the meantime, described Frederick's forays into northern Italy as injurious to the prospects of a new crusade. The one significant military victory of the imperial forces was the Battle of Cortenova in 1237. In the aftermath of Cortenova some of the formerly belligerent Lombard city-states permitted the presence of imperial vicar generals in their midst, but ultimately Frederick's refusal to come to terms with Milan, from which he demanded unconditional surrender, led to a reinvigoration of Lombard opposition.

The relationship between the papacy and the empire can best be described as opportunistic during this period: when Gregory, who spent much of the decade in exile due to the hostility of the Roman nobles, needed Frederick's aid to oppose his enemy, he did not hesitate to reconcile with the emperor and remind him of his role of defender of the church. Similarly, when the emperor's son Henry rebelled in 1235, allying himself with the Lombard communes against his father, Frederick sought the pope's support, since a papal decision in favor of the son could have resulted in the father's deposition.

In Lombardy, Gregory did not explicitly promote rebellion against imperial rule, but he was able to use his role as mediator of the imperial-Lombard conflict to thwart Frederick's ambitions there. For example, his legate, Cardinal Bishop James of Palestrina, was instrumental in luring Piacenza, site of a proposed imperial diet, from the imperial camp in 1236—an event that later becomes proof, in imperial letters to Christian princes, of Gregory's lack of impartiality, his intention to damage imperial rights, and his ineligibility to stand in judgment of the emperor.

By the middle of the decade, Gregory had renewed his attacks against Frederick on the issue of the treatment of the Sicilian church and the many vacancies which, according to the pope, were the result of Frederick's interference in ecclesiastical elections. Frederick had also angered Gregory by arranging a marriage between his son Enzo and the heiress of Sardinia. The papacy claimed sovereignty over that island dating back to the Donation of Constantine.

On Palm Sunday in 1239, Pope Gregory excommunicated Frederick for the second time. Frederick responded by calling for a council of princes and prelates to judge the worthiness of Gregory to occupy the papal cathedra. Lomax has shown how the imperial encyclical *Levate* carefully constructs a case of heresy against Gregory, the only charge that laymen could legally bring against clerics. According to Lomax, "the whole of *Levate* is built to the point at which the emperor could justifiably propose that Gregory be subjected to human judgment, with the good result of removing the Pope from the papal dignity."[32] The pope moved to depose the emperor.

The final decade of Frederick's reign, which is not the subject of the present study, was one of intense conflict between the two powers. It is a period in which the desire for conciliation, motivated especially by the failure of Louis IX in the Holy Land and fear of a Tartar invasion, was undermined by mistrust and missed cues on the part of the papacy and the empire. Hostility was exacerbated when a ship full of cardinals, en route to a general council to judge the emperor, was captured by the Sicilian and Pisan fleets on May 3, 1241. More than a hundred prelates were subjected to harsh treatment, and those most inimical to imperial ambitions were hauled off to prison in Apulia—a move that did little to further Frederick's attempt to win the support of the Roman cardinals. In August 1241, with Frederick poised to enter the gates of Rome, Pope Gregory died. Intense negotiations followed between the cardinals and the emperor, and eventually a compromise was reached, but Pope Celestine IV died within three weeks of his election.

All Christendom rejoiced at the election of Sinibaldo dei Fieschi, who took the name Innocent IV, in June 1243. Innocent was a renowned canonist for whom Frederick's conception of absolute and autonomous rule within his kingdom was "wholly inimical to the hierarchical authority of the Holy See."[33] He maintained negotiations with Frederick, mostly at the behest of Louis IX, who sought imperial assistance to sustain his crusade effort. Innocent even promised a meeting with the emperor at Narni in 1244. But instead, he fled the Italian peninsula and established residence in Lyons. At a Christmas sermon, Innocent announced that a general council would take place on June 24 of the following year, to judge the emperor. Frederick may have been willing, at this point and later in the decade, to accede to the demands of the pope: to restore papal lands, free the imprisoned cardinals, make amends for damages, undertake a three-year crusade to the Holy Land, and permit papal mediation of the Lombard question. In spite of assurances of Frederick's sincerity by other European princes, Frederick was accused at the council of perjury, violation of the peace, sacrilege, and heresy, and was deposed on July 17, 1245. Given the infamous and notorious nature of his crimes, no formal juridical examination was deemed necessary. Frederick died at Castel Fiorentino in Apulia on December 13, 1250, excommunicate, in a state of open rebellion against the papacy, and, according to Matthew Paris, wearing the robes of a Cistercian monk.

NOTES

1. Honorius's text reads, "Quum enim advocatus Ecclesie idem intelligi debat quam defensor, si defensoris omittis officium, nomen improprie ritenes advocati." *Miranda tuis,* J.-L. A. Huillard-Bréholles, *Historia diplomatica Friderici Secundi* 2.2 (Paris: H. Plon, 1852-1861) 589-99. Unfortunately, Frederick's letter is not extant, but its content is made fairly clear in *Miranda tuis.*

2. Useful works on the history of the papal-imperial relationship are David Abulafia, *Frederick II: A Medieval Emperor* (New York: Penguin, 1988); Eduard Jordan, *L' Allemagne et l'Italie aux XIIe et XIIIe siècles* (Paris: Presses

Universitaires de France, 1939); Ernst Kantorowicz, *Frederick the Second 1194-1250*, Trans. E. O. Lorimer (New York: Frederick Ungar Publishing, 1957), and *Kaiser Friedrich der Zweite* 2 (Munich: Georg Bondi, 1931), which contains invaluable notes not included in the English edition; John Phillip Lomax II, *"Ingratus" or "Indignus": Canonistic Argument in the Conflict between Pope Gregory IX and Emperor Frederick II*, diss., University of Kansas, 1987; I. S. Robinson, *The Papacy 1073-1198: Continuity and Innovation* (New York: Cambridge University Press, 1990); Steven Runciman, *A History of the Crusades* 3, *The Kingdom of Acre and the Later Crusades* (New York: Cambridge University Press, 1987); Brian Tierney and Sidney Painter, *Western Europe in the Middle Ages, 300-1475* (New York: Alfred A. Knopf, 1970), and Thomas Curtis Van Cleve, *The Emperor Frederick II of Hohenstaufen, Immutator Mundi* (Oxford: Clarendon Press, 1972).

3. Most recently, James A. Brundage, *Medieval Canon Law* (New York: Longman, 1995) 177. Brundage writes of the period: "It also produced massive amounts of new law and new legal doctrines nearly everywhere in the Latin West. . . . Canon law, too, grew enormously in volume and complexity during the period. The thirteenth-century *ius novum* comprised thousands of papal decretals, the hundreds of constitutions adopted by three great general councils (the Fourth Lateran in 1215, the First Council of Lyon in 1245, and the Second Council of Lyon in 1274), as well as the canons that countless provincial and local councils and synods adopted" (164-65).

4. 'The identification of natural law with divine law was always strongly insisted upon by the canonists. This identification was so generally known and understood that we find no very lengthy discussions on the topic. The usual statement simply ran: "Jus naturale, id est, jus divinum."' Walter Ullmann, *Medieval Papalism* (London: Methuen, 1949) 40.

5. I am well aware of the dangers of approaching a discipline like canon law without formal training in the field, but the impact of the law on epistolary language and argument is extremely important. I have consulted Harold J. Berman, *Law and Revolution: The Formation of the Western Legal Tradition* (Cambridge, MA: Harvard University Press, 1983); Brundage, *Medieval Canon Law;* R. W. Carlyle and A. J. Carlyle, *A History of Medieval Political Theory in the West* 5, *The Political Theory of the Thirteenth Century* (1938. London: W. Blackwood, 1950); Amleto Giovanni Cicognani, *Canon Law.* Trans. Joseph M. O'Hara and Francis J. Brennan, 2nd ed. (Westminster: Newman Bookshop, 1934); Gabriel Le Bras, Charles Lefebre and Jacqueline Rambaud, *Histoire du Droit et des Institutions de l'Eglise en Occident, L' Age Classique, 1140-1378,* Sources et théorie du droit 7 (Paris: Sirey, 1965); Kenneth Pennington, *Pope*

and Bishops: The Papal Monarchy in the Twelfth and Thirteenth Centuries (Philadelphia: University of Pennsylvania Press, 1984); Brian Tierney, "The Continuity of Papal Political Theory in the Thirteenth Century," *Medieval Studies* 27 (1965): 227-45; Walter Ullmann, *A History of Political Thought in the Middle Ages* (Baltimore: Penguin Books, 1965), *A Short History of the Papacy in the Middle Ages*, 2nd ed. (London: Methuen, 1972); *Medieval Papalism: The Political Theories of the Medieval Canonists* (London: Methuen, 1949), and *The Growth of Papal Government in the Middle Ages* (London: Methuen, 1955), and John A. Watt, "The Theory of Papal Monarchy in the Thirteenth Century," *Traditio* 20 (1964): 179-317.

6. Helena Tillmann, *Pope Innocent III,* Trans. Walter Sax (New York: North-Holland Publishing Co., 1980) 85. Tillmann writes: "By the ecclesiastical privileges granted to William I by Hadrian IV in the treaty of Benevento of 1156, a unique position had been conceded to the kingdom in ecclesiastical matters. The appointment to bishoprics and abbacies lay in the king's hands owing to this unrestricted right to reject any candidate elected by the chapters and convents, and owing to the stipulation that the voting return had to be kept secret until the king had been informed. Appeals to the pope were not permitted in Sicily, and in other parts of the kingdom they were liable to restrictions. No legate was allowed to be sent to the island without request by the king. It was for the king to decide whether priests from Sicily summoned to the Apostolic See could obey the summons. When the privilege was renewed by Celestine III, Tancred, the 'usurper', had to acquiesce in considerably reduced rights, but had yet retained important prerogatives as to legation and ecclesiastical elections. Henry VI and Constance did not recognize Tancred's concordat. In gruff, insulting terms Constance on one occasion entered a protest against an infringement of her and her husband's ecclesiastical prerogatives by Celestine III. (85).

7. Robinson 396-97.

8. The bibliography on Innocent III is vast, including C. R. Cheney, *Innocent III and England,* Päpste und Papsttum 9 (Stuttgart: Anton Hiersemann, 1976), and "The Letters of Pope Innocent III," *Bulletin of the John Rylands Library* 35 (1952): 23-43; Raymond Foreville, *Le Pape Innocent III et la France,* Päpste und Papsttum 26 (Stuttgart: Anton Hiersemann, 1992); Michele Maccarone, *Studi su Innocenzo III,* Italia sacra, Studi e documenti di storia ecclesiastica 17 (Padua: Antenore, 1972); Colin Morris, *The Papal Monarchy: The Western Church from 1050 to 1250* (Oxford: Clarendon Press, 1989); Pennington, *Pope and Bishops,* and "Pope Innocent III's View on Church and State: A Gloss to *Per venerabilem,*" *Law, Church and Society: Essays in Honor of Stephan Kuttner,* Eds. Kenneth Pennington and Robert Somerville (Philadelphia: University of Pennsylvania Press, 1977) 49-67, as well as the rest of that volume, and Helena Tillmann.

More generally, on the papal chancery see Harry Bresslau, *Handbuch der Urkundenlehre* 1 (Berlin: Walter De Gruyter, 1958); C. R. Cheney, *The Study of the Medieval Papal Chancery,* The Second Edwards Lecture Delivered within the University of Glasgow on December 7, 1964 (Glasgow: Jackson, 1966); C. R. and Mary G. Cheney, Eds. *The Letters of Pope Innocent III (1198-1216) Concerning England and Wales. A Calendar with an Appendix of Texts* (Oxford: Clarendon Press, 1967), especially the Introduction (ix-xxviii), and Reginald L. Poole, *Lectures on the History of the Papal Chancery* (Cambridge: University Press, 1915).

9. Again quoting Tillmann, "In the last days of her life, under pressure perhaps of the disturbances prevailing in the kingdom at that time or perhaps in presentiment of her imminent death, Constance waived the extraordinary prerogatives of the Norman kings. Only in the question of elections did Innocent make a concession" (86). Innocent's concessions are preserved in *Nec novum,* addressed to Constance and Frederick on November 1198. The passage reads as follows: "Sede vacante capitulum significabit vobis et vestris heredibus obitum decessoris. Deinde convenientes in unum, invocata spiritus sancti gratia secundum Deum eligent canonice personam idoneam, cui requisitum a vobis prebere debeatis assensum, et electionem factam non different publicare. Electionem vero factam et publicatam denunciabunt vobis et vestrum requirent assensum." Othmar Hageneder and Anton Haidacher, Eds., *Die Register Innocenz' III* 2, Publikationen der Abteilung für historische Studien des Österreichischen Kulturinstituts in Rom, 2nd ser., sect. 1 (Graz: Hermann Bohlaus, 1964) 618.

10. Van Cleve 47.

11. Van Cleve 61.

12. Cheney, *Innocent III* 335.

13. Cheney, *Innocent III* 355. Ullmann writes that "papal vassalage of England was preceded by the enfeoffments of other countries. Bulgaria under its King Joannitza had become a papal fief. The Spanish peninsula became of particular importance for Europe. Aragon under its King Peter II renewed the arrangements which had started in 1089, but had lapsed in the course of the twelfth century, according to which the country was to be a papal fief. In 1204 he [Peter] was crowned a papal vassal by Innocent himself who also obtained the king's promise of free and canonical elections. Portugal as well as Castile renewed feudal contracts with the papacy. . . . In fact, the papacy in the early thirteenth century counted a greater number of vassals than any other European power" (Ullmann, *A Short* 114-15).

14. Lomax 117.

15. J. N. D. Kelly, *The Oxford Dictionary of Popes* (New York: Oxford University Press, 1986) 189.

16. "And Innocent himself ordered the composition of a new imperial rite that finally developed the plenitude of power in symbolic fullness, and sharply accentuated the role of the pope as the sole organ that dispensed imperial power" (Ullmann, *A Short* 224).

17. Tillmann 152.

18. Abulafia 161-62.

19. The passage "nullus manum vel pedem abseque tuo movet imperio" occurs in *Si memoriam,* in Huillard-Bréholles, 4.2, 914-23.

20. Lomax 152.

21. Honorius's act, justified in his mind by Frederick's interference in the process of filling empty episcopates, violates the letter of Innocent's concessions to Constance and Frederick (see note 9 above).

22. Van Cleve 180.

23. Van Cleve 187. Abulafia offers a different interpretation of Frederick's intentions at Cremona. "Naturally, the new emperor also wished to show himself to his Lombard subjects. But the purpose of the emperor was in this respect ceremonial rather than constitutional. . . . Frederick and the Pope had a common objective, the crusade. What is striking in 1226 is the trust between emperor and Pope" (158).

24. Abulafia 162.

25. Abulafia 164-65.

26. Berman 203.

27. Runciman adds that Frederick's crusade brought no real benefits to Christians in the Outremer, or even to the emperor. "In fact the recovery of Jerusalem was of little profit to the kingdom. Owing to Frederick's hurried departure it remained an open city. It was impossible to police the road up from the coast; and Moslem bandits continually robbed and even killed pilgrims. A few weeks after Frederick had left the country fanatical Moslem imams in Hebron and Nablus organized a raid against Jerusalem itself. Frederick's main legacy, both in Cyprus and in the kingdom of Jerusalem, was a bitter civil war" (193-94).

28. Berman 425-26.

29. James M. Powell, Ed. and Trans., *The "Liber Augustalis" or "Constitutions of Melfi" Promulgated by the Emperor Frederick II for the Kingdom of Sicily in 1231* (Syracuse: Syracuse University Press, 1971) xxiii.

30. *Sive qui* is in Huillard-Bréholles, 4.1, 290.

31. The translation, with some modifications, is from Kantorowicz, *Frederick* 261. The text (Huillard-Bréholles, 4.1, 289) reads: "Intelleximus siquidem quod vel proprio motu vel motus seductus inconsultis consiliis perversorum novas edere constitutiones intendis, ex quibus necessario sequitur ut dicaris Ecclesie persecutor et obrutor publice libertatis. . . . Sane si id ex te forte moveris, tememus multum Dei gratiam tibi esse subtractam, dum sic patenter famam propriam negligis et salutem; si vero impulsus ab aliis, miramur quod talibus consiliariis acquiescis qui spiritu vexati nequitie te intendunt Deo et hominibus constituere inimicum. . . ."

32. Lomax 427-29.

33. *Eger cui lenia,* long attributed to Innocent IV but now considered the work of the most radical elements of his curia, states, "We rule upon the earth with *plenitudo potestatis* of the King of Kings, which was bestowed upon the Apostles and upon us without limitation, and with absolute authority to bind and loose, and thereby nothing is excluded" (translation from Van Cleve 488). See Peter Herde, "Ein Pamphlet der päpstliche Kurie gegen Kaiser Friedrich II. von 1245/46 (*Eger cui lenia*)," *Deutches Achiv für die Erforschung des Mittelalters* 23 (1967): 468-538.

PART 2

Persuasion and Power at the Papal Chancery

CHAPTER 4

Elevated Prose Style and Power at the Chancery of Innocent III

This chapter and the two that follow explore persuasive language in letters of popes Innocent III (1198-1216), Honorius III (1216-1227), and Gregory IX (1227-1241). Because of the importance of the Roman church in thirteenth-century politics, and the eminence of many papal chancellors, letters from the popes were collected and preserved not only as attestations of grants, privileges, and directives, but also as models of epistolography in courts and bishoprics that were less illustrious but no less ambitious about asserting and protecting their own prerogatives and rights. In the case of Innocent III, over 5,000 collected letters, and hundreds that were not incorporated into collections, have survived in libraries throughout Europe.[1]

Strife was abhorrent in a society unified by love, a society that had as its principal objective the salvation of mankind. Yet the opposition that each pope faced might be viewed as one of the more stable facets of the forty-three years their pontificates spanned. Names and faces changed but issues of conflict were, to a large extent, structured along legal/institutional lines: there was strife within the church, between church and state, between princes, and between princes and their subjects. Increasingly, in the thirteenth century, the conflict could not, in any satisfactory way, be reduced to simple syllogisms or straightforward assertions of jurisdictional power. The exchanges between the holy fathers and secular rulers in this period pitted ideological assertions against the claims of history, and interpretations of actions premised on a spiritual understanding against those premised on the material consequences of those actions. The chanceries countered opposition in different ways: reactions depended on each pope's vision of Christendom, on the way in which each wielded an increasingly powerful legal arsenal, and to a lesser extent on the personnel of the chanceries. As a rule, the effort was made to seek acquiescence through persuasion, exhortation, and entreaty before applying legal remedies. As Innocent writes to King Richard, "As a prudent and discreet man, choose . . . to find in us, not a teacher's sternness, but a mother's love,"[2] although such appeals were generally insufficient to resolve serious disputes.

Pope Innocent III, who dominated Christendom from 1198 to 1216, renewed the language of papal authority. The pope "pushed the papacy in new directions, created new justifications for the exercise of papal authority, and used older justifications in new ways."[3] Despite Innocent's singular importance in reformulating the language of papal power, our knowledge of his personal intervention in the production of his chancery is limited. Although the chancery had not yet become so rigid a bureaucracy that the "unmediated influence" of a pope was rare or improbable, it remains difficult to prove that Innocent dictated any specific letter.[4] The standard description of the epistolary language of Pope Innocent's chancery is that it successfully weds two trends converging on Rome at the beginning of the thirteenth century: the logical structures of the canonists and the verbal ornament associated with the Cistercians in particular.[5] This chapter explores both aspects of Innocent's renewal of the language of papal authority in two letters issued from the chancery. The first letter, *Quanto personam,* is characteristic of his logical and sometimes extravagant legal exegesis. In the second letter, *Apostolica sedes,* the Innocentian chancery's use of the elevated prose style, an essential component and indeed a stylistic correlative of traditional persuasive strategies of epistolography, comes into sharper focus. My objective, particularly in the discussion of *Apostolica sedes,* is to suggest that Innocent's style functions as an integral component of an innovative and robust persuasive strategy. In Innocentian letters the elevated prose style does not merely serve as embellishment or blandishment; it is patterned to reflect a vision of Christian society animated by papal love and governed by papal vigilance. The style itself became a challenge to the secular and ecclesiastical officials of Latin Christendom, a challenge of excellence and of supremacy.

The logical rigor of Innocent's letters, as well as the digressions on the law and its meaning (which found their way into the decretal collections under the pope's watchful eye), have always been attributed to his legal training. Cheney speaks of "the young pope, fresh from his legal studies,"[6] and his contemporaries referred to him with epithets like "nostri temporis Salomon" and "pater iuris."[7] Innocent's innovative grafting of the language of law onto the elevated prose style is of fundamental importance to his epistolary approach and to that of his successors. The maturation of canon law galvanized the language of Rome. Words had an enhanced semantic value when they issued from the Roman chancery—Biblical phrases were freighted with legal conviction. Even common metaphors carried legal significance in papal letters.[8] At the Innocentian chancery the elevated prose style becomes a language of power.

In papal letters, wrongdoing cannot be isolated from the moral category of sin. Innocent provides a sense of the medieval understanding of wrongdoing in a famous passage in the letter *Novit ille*. The letter, addressed to the bishops of France in April or May 1204, explains the pretext for papal intervention in the threatened war between King Philip II of France and King John of England; the war is not a feudal power struggle but an issue of sin.

> Let no man, therefore, imagine that we intend to diminish or disturb the king's jurisdiction and power. . . . For we do not intend to judge concerning a fief, judgment on which belongs to him—but concerning sin [sed decernere de peccato], a judgment which unquestionably belongs to us, and which we can and should exercise against anyone. . . . There is no man of sound mind but knows that it belongs to our office to rebuke any Christian for any mortal sin. . . . Though we are empowered to proceed thus in respect of any criminal sin so that we may recall the sinner from error to truth and from vice to virtue, yet we are specially so empowered when it is a sin against peace. . . .[9]

Political implications of the statement aside, its ramifications for the language and arguments appropriate to a situation of conflict are immense. The overwhelming tendency to treat conflict as sin denies its validity, and casts its elimination as more important than its resolution. Sin is not rationally motivated: it is the work of Satan and his agents, of those who are excluded from the community of the church and salvation. This attitude is reflected in the persuasive approach long associated with the epistolary form, especially the prevailing strategy of medieval writers to seek the adherence of the addressee rather than dwell on the differences that divide the parties. The reasons for which the erring party has acted are treated as obstacles to an ardently desired reconciliation. While expressions of affection and esteem and the principle that shows the appropriate course of action are prominent in letters, discussions of contentious issues are abbreviated and devoid of nuance. As the passage cited above illustrates, conflict is reduced to figures like antithesis—sanity/insanity, truth/error, virtue/vice, and peace/war. When secular rulers found themselves at odds with the Roman church, their complaints were regarded as suspect. When the Frederican chancery elaborates the reasons for its policies, and, even more audaciously, dares to question papal intentions, Pope Gregory interprets the act as a threat to Christendom.

To suggest that papal letters are documents that present plausible arguments intended to move a public to adopt a certain interpretation of events, or in other words, that they are "rhetorical" documents, poses some vexatious problems. The pope himself did not regard them as such: as Christ's vicar he acted not as pure man but as true God. From his mouth issued words of verity, not mere plausibility. A formulaic closing to papal epistles includes the phrase "nullis litteris veritati et justitiae praejudicantibus a sede apostolic impetratis" (no letters obtained from the Apostolic See [being] prejudicial to the truth or to justice).[10] But examined from the perspective of their reception, papal words were not perceived as divinely inspired, either by princes or by prelates. Papal missives—and in some cases even legal verdicts—were viewed as strong and eloquently argued statements of the will of the pontiff, as King Louis's indignant dismissal of Gregory's plan to depose the emperor, quoted in Chapter 2, illustrates.

Even when his commands were disobeyed, his entreaties ignored, and his threats fended off, Innocent's language was greatly admired and emulated, and it spurred innovation in the language and the structure of other chanceries' appeals.[11] The language of Innocent's letters differs quite markedly depending on the quality and size of the intended public, as well as the subject matter. The sentences, like those of his most accomplished contemporaries, are discrete set-pieces that orchestrate ideas at many levels. Some are long, with significance posited in the density and sophistication of the verbal patterning. Sentences accumulate meaning as they progress, the essential point introduced at the beginning of the sentence, then elaborated, modified, or ornamented in a trail of clauses.[12] Legalistic letters, intended for a limited number of clerics, employ a relatively complex syntax. The more strictly emotional appeals can be divided into two groups: those intended for a limited and intimate public and those composed to be read (and probably spontaneously translated into the vernacular) before a large public. In both categories parallel clauses and coordination are favored over subordination.

Quanto personam deals with church discipline, one of Innocent's primary concerns, and Tillmann argues that because of the subject matter, Innocent himself may have been personally involved in the decision and justification that the letter conveys.[13] In a move that was not infrequent at the end of the twelfth century, Conrad of Querfort, a powerful German bishop who had formerly served as chancellor to Henry VI, transferred himself from the episcopal see of Hildesheim to the wealthier diocese of Würzburg without papal permission.[14] He is directed, in *Quanto personam*, to abandon the cathedra at Würzburg at once; nor may he return to his former see. Issued from Rome on August 21, 1198, and addressed to five German bishops, *Quanto personam* contains a fundamentally important digression on papal plenitude of power, although the term is never used. In fact, during the first four years of the Innocentian papacy, the articulation of papal *plenitudo potentatis* is frequent, even in the "preambles to many comparatively unimportant letters."[15]

The exordium of *Quanto personam* focuses on the issue of church discipline, born of the love and duty that bind the pope and the entire church hierarchy to the errant bishop, and the sense that all Christians are imperiled by the former bishop's sinful behavior.

Quanto personam venerabilis fratris nostri . . . Hildesemenis quondam episcopi sinceriori diligebamus affectu, tanto securius sperabamus, quod nichil adversus matrem suam, Romanam ecclesiam, in prejudicium sui ordinis et ecclesiastice discipline dispendium attemptaret.

As much as we have loved with very sincere affection the person of our venerable brother . . . formerly bishop of Hildesheim, so we

> hoped, with greater certainty, that he would not attempt anything
> against his mother, the church of Rome, that imperiled his orders and
> the discipline of the church.

The exordium is the part of the letter that tends to be most elaborately
styled. Formulas existed for the various types of pronouncements made
at the opening of a document, *tanto . . . quanto* being a standard
formula to register disequilibrium and a sense of dissatisfaction with
the state of things.[16] The development of exordia that are strictly
pertinent to the issues raised in the body of the letter is an epistolary
innovation attributed to Innocent and his chancery, although Innocent's
exordia also tend to be more personal than those of his successors.

In the statement that follows, the pope asserts that he has obtained
the necessary evidence to issue his judgment from the testimony of
reliable witnesses as well as the guilty bishop himself. The premise for
papal intervention is provided by a commonplace metaphor of the
twelfth century: the relationship that binds the bishop to his church is a
marriage. In the case of Conrad, "the church of Hildesheim to which he
was bound by a spiritual marriage has been abandoned" [ipse relicta
Hildesemensi ecclesia, cui fuerat spirituali coniugio copulatus]. The
metaphor becomes the opening for a unique and unprecedented
exposition on the nature of papal authority over the ecclesiastical
hierarchy, in which Innocent demonstrates that papal authority partakes
of divine authority. His demonstration consists of a deduction from a
theological and legal axiom found in Matthew 19:6 and Mark 10:9:
"What God has joined, no man may separate" [Quos Deus coniunxit,
homo non separet]. Since, as Scripture testifies, only God has the power
to bind and loose, then in conceding that power to His vicar on earth, it
follows that the pope's authority is divine and not merely human.

> Potestatem enim transferendi pontifices ita sibi retinuit Dominus et
> Magister, quod soli beato Petro vicario suo et per ipsum
> successoribus suis et nobis ipsis, qui locum eius licet indigni tenemus
> in terris, speciali privilegio prebuit et concessit. . . . Non enim homo
> sed Deus separat, quod Romanus pontifex, qui non puri hominis sed
> veri Dei vicem gerit in terris, ecclesiarum necessitate vel utilitate
> pensata, non humana sed divina potius auctoritate dissolvit.

> The power of transferring bishops the Lord and Master thus retained
> for himself, in that only to Saint Peter his vicar, and to Peter's own
> successors and to us who, however unworthy, hold his place on earth,
> He granted and conceded the special privilege. . . . In fact, not man
> but God loosens, in that the pope, who acts on earth not as pure man
> but as the vicar of the true God, loosens, weighing the necessity or
> utility of the Church, wielding not human but rather divine authority.

From the juxtaposition of the metaphor (the bishop's marriage to his church that is sanctioned by God), and the Biblical law (what God has joined, no man may separate), Innocent deduces a radically new description of papal authority. Pennington refers to the configuration as a "luminous mosaic"[17]—if the external structure is provided by human logic, the premises themselves are drawn from spiritual metaphors and the revealed Word.

Nor is Innocent's excursus on the nature of papal power essential to the message of *Quanto personam*. A rapid examination of the remainder of the letter is useful to understand the context of Innocent's theoretical elaboration. The narration, which follows directly after the exordium, and precedes the syllogistic deduction on the nature of papal power cited above, consists of a brief statement that Conrad has abandoned his church at Hildesheim for the episcopal seat at Würzburg. Conrad's offense—that is, the abandonment of one episcopal see for another without papal authorization—is not discussed in any detail. In this letter of correction, the particulars of the transfer are completely insignificant.

Conrad of Querfort had broken church discipline. The need for punishment is cited lest the errant bishop become an example to others who might presume as he has. An allusion to Paul's call to readily punish those who are disobedient to Christ's rule in 2 Corinthians 10:6 further justifies papal intervention. The bishop is not merely disobedient to the church, thereby threatening himself and his order (indeed, all Christianity, as the exordium states), but he is guilty of the sin of idolatry because he has preferred his own counsel to the rule of God and His church.

The letter concludes with instructions to the five German bishops: excommunication is ordered if the bishop does not immediately yield to ecclesiastical authority. In fact, despite the letter's demonstration of the divine nature of papal authority, Innocent's judgment was, after a lengthy negotiation, set aside. As Cheney notes, "The most striking of Innocent III's letters on political theory which found their way into the law-books . . . bore little or no fruit at the time."[18]

Quanto personam is representative of Innocent's legalistic style. The premises of papal authority and judgment are provided by canonical language and Scripture. Ornament is limited to the observation of the *cursus*. The five Biblical passages cited and alluded to in the text stand as irrefutable propositions from which papal arguments proceed. Nor is the characterization of a bishop's nomination to a see as a marriage in any way ornamental; it serves to describe and clarify the sacramental character of investiture.

That the pope operated within what might be called a legal "industry" in the late twelfth and early thirteenth centuries had the effect of diffusing and, eventually, ratifying his language of papal authority. In 1210, Innocent himself sent a collection of letters from the first twelve years of his pontificate to Bologna, the foremost university of both laws, and he treats statements of authority like those found in *Quanto personam* and *Novit ille* as canonical in the latter years of his papacy.[19]

Other important letters eschew the legal and make essentially personal, spiritual, and esthetic appeals. Usually addressed to an individual or a small public, the syntax is characterized by an interlacing of clauses and the phonic patterns which scholars have again associated with Innocent himself.[20] Innocent exploits the expressive potential of the elevated prose style to redefine the status of the addressee in the context of his conception of Christendom, a society animated by papal love and governed by papal vigilance. The pope, the keystone of a fragile social structure, alone guaranteed peace, justice, the salvation of all Christians, and the recovery of the Holy Land. The elevated prose style itself becomes a politicized language that translates Innocent's vision of papal sovereignty by means of lexical repetitions, structural, phonic, and rhythmic parallel patterns, and Biblical citations. Even if these messages were not received as divinely inspired and inviolable, they became the standard and the challenge that other chanceries had to meet if they were to establish a successful dialog with the Rome.

The style is illustrated especially well in *Apostolica sedes,* addressed to King Richard of England (1189-1198), and dated April 28, 1199. It concerns Richard's denial of his half-brother Geoffrey's temporalities. Geoffrey, Archbishop of York, was an illegitimate son of Henry II who had already established a reputation as unruly in his relations with the cathedral chapter of York—which led to his temporary suspension by Pope Celestine III (1191-98)—and with his half-brothers, Richard and John. Failing to receive satisfaction from Richard, Geoffrey appealed to the pope who could not, as a matter of principle, recognize that the archbishop himself might be at fault.

In the exordium, Innocent describes the Apostolic See as the devoted protector, the mother and *magister* of the faithful and of her dear son and pupil Richard. Innocent seeks to persuade Richard to yield on the issue by drawing on the affection that binds pope and prince, an affection that also requires the pope to direct the prince on the paths of righteousness.

> Apostolica sedes universorum Christi fidelium mater et magistra, non ab homine sed deo potius constituta, tunc vere matris affectum et magisterii redolet disciplinam, cum ad benignitatem gratie diligit filios et discipulos ad justitie dirigit equitatem.[21]

> The Apostolic See, mother and teacher of all the faithful of Christ, constituted not by man but by God, most truly exercises its maternal affection and its educative discipline when it loves its sons with a kindly graciousness and guides its pupils with a rule of justice.

The exordium is ornamented by the alliterative repetition of the pope's roles (universorum Christi fidelium mater et magistra; matris affectum et magisterii . . . disciplinam) and by a chiastic figure that incorporates phonic play on the verbs *diligit* and *dirigit* (ad benignitatem gratie diligit filios et discipulos ad justitie dirigit). The fulfillment of one role cannot be achieved except through the fulfillment of the other.

The power of binding and loosing is immediately introduced as one of the mother-master's responsibilities, as much so as the nurturing of the flock. It is not up to Richard to judge or interfere with an archbishop's abilities to perform his office, but to Innocent.

> Non enim potest vel dissimulare matrem vel magisterium qualibet occasione negligere, que a domino in signum dilectionis oves dominicas pascendas in beato Petro recepit et ligandi et solvendi ab eodem et in eodem obtinuit potestatem.

It [the papacy] cannot for any reason either ignore its role as mother
or neglect its role as teacher; for from the Lord through St. Peter it
has received, as a token of love, the Lord's sheep to feed, and from
the same Lord through St. Peter it has been given the power of
binding and loosing.

The admonition also serves to remind Richard that a pope has the
authority to release royal subjects of oaths of fealty, a warning that
takes the form of a specific threat at the end of the letter.

Richard himself had exhorted Innocent, at the time of the latter's
ascension to the papal cathedra, to pursue justice vigorously, and
Innocent is now merely carrying out Richard's dearest wish. The pope's
reminders of this "salutary counsel" at several points in the letter betray
more than a hint of irony. Evidence of Richard's unjust treatment has
been provided by the victim himself. The pope had granted Geoffrey a
hearing "moved . . . by concern for our pastoral office and recalling the
substance of your royal advice."

In spite of the irony and the admonitory interjections, the essential
persuasive force of the pope's appeal is provided by a highly emotional,
esthetic evocation of the harmonious society over which he presides.
Throughout the letter, Innocent implies that whatever hurts Richard is
even more painful to the mother church (which includes the
archbishop), reinforcing the symbolic empathy that unites pope, king,
and archbishop. The pope seeks justice for all three:

Volentes itaque ipsum tanquam fratrem nostrum et ecclesie filium
diligere ad gratiam, et te tanquam catholicum principem et apostolice
sedis filium specialem ad justitam dirigere conservandam, imo
directum potius exhortari, cum in contemptum eius cuius minister
existit, et apostolice sedis injuriam, que ipsum in partem sollicitudinis
evocavit, et tuam etiam, ut prosequamur verum, verecundiam, cuius
est frater, redundet ministrum dei sollicitudinis nostre consortem et
regali stirpe progenitum mendicare: serenitatem regiam omni
affectione qua possumus rogandam duximus et monendam quatinus
tam nos quam te ipsum ab huius onore difficultatis absolvas et a labiis
liberes detractorum, qui non solum que perperam attemptantur ad
detractionem assumunt, sed etiam, secundum prophetam, exacuerunt
ut gladium linguas suas, tetenderunt arcum rem amaram, ut sagittent
innoxios in occultis.

Because we wished, therefore, to show him a gracious affection as
our brother and a son of the Church, and to guide you as a catholic
prince, and a specially dear son of the Apostolic See,—nay, both to
guide and exhort you—to uphold justice; and because the destitution
of a servant of God, a partner in our own responsibility, and a man of
royal lineage, causes dishonor to Him whose servant he is, and injury
to the Apostolic See which called him to share its duty, and (not to
shirk the truth) shame to yourself as his brother, we have thought fit,
with all possible affection, to beg and warn Your Majesty to free us
and yourself from the weight of this burden and from the abuse of
slanderers, who seize not on misdeeds only as material for calumny
but, in the words of the prophet, "have whetted their tongues like a
sword and bent their bows to shoot arrows, even bitter words, at the
perfect."

The sentence opens with clauses describing papal responsibility to both
the impoverished archbishop (ipsum tanquam fratrem nostrum et
ecclesie filium) and the recalcitrant king (te tanquam catholicum
principem et apostolice sedis filium specialem), which are distributed to
make a bipartite frame (Volentes itaque . . . diligere ad gratiam . . . ad
justitam dirigere conservandam) around the archbishop and king, a
frame reinforced by anaphora (tanquam . . . tanquam) and an echo of
the verbal play of the exordium (diligere ad gratiam . . . ad justitiam
dirigere). The structure of the discourse mirrors Innocent's vision of
himself as mother/master and keystone of a fragile social edifice in
which each constituent part affects and is affected by every other part.
The opening expression of papal duty toward archbishop and king is
amplified with the consequences of Richard's error: Geoffrey's
misfortune redounds to Richard's shame and to the discredit of
Innocent, for the three men are bound by moral law and by mutual love
(cum in contemptum eius cuius minister existit, et apostolice sedis
iniuriam, que ipsum in partem sollicitudinis evocavit, et tuam etiam, ut
prosequamur verum, verecundiam, cuius est frater, redundet ministrum
dei sollicitudinis nostre consortem et regali stirpe progenitum
mendicare). The archbishop, a priest and a man of royal blood, has been
reduced to penury because of Richard, and the holy father seeks redress
of the error that does harm to all. Again the phrases referring to the
pope and king are juxtaposed and inseparable (serenitatem regiam omni
affectione qua possumus rogandam duximus et monendam quatinus

tam nos quam te ipsum ab huius onore difficultatis absolvas). The enemy is not the Archbishop of York, whom Innocent describes as Richard's "brother in exile." The sentence concludes with a second clarification of the consequences of Richard's crime: it nourishes the slanderers, the wicked voices of those who have been excluded from the fraternity of Christian love, who prey on weakness and seize on misdeeds as material for calumny, and who, in the words of the prophet, "have whetted their tongues like a sword and bent their bows to shoot their arrows, even bitter words, that they may shoot in secret at the perfect (innoxios)." [Psalm 64:3-4] The importance of error lies in its elimination. More significant than Richard's error is his place in the edifice of Christian society, and this is the message that Innocent chooses to emphasize. It is only when the sinner is excommunicate and alienated from the community of the church that this pretense is abandoned and blame is squarely placed where it belongs.

In this case Innocent repeats that he regards Richard as a sage ruler and a beloved son, and that he trusts Richard will zealously redress the wrong. The prose resounds with the benefits and harmony that would result from Richard's obedience.

> Attendas igitur quanta nos infamia, quanta te detractio sequeretur, si vel justa petitio exulis non introiret in aures nostras, vel te fratris exilium non moveret; et eundem archiepiscopum ob reverentiam apostolice sedis, que te tanquam filium diligit specialem et in hoc et maioribus de celsitudinis tue sinceritate confidit, in plenitudinem gratie regalis admittas, et diligas sicut fratrem et velut Christi ministrum honores, ut in uno et eodem negotio deum tibi reddas propicium, consulas apostolice sedis honori, tue saluti provideas, et fratri subvenias exultanti.

> Reflect, therefore, what infamy would attach to us and what obloquy to you, if we should not listen to an exile's just petition or if you should be unaffected by your brother's banishment. From respect, therefore, for the Apostolic See which loves you as a specially dear son and trusts your Majesty's integrity both in this and more important matters, receive the archbishop fully into your royal favour, love him as a brother, and honour him as Christ's servant; and thus simultaneously you will win the favour of God, guard the honor of

the Apostolic See, provide for your own salvation, and help a brother
in exile.

Each clause and phrase adds to the complex structure of mutually
beneficial bonds of kinship, love, and sanctity. Between the hortatory
subjunctive at the opening (attendas), and the imperfect subjunctive
verb that expresses its consequence at the end of the second clause
(sequeretur), both the pope and the king are portrayed as imperiled, the
fate of the two powers linked by the repetition of *quanta*. The
concatenation continues in the next two clauses, again linked by
anaphora (si vel . . . vel), again binding the fates of the persons of pope,
king, and exiled archbishop, brother of the king (si vel justa petitio
exulis non introiret in aures nostras, vel te fratris exilium non moveret).
And between the object (eundem archiepiscopum) and the instructions
to the king (in plenitudinem gratie regalis admittas, et diligas sicut
fratrem et velut Christi ministrum honores), phrases accumulate
expressing the special relationship between sovereign and pope (ob
reverentiam apostolice sedis, que te tanquam filium diligit specialem et
in hoc et maioribus de celsitudinis tue sinceritate confidit). These bonds
are inviolable and compel a course of action that will yield magnificent
results (ut in uno et eodem negotio deum tibi reddas propicium,
consulas apostolice sedis honori, tue saluti provideas, et fratri subvenias
exultanti). The message of this highly synthetic prose cannot be
isolated in a legal phrase, Biblical citation, or rhetorical figure. Its
charm is more complex, reflecting the contrapuntal harmony composed
of pope, king, archbishop, and implicitly, all Christians. The
esthetically and emotionally wrought prose is intended to dictate a
course of action from which Richard may not deviate.

Should rhetorical persuasion fail, however, Innocent has another
means of coercion at his disposal. The Archbishop of Rouen (formerly
King Richard's justiciar), and the Cistercian Abbot of Perseigne (the
king's confessor), have been designated to settle the differences
between Richard and Geoffrey, and, failing that (at least in the second
of two versions of this letter), first York, then all England will
immediately be placed under sentence of interdict.

In the conclusion to the letter Innocent appeals once again to
Richard's wisdom, urging him to choose the embrace of the mother
over the harsher measures of the master. Again the passionate bond
between pope and king is sounded, "sine multa molestatione nostra te

molestare non possumus" [we cannot cause you pain without much pain to ourselves], and syntactically echoed. This matter is, first and foremost, a question of Richard's salvation.

Unfortunately Pope Innocent's salutary admonition arrived too late to help Richard; unbeknownst to the pope, the king had been dead for three weeks when the letter was composed.

The two letters discussed in this chapter, while not representative of the entire range of the Innocentian chancery, do illustrate the gauntlet that the papal chancery tossed out to Latin Christendom. Innocent's imagery and demonstration of papal plenitude of power reinvigorated the language of papal authority. In *Apostolica sedes* the papal vision of Christendom is subtly patterned into a language of power that incorporates within it all Christendom and leaves little legitimacy for opposition. The style, in conjunction with the enthymemic form of the traditional letter, becomes a celebration of a vision of papal sovereignty. To defend conflict or to question the motives of the papal mother/master represents an offense that threatens to destabilize the whole. The elevated prose style is not a language that permitted difference or furthered the resolution of conflict. At the Innocentian chancery, it is a language appropriated by the Roman church to express its vision of Christendom.

NOTES

1. The statistic is from C. R. Cheney, "The Letters of Innocent III," *Bulletin of the John Rylands Library* 35 (1952-53): 23. The chief personnel of the papal chancery are listed in Harry Bresslau, *Handbuch der Urkundenlehre* 1 (Berlin: Walter De Gruyter, 1958) 248-50. Evidence of the prominence of the papal chancellors is provided by the that fact that in the course of the twelfth century, five chancellors acceded to the papal throne. See Chapter 2, note 3 in this volume for bibliography on the medieval papal chancery.

2. The text and translation of *Apostolica sedes* are found in C. R. Cheney and W. H. Semple, Eds. and Trans., *Selected Letters of Pope Innocent III Concerning England (1198-1216)* (New York: Thomas Nelson and Sons Ltd., 1953) 10-14.

3. Kenneth Pennington, "Innocent III and the Divine Authority of the Pope," *Pope and Bishops* (Philadelphia: University of Pennsylvania Press, 1984) 13.

4. Cheney, noting "stylistic likenesses" between certain papal communications and Innocent's earlier theological works, does allow "that Innocent himself drafted many of the letters" ("The Letters" 35).

5. Hans Martin Schaller, "Die Kanzlei Kaiser Friedrichs II. Ihr Personal und ihr Sprachstil 2," *Archiv für Diplomatik* 4 (1958): 279. Cheney quotes Fliche, who describes Innocent's letters as written in "a studied style, full of imagery, fertile in antithesis, rich in reminiscences of the liturgy and of the Old and New Testaments, with passages from profane authors, notably Horace and Ovid, and with scriptural comparisons which are sometimes rather forced." Cheney continues, "Moreover, the letters of Innocent's immediate predecessors do not show so markedly these features. The same school of rhetoric had produced their tropes, but they very seldom develop—as the Innocentian letters sometimes do—into a little theological or moral essay" ("The Letters" 35).

6. Cheney, "The Letters" 41.

7. Pennington offers a brief overview of Innocent's education in the opening of "Pope Innocent III's Views on Church and State: A Gloss to *Per Venerabilem*," *Law, Church, and Society: Essays in Honor of Stephen Kuttner,* Eds. Kenneth Pennington and Robert Somerville (Philadelphia: University of Pennsylvania Press, 1977) 51-54. The epithets are from Pennington, who also includes a discussion of biographical and technical evidence that casts doubt on the common assumption that Innocent was thoroughly trained in law.

8. Writing of a charge of ingratitude in the papal encyclical of excommunication of 1239, Lomax explains that an emotional metaphor of the church as nourishing mother also functioned legally. "The Pope echoed the language of the law with many words that were not in themselves juristic terms of art but that carried distinct legal connotations: *mater, excipere, filius, lactare,* and so on." John Phillip Lomax, *"Ingratus" or "Indignus": Canonistic Argument in the Conflict between Pope Gregory IX and Emperor Frederick II,* Diss., University of Kansas, 1987, 194.

9. The translation of *Novit ille* is from Cheney and Semple 63-68. For further discussion of the document see Cheney, *Innocent III and England,* Päpste und Papsttum 9 (Stuttgart: Anton Hiersemann, 1976) 289-91; also Walter Ullmann, *Medieval Papalism: The Political Theories of the Medieval Canonists* (London: Methuen, 1949) 103-04. I would like thank Professor James A. Brundage, who generously assisted me on this question.

France and England had been at war since the release from captivity of Richard in 1194, and the pope had previously enjoined John to go directly to Philip with his complaint and in that manner to resolve the conflict between themselves. For a discussion of the procedure of the "charitable admonition" in

Matthew 18:15-17 ("If your brother shall trespass against thee, go and rebuke him between thee and him alone; if he shall hear thee, thou hast gained a brother. But if he will not hear thee, then take with thee one or two more, that in the mouth of two or three witnesses every word may be established. But if he shall neglect to hear them, tell it unto the church. But if he neglect to hear the church let him be unto thee as a heathen man and a publican"), see James A. Brundage, *Medieval Canon Law* (New York: Longman, 1995) 143.

10. This is pointed out by Cheney, "The Letters" 32. See, for example, the letter dated March 7, 1212, addressed to the Bishop of Magolona. J.-P. Migne, Ed., *Patrologie Cursus Completus,* Series Latina 216 (Paris: Garnier, 1958-1974) Col. 549.

11. Emmy Heller, "Zur Frage des kurialen Stileinflusses in der sizilische Kanzlei Friedrichs II.," *Deutsches Archiv für die Erforschung des Mittelalters,* 19.2 (1963): 434-35. According to Heller, there is no conclusive evidence that a collection of Innocentian letters ever existed in the Frederican chancery. See, also, Schaller, "Die Kanzlei 2" 279.

12. Janet Martin, "Classicism and Style in Latin Literature," *Renaissance and Renewal in the Twelfth Century,* Eds. R. L. Benson, G. Constable, and C. Lanham (Cambridge, MA: Harvard University Press, 1982) 544-45, contrasts the classical and medieval sentence.

13. Helena Tillmann, *Pope Innocent III,* Trans. Walter Sax (New York: North-Holland Publishing Co., 1980) 60.

14. *Quanto personam* is in Othmar Hageneder and Anton Haidacher, Eds., *Die Register Innocenz' III* 1. Publikationen der Abteilung für historische Studien des Österreichischen Kulturinstituts in Rom, 2nd ser., sect. 1 (Graz: Hermann Bohlaus, 1964) 495-97.

15. Cheney, "The Letters" 41.

16. Schaller, "Die Kanzlei 2" 319. Schaller and others have shown that variation by an individual secretary of the chancery was usually limited to the exordium and the narration. Schaller, "Die Kanzlei 2" 295.

17. Pennington, "Innocent III and the Divine" 39.

18. Cheney, "The Letters" 42.

19. Pennington, "Innocent and the Divine" 15-24. Pennington shows how the language of *Quanto personam* was interpreted and inflated by the legal scholar Laurentius Hispanus (ca. 1215).

20. Cheney, "The Letters": "minor points emerge in a taste for parallels between words of similar sounds (parachesis): thus, *affectus* and *effectus, servire* and *sevire,* and for transpositions of epithets: thus *fidelitas devota et fidelis devotio, non solum discretionis spiritum verum etiam discretionem*

spiritus, unitatis concordiam et concordie unitatem, culpabiliter durum et dure culpabiliem. These would not attract much notice were they not closely paralleled in Innocent's sermons and other treatises: for example, *O superba praesumptio et praesumptuosa superbia*" (37).

21. The text and translation of *Apostolica sedes* is taken from Cheney and Semple 10-4. The translation has been modified at certain points in order to represent the Latin text as faithfully as possible.

CHAPTER 5

Harmony and Conflict at the Chancery of Honorius III

Innocent's successor, Cardinal Cencius Sevelli, became Pope Honorius III on July 24, 1216. Honorius was neither a jurist nor a judge. His letters are animated by the features that make crusade predication readily comprehensible to large audiences: they are accented with verbal, phonic, and rhythmic repetition and laced with exclamations expressing papal love, affection, fear, horror, and disappointment. The sentences have a clear and natural order.

Schaller argues that the two leading exponents of the elevated prose style, Innocent III and Honorius III, actually represent opposite poles when it comes to epistolary persuasion.[1] Despite the pathos of Innocent's letters, writes Schaller, the emphasis is on concrete facts, not feelings. Innocent's appeals are contoured by his idea of the papal office. Whether the chancery is addressing an individual or all Christendom, the person and office of the pope emerges as the instrument of renewal and reform. Innocent seeks to persuade with praise and affection and a verbal musicality that expresses the joy of his vision of Christian society, a fraternity bound by love and law that ensures universal salvation. And as *Quanto personam* exemplifies, Innocent interpolates "demonstrations" of his power, even where they are not strictly pertinent to the issue at hand. Honorius, on the other hand, guides his flock with spiritual allegories. His appeals are less self-referential: he judges and defends actions in view of the soul's salvation. Sin is ascribed to the sinner and, at least in Frederick's case, there is a sense that the sinner, through prayer and meditation, may recognize the Truth and correct the error of his ways. The difference in style between the two popes is particularly striking in their exhortations to take up the cross because of their dissimilar conceptions of the Christian mission in the Holy Land. While Innocent viewed the crusader's bound duty as that of a vassal to his lord, Honorius envisioned the crusade as a matter of the heart and the soul.[2] Christians went to war in the Holy Land to be redeemed.

The elevated prose style is a correlative to the traditional epistolary appeal, and a fuller understanding of its use by the Honorian chancery, which is, perhaps, less idiosyncratic than that of either his predecessor Innocent III, or his successor, Gregory IX, will shed light on the new direction of epistolary persuasion. Although there is no evidence that the letters composed at the Honorian chancery challenged the emperor in new or extraordinary ways, it is during his pontificate that a new style begins to take form at the imperial chancery. It seems likely that the political and legal conflicts of the period, and Honorius's apparent willingness to permit the "sinner" to explain himself, promoted the development of a new epistolary appeal in which events are justified in terms of the contingencies of the situation rather than glossed on the basis of abstract and universal principles.

Justus Dominus, sent to the lords of Christendom in 1223, is typical of the Honorian chancery. The letter announces that negotiations for the crusade have been renewed between the pope and the emperor. The epistle opens with a pronouncement on the mysterious ways of divine justice.

> Justus Dominus in omnibus viis suis qui unicuique pro meritis condigna retributione respondet, circa negotium Terre sancte spem populi christiani fovit aliquando prosperis et interdum debilitavit adversis.[3]

> God, just in all His ways, treats with worthy retribution each man according to his merits. At times He fosters with good fortune the hope of the Christian people for the Holy Land, at times He weakens their hope with adversity.

The strategically important city of Damietta had been lost to the Christians because of the inept leadership of Cardinal Pelagius as well as (at least in the mind of many) Frederick's failure to act on his crusade vow. Although it is a devastating loss, Honorius exhorts

Christians not to despair, for God is as just as He is mysterious. The elusiveness of the victory at Damietta is offered as a poignant illustration of divine justice. Honorius's laments are joined anaphorically (O quantum . . . videbatur . . . O quantum. . . credebatur), the second part branching into four new phrases joined by anaphora (post . . . post . . . post . . . postea).[4]

> O quantum christicolis videbatur arridere prosperitas! O quantum illuxisse credebatur fidelibus felicium aurora successuum, quando crucesignatorum exercitus Egyptum aggrediens post turrim captam, post transitum fluminis, post hostes exterritos, in adversariorum stationibus castra fixit et Damiatam que robur censebatur Egypti duris obsidionis angustiis coarctavit! Postea memorat infelicem exercitus christiani casum amissionemque Damiatae, et inde ita pergit. . . .

> O how prosperity seemed to smile on the dear children of Christ! O how the dawn was believed by the faithful to shine on happy success; when the army of crusaders attacking Egypt, after capturing the tower, after crossing the river, after expelling the enemy, set up camp in enemy territory and pressed upon Damietta whose strength is measured in hard Egyptian obsidian. After which, the army remembers the unfortunate defeat of the Christians and the loss of Damietta, and thus it continued. . . .

Honorius deepens the pathos by describing the crusaders not as brave and mighty soldiers but as *christicolis,* humble and devout children of Christ who eagerly embrace sacrifice. The use of anaphora controls and intensifies the pope's lament by structuring the catalog of hopeful signs and heroic actions and projecting a victory that is the only appropriate consummation of so glorious a project. Anaphora spurs the audience toward the pathetic letdown of the final sentence. Christian failure is not merely anticlimactic, it is painful and wrong in view of our expectations. The pope suffers the same humiliation as other Christians, yet his understanding of the deeper, spiritual meaning of the event allows him to take heart and rally.

In the narration the pope announces Frederick's renewed promise to lead a crusade within two years' time. The marriage of Frederick to Isabella-Yolanda, daughter of John of Brienne, Regent King of

Jerusalem, is publicized, and Honorius interprets this marriage as a sign of blessing for Frederick's proposed crusade.

> Sane probabili presumptione tenemus quod cum a Domino factum est istud ut votis fidelium optate rei successus exsolvat quod preconcepte spei preludia promiserunt, ad sui restaurationem negotii tuum et aliorum regum ac principum animos ipse filius summi regis accendet, qui de secreto patris in publicum egressus est ad servos, ad ima descendit ut subditis ad summa pararet ascensum, sub testa nostre mortalitatis figulus in terris visus et cum hominibus conversatus.

> Quite reasonably we hold with assurance that God performed this marriage so that He might requite the vows of the faithful with the longed-for happy result, which the hopeful opening scenes had previously promised. The Son of the Highest King, who departed from the mystery of the Father and openly came forth to a state of subjection, who descended in order to prepare for the lowly to ascend to the heavens, who in mortal clay lived among men on earth, ignites your soul and those of other kings and princes for the redress of his operation.

The marriage becomes an index of the divine will to complete His mission in the Holy Land. It is invoked alongside the greater mystery of Christ's incarnation and cited as evidence of His will in an exhortation for Christians to believe and to act. In this sentence the play of contraries (of concealment and exposure, of heavenly and earthly kings, of descent and ascent) and alliteration (probabili presumptione . . . preconcepte spei preludia promiserunt, accendet and ascensum) reinforce and embellish sacred mystery.

Justus Dominus is entirely typical of traditional medieval epistolary rhetoric, and the type of pronouncement one would expect of a chancery directed by Thomas of Capua.[5] The exordium confers meaning on all the events recounted in the letter. It offers hope in the face of the Christian defeat at Damietta. Christian failure is not analyzed or explained: the details of the operation are reduced to a series of poignant moments intended to reenact our plunge from elation to despair. The nuptials of the emperor, announced in the narration, function as a confirmation of God's blessing on Frederick, the man whom He has chosen to lead the Christian army to victory, for, as the exordium tells us, God treats each man according to his merits.

Syntactic complexity is not desired; words are arranged to make pleasurable verbal harmonies, or in this case, painful cadences.

Celestis altitudo, addressed to Frederick by Honorius in January 1227, again illustrates the practice of enhancing the persuasiveness of an appeal by interpreting its spiritual significance. The pope requests grain to feed the Romans in a season of famine. The matter is more mundane and immediate than the conquest of the Holy Land, and Honorius's appeal to Frederick is at once based on the salvation of his soul and more pragmatic arguments like the charity that every man naturally owes his brother, the memory of Frederick's ancestors' largesse, the gratitude that the Roman people will show Frederick when he responds generously, and, most significantly, the fact that the good will of the papacy depends on a beneficent imperial response.

A poor harvest is explained as God's way of instructing men on Christian charity, making the emperor's donation of wheat a spiritual imperative. The exordium is structured around verbal figures, in this case anaphora (nunc . . . nunc . . .) and polyptoton (egentes faciens habundare, habundentes egere).

Celestis altitudo consilii alta et ineffabili pietate universa disponens rerum vicissitudines non sine dispositione certe rationis alternat, nunc egentes faciens habundare, nunc habundantes egere, ut humana conditio per alternationem huiusmodi seculi sui status instabilitatem agnoscat, et alter alteri compatienti subveniens impleat legem Christi, quia jubemur proximos nostros diligere et alter alterius honera supportare.[6]

The loftiness of celestial purpose, disposing the inconstancy of things with ineffable universal mercy, does not alternate without a definite purpose, now making what is scarce abundant, now what is abundant scarce, so that humankind might know by vicissitudes the instability of its own state, and each man might compassionately fulfill the law of Christ by succoring his brother, because we are ordered to love our neighbor and to uphold one another's honor.

The polyptoton within an anaphora becomes a verbal icon of mutability in the unchanging empyrean, a theme reinforced by verbal play on *altus* and *alter.*

The remainder of the letter presents a series of reasons why Frederick should react charitably in this time of distress; those who hoard grain and claim indigence will be damned. A scene of the desperation of the Roman people and of Honorius's sorrow at his own inability to relieve the hunger adds pathos.

> Urgente igitur necessariorum inopia, confluunt ad nos populi multitudo quos sine lacrymis audire non possumus, alimenta deposcens, et nec aliter quam si lapides convertere possimus in panem aut in farinam terre pulverem commutare.

> Consequently, with this pressing scarcity of necessities, a multitude of people, whom we cannot hear without weeping, converge on us. They beseech us for food, as if we could convert stones to bread and dust to flour.

Honorius reminds Frederick of the liberality of his predecessors who had responded to the entreaties by popes Alexander and Lucius in times of famine, and he assumes that Frederick will demonstrate the same generosity and compassion. The letter closes with a threat: the faith and goodwill which the papacy has always shown to Frederick depends upon his munificence, and will be withdrawn should the emperor harden his heart in this time of distress. But again, the essential spiritual message, the most important reason for Frederick to respond to the papal appeal, is stated in the exordium.

Non dubitat, written in January 1227, shortly before the pope's death, highlights another contrast between Honorius and his predecessor. In the letter Honorius admonishes Frederick for alienating his father-in-law, John of Brienne, formerly the Regent King of Jerusalem, and announces that he is sending an envoy to settle the matter. Frederick had claimed the title of King of Jerusalem for himself on the eve of his marriage to John's daughter, Isabella-Yolanda. The papacy did not recognize Frederick's title until 1231. Honorius's protest opens:

> Non dubitat, sicut credimus, tua serenitas quin te sincero diligamus affectu et quin ad incrementum tui honoris ac nominis aspiremus: unde cum ea tue celsitudini suademus que ad honorem tuum novimus pertinere, debes suasiones nostras gratanter accipere ac eis

acquiescere reverenter. Sane charissimo in Christo filio nostro Johanne illustri rege Hierosolymitano tue sublimitati affinitate conjuncto, communis fuit omnium vox et opinio, quod quasi in immensum successisset eidem et quod Deus ipsam sublimitatem eius per affinitatem tanti principis magnifice sublimasset. Nec mirum si hoc homines crediderunt, considerantes hinc excellentie tue potentiam, cui esse facile cognoscebant non solum in sua sublimitate conservare sublimes, sed etiam humiles novis honoribus sublimare, illinc vero strenuitatem et industriam dicti regis, non solum dignam ut ei suum conservares honorem, sed ut illum etiam ampliares.[7]

There is no doubt, as we believe, that we love your highness with sincere affection and that we aspire to enhance your honor and name: whence, when we urge your highness in that way we know to pertain to your honor, you ought to gratefully accept our exhortations and reverently acquiesce to them. Given that our son John, beloved of Christ, illustrious king of Jerusalem, is related to your highness by marriage, the voice of all and the common opinion was that it seemed as if it had come about on high, and that God himself had exalted John's majesty because of the likeness of such magnificent princes. Nor was it astonishing that men believed this, considering the authority of your excellency, which they knew made it easy for you not only to promote your own eminence, but also to elevate the humble with new honors, and thus with what is called the zeal and industry of a king, you would not only preserve worthy honor as he does, but you would even increase it.

The interpretation with which papal secretaries had previously, in *Justus Dominus,* endowed Frederick's marriage to Isabella-Yolanda, is now attributed to the people—and the transfer allows the pope to avoid a direct attack against Frederick, at least in the opening salvo of his letter. On the contrary, phonic and verbal repetition (Non . . . quin . . . quin; honoris . . . honorem; suademus . . . suasiones; accipere ac . . . acquiescere; charissimo in Christo conjuncto, communis; omnium vox et opinio; successisset . . . sublimitatem . . . sublimasset; crediderunt, considerantes . . . cui . . . cognoscebant; non solum in sua sublimitate conservare sublimes, sed . . . sublimare) resound the glad tidings of papal love and concern for Frederick's nobility. The ornament is a guarantee of the solemnity, honor, and respect with which the papacy regards its prince.

"But behold!" Honorius expresses his surprise that those expectations, so widely shared, have been thwarted by Frederick, and that a king who had counted on elevation through the marriage of his daughter to the emperor has instead been treated shabbily. In a passage that calls to mind Innocent's *Post miserabile,* where the voice of the infidel mocks and jeers Christian cowardice,[8] Honorius invokes the voice of the people.

> Omnes qui hec audiunt vehementer admirantur et dicunt "Que est hec imperialis industrie providentia alienasse a se tante prudentie, tante strenuitatis, tante industrie, tanti consilii virum et tanto sibi vinculo copulatum, de quo poterat tanquam de semet ipso confidere, cuius honorem et statum deberet proprium reputare? Cui fiducilius poterit regnum Hierosolymitanum committere? Quis fidelibus ibi existentibus gratiosior? Quis terribilior infidelibus? Quis utilior toti negotio Terre Sancte?" . . . Hec et similia parvi loquuntur et magni, admirantes super huiusmodi facto et illud, ut loquamur verius, detestantes.

> All who heard this were astonished and said, "Where is the foresight in the emperor's actions that have alienated from himself so much prudence, so much alacrity, so much industry; a man of such deliberation, who is thus united with him, in whom he might confide as if with himself, whose honor and condition he should regard like his own? Whom could he commission more confidently than the King of Jerusalem? Who is more beloved to the faithful there? Who more terrible to the infidel? Who more useful to whole Holy Land enterprise?" . . . This and similar words were said by the small and great, wondering over this kind of event and, to speak more truly, abhorring it.

Honorius continues with an evocation of the situation in the Holy Land, and emphasizes the absurdity of the imperial insult to John, given the common Christian goal of reclaiming the land where Christ had walked. We may assume that Frederick and John were reconciled, at least briefly, during the last months of 1227, because the latter, "'moved by natural piety', expressed his willingness to release to

Frederick the 50,000 silver marks given him by Philip Augustus to be employed in the recovery of the Holy Land."[9] Ultimately, however, they were so far from rapprochement that when Pope Gregory sought a military commander to lead the invasion of the Kingdom of Sicily to oust Frederick, he turned to John, and John accepted the commission.

Justus Dominus, Celestis altitudo, and *Non dubitat* adhere to the traditional persuasive strategy of the *artes dictandi.* Persuasion is balanced between the vigor of the major premise of the letter and the expression of goodwill between the parties. Ornamentation further enhances the appeal. Secondary reasons, including the approbation or disapproval of others, reinforce the main argument. To the extent that the addressee was willing to attend and heed the papal will, the approach was effective. But even fortified by the holy father's words of praise and affection, or a logical legerdemain like that contained in *Quanto personam,* such appeals fell short when the vision and goals of the correspondents did not coincide, and were even less effective where there was serious conflict or deep distrust between the parties. When persuasion fails, stronger measures are invoked, and many letters issued from the papacy conclude with a threat of legal redress if the desired action is not promptly executed.

By 1225, the imperial posture of humility and gratitude vis-à-vis the supreme pontiff that characterizes letters written on the eve of the coronation and immediately thereafter is abandoned. The imperial chancery experimented with a more aggressive tone as Frederick saw his ambitions outside the Kingdom of Sicily thwarted by the papacy. Van Cleve writes that the imperial chancery began to portray the pope was "not as a bona-fide spiritual leader, but as a temporal rival demanding supervisory rights over all states and all temporal po'icies."[10] After 1225 Frederick's alliance with the church becomes one of accommodation based on self-interest, expressed respectfully, and even celebrated in the ongoing epistolary exchange, but periodically interrupted by manifestos intended to drive a stake into the heart of the thirteenth-century doctrine of papal plenitude of power.

In a letter that is not extant, Frederick challenged papal objections to his treatment of the Sicilian church during the years that followed the Roman coronation, and, more audaciously, the emperor raised doubts about papal tutelage of the Kingdom of Sicily during his minority.[11] It was the opening salvo of a new phase of the ongoing struggle that pitted secular rulers against a Roman church that sought both to reform ecclesiastical jurisdiction in Latin Christendom and define the jurisdiction of the secular rulers in its own terms. This reform was attempted in various ways including consultations, epistolary exchanges between the parties, appeals for support addressed to other princes and prelates of Christian Europe, legal and spiritual measures like interdiction, excommunication, and deposition, and military battles. From the conflict, an important secondary debate about the appropriate method to interpret events emerged, as the papal-imperial correspondence of the 1230s makes clear.

Miranda tuis, directed to the emperor in May or June 1226, launches a two-pronged attack: Frederick's ingratitude is thoroughly denounced in language that is bitter and laden with pain, and the pope responds directly to Frederick's provocative thesis with a detailed accounting of papal assistance provided to Frederick during his minority and afterwards. According to the papal letter, the emperor's ingratitude has numbed his heart and distorted his reason, which the particulars of the narration prove. It opens with an ironic statement of astonishment: "Miranda tuis sensibus nostra venit epistola ut scripsisti, sed mirabilior tua nostris" [As you wrote that our letter is astounding for you, we read yours with even greater astonishment].

Frederick's examination of church charters and his presumption in reassessing church history in Sicily during his minority are sinful exhibitions of pride. Honorius begs Frederick to adopt a more humble and obedient posture.

> Recogita, fili karissime, et intra claustra tui pectoris frequenti meditatione revolve quam parvum, quam depressum te illie summus pontifex post obitum matris accepit, quam grandem quamque promotum in sua morte reliquit.

> Dearest son, reconsider, turning with frequent meditation to the innermost chamber of your breast, how small, how low you were after the death of your mother, when the high pope took you up, and how grand and elevated he left you at his death.

The pope's supplication is structured anaphorically (quam parvum . . . quam depressum . . . quam grandem quamque promotum) and antithetically (parvum . . . depressum . . . grandem . . . promotum; te. . . ille summus pontifex; post obitum matris . . . in sua morte; accepit . . .

reliquit), and laced with alliteration and assonance—but it seems likely that the ornament and the traditional exhortation of humility failed to move Frederick.

Honorius will counter Frederick's arguments with evidence from the papal archives.[12] It has been suggested that Honorius, in his willingness to seek common ground with the emperor, demonstrates an unusual degree of pragmatism.[13] Whether it is his pragmatism or his faith in Frederick, the vitality of the letter is provided by Honorius's belief that a rational exchange is possible. As Frederick's father and master, he must make him understand the Truth within him. Honorius demands to know why the emperor's account of events is so seriously distorted.

> Unde igitur tam contraria istis, tam novella processit opinio? Unde presumptio tam adversa et tam repentina prorupit? Si enim frequens missio litterarum comitem conscientiam mittentis habebat, cum nulla subsecuta sit causa nove scientie nec scientia nove cause, calumpniose impungitur quod evidentia facti non patitur? Cur sub quodam involucro duplicitatis infertur quod rei simplicitas non admittit?

> From whence does such contradiction, so new an opinion, proceed? From whence does such a presumption, so adverse and so sudden, come forth? If truly, the frequent exchange of letters expressed the conscience of the sender, when nothing subsequent is the cause of this new "science" nor "science" of this new complaint, why attack with calumnies what the evidence of fact does not permit? Why does [your contradiction] hide beneath a cover of duplicity that which the simplicity of the situation does not admit?

Facti evidentia is a legal, procedural term, but its significance extends beyond the legal and forms the basis of persuasive argument as well.[14] Honorius's use of *scientia* is mocking and ironic; this is a *scientia* that is not based on *facti evidentia;* it is opinion or conjecture. His outright rejection of *novella opinio* becomes a clarion call in the epistolary battle that is beginning: from Honorius's standpoint, there can be no such rewriting of history, no questioning of motives.[15] The pope's anger is conveyed by the sharp rhetorical questions, repetition, and figures like polyptoton and antithesis that reinforce the tone of ridicule

(Unde . . . tam . . . tam . . . processit. Unde presumptio tam . . . prorupit
. . . missio litterarum comitem conscientiam mittentis habebat . . . causa
nove scientie nec scientia nove cause). The opposition between
involucro duplicitatis and *rei simplicitas* encapsulates Honorius's
condemnation of imperial rhetoric.

Yet another torrent of outraged indignation at Frederick's failure to
perceive that his election depends entirely upon the benevolence of the
papacy follows. Frederick's ingratitude will undermine his relations
with others.

> Ha Deus! que in tali filio spei reliquie aliis relinquuntur, si mater tam
> diligens desperare cogatur? Ha Deus! que in tali pupillo fragmenta
> favoris ceteri colligent, si tutrix tam utilis iaculis detractionis
> impetitur? Ha Deus! quot et quantos labores amisit Ecclesia, si
> palmes quem multo sudore plantavit et coluit in amaritudinem vitis
> convertitur aliene, cum sit minoris dispendii fructus nullos producere
> quam nocivos! O quam uberes lacrymas, quam amaras felicis
> recordationis Innocentius papa predecessor noster multoties pro te
> fudit! O quanta sollicitudine laboravit ut te a nocentium eriperet
> manibus et insidiantium laqueis liberaret et quasi de mortis faucibus
> extorqueret! Ecce quid retributionis eidem imperialis excellentia
> affert! Ecce quid regalis magnificentia recompensat, dum pupilli vite
> insidiator occultus dicitur et bonorum tacitus spoliator!

> Ha Deus! what shreds of hope are left for others in such a son if such
> a loving mother is forced to despair? Ha Deus! what fragments of
> favor may be gleaned from such a ward, if so useful a tutrix is
> attacked with ravaging blows? Ha Deus! how many and what labors
> the church wasted, if the young shoot that it planted and cultivated
> with much effort is perversely changed into a bitter vine, when it
> takes less expense to grow none than harmful fruit? Oh what great
> tears, what bitter tears Pope Innocent our predecessor of happy
> memory so often shed for you! Oh with what great care did he labor
> so that you would be snatched from harm's hands, liberated from
> evil's snares and virtually wrenched from death's jaws. Look at the
> excellence of the imperial appreciation you offer to him! This is the
> regal magnificence with which you repay him, as if he were a man
> who lay in ambush for the pupil to secretly despoil him of his goods.

The church patiently cultivated its vines but she harvested bitter fruit. Papal care for the young Frederick is expressed in an accumulation intended to heighten the emotional response to the situation, and the generic descriptions of cultivation are amplified almost to the point of absurdity in the last clause (cum sit minoris dispendii fructus nullos producere quam nocivos). The great Innocent is portrayed as the child's protector, who labored for him, snatched him from danger, and guarded him from evil. Honorius begs Frederick to understand the truth about his elevation in stark and dramatic terms. The passage is richly illustrated with the verbal and phonic ornament (Ha Deus! que in tali filio . . . Ha Deus! que in tali pupilo; reliquie . . . relinquuntur; diligens desperare; cogatur . . . ceteri colligent, fragmenta favoris), endowing the pope's reproachful words with a musical quality intended, perhaps, to stir the emperor's soul.

Miranda tuis continues with a historical narrative, some of which I include here to show how soberly and thoroughly each event is treated. It is only occasionally punctuated with angry and threatening exclamations. Honorius uses his reading of recent history to appeal to the reason of the emperor, to attempt to teach and to make Frederick aware of the consequences of the disobedience of his imperial predecessors. The details are more precise and extensive than in the preceding passages.

With respect to the succession of the imperial crown, which Frederick's letter must have claimed was nearly lost to the youth after his father's death because of Innocent's political machinations, Honorius reminds Frederick that the emperor is elected by the Palatine princes, not selected by the pope, and that Philip of Swabia had failed to secure the election of the child. The German princes had instead chosen Otto, and it was the papacy that rescued Frederick from the perilous seas into which he had been tossed by the election of the impious Otto, and the papacy that had provided for him at every point. The description of both the procedure of imperial elections and the events that took place gives a sense of the cautionary tone of the letter.

Circa hominem si quidem alienum quem in patris tui sede, si tamen sedes patris dici debeat que non successionis, sed electionis jure defertur, erectum fuisse per Ecclesiam predixeras, tua utinam adversus Ecclesiam substitisset inventio, eo quo veritas negata de publicis minus reliquit fidei de occultis. Nullum enim angulum latet imperii quod, imperatore Henrico defuncto, quidam Philippo duci Suevie, quidam Ottoni postmodum imperatori divisis, voluntatibus adheserunt. . . . Predicto tandem Philippo sublato de medio, Ottoni quem omnium principium roborata consensibus presentabat electio, nec expedivit ne licuit diadema imperii denegrare: qui procul dubio, ut scripsisti, subito factus ingratus tergum, non faciem vertit Ecclesie, immemor preceptorum et quamvis eam multis provocaverit offensis, dissimulabat eas utcumque misericordis Ecclesie patientia consueta.

Concerning the other man whom you claimed to have been elevated by the church to the throne of your father, if indeed that which is legally conferred by election may be called a hereditary throne, I only wish your invention against the church might be sustained, for the more the truth is denied in public, the more tightly it is held by the faithful in secret. Truly the point is not concealed from your majesty that, the emperor Henry dead, a certain Philip, duke of Swabia, shortly thereafter, was contested by a certain Otto. The above mentioned Philip succumbed suddenly; the election of Otto was supported by all the princes, lest the crown be allowed to grow weak, Otto, who, as you have written, with acts of ingratitude immediately turned not his face but his back to the church, and oblivious to his masters, provoked the church with many offenses, and hid these in one way or another from the long-standing suffering of the merciful church.

Other points of contention are addressed, including the agreement on filling the bishoprics in the Sicilian church, the ecclesiastical officials accused of criminal behavior by Frederick, the renewal of the law of Sicily, and the fact that the crusade vow remains unfulfilled. The church's right to protect its prerogatives and patrimony is vigorously defended, and Honorius pleads that Frederick understand the role of his ancestors in defending the church.

Verum si scripta tua et genitricis tue manu sollicitudinis revolvisses, si sanctorum etiam patrum constitutiones adverteres, non culpares Ecclesiam circa defensionem ecclesiastice libertatis, cum non debeat de justicie persecutione morderi qui contendere nititur de abusu. Asseris nos insuper preter formam communiter requisitam, te inconsulto quibusdam regni ecclesiis prefecisse personas vacantibus,

que profecto minus esset informis per quam apostolice Sedis
judicium ex tue voluntatis arbitrio dependeret.

Truly if you turned, on your own, to your writings and the writings of
your solicitous paternal ancestors, if you heeded the constitutions of
your holy fathers, you would not blame the church for defending its
liberty, since the man who strives to counter abuse in the pursuit of
justice does not injure reputations. You claim that we, against
custom, preferred men to certain vacant churches in the kingdom
without consulting you, which no doubt is less heinous than if the
judgment of the Apostolic See depended on your own exercise of
will.

Honorius does not write to incite an emotional response, but to set the
historical record straight, based on the evidence of fact. Nevertheless,
he warns that just as the hand of God can elevate, so can it bring down
the proud.

Quia vero non est abbreviata manus Domini adeo quod non possit
sublimitatem incurvare potentum et altitudinem humiliare virorum,
nunc cum felicium tuis votis successum splendor illuxerit, in sereno
humilitatem non deseras quam in nubilo pretendebas.

The hand of the Lord has not yet become so weak that it is unable to
destroy the haughty and to humble the arrogance of the mighty. In the
lustrous moment of success, therefore, do not depart from the
humility that you displayed in adversity.[16]

Honorius, Frederick's father and master, implores his pupil to recognize
the truth within his mind and heart, and to return to the paths of
righteousness. At the conclusion, Honorius reminds Frederick of the
glorious deeds of his ancestors once again, and again protests
Frederick's unworthiness and essential lack of honesty.[17]

From the first to the last sentence of this long and bitter letter,
Miranda tuis attacks Frederick's interpretation of recent history.
Honorius's premise is that there can be no *novella opinio,* no
interpretation of recent events other than that which he has taken pains
to recount. Unless Frederick obediently embraces his role of *advocatus*
and *defensor ecclesiae,* he runs the risk of losing his high office (the

text reads, "Quum enim advocatus Ecclesie idem intelligi debat quam defensor, si defensoris omittis officium, nomen improprie ritenes advocati"). While Honorius sets the record straight, his intention is much more profound. He seeks to humble the emperor, to lead Frederick back to the posture and rhetoric of submission and gratitude that the emperor displayed at the time of his coronation in 1220. If Frederick is truly worthy of his office, then his own mind and heart will teach him that ingratitude has perverted his perception and reason and that it threatens his salvation.

We do not have the imperial letter that angered Honorius, but many epistles of the second half of the 1220s are remarkable for the way in which detailed accounts of events function to justify actions taken or proposed. The role of Honorius in spurring the development of a new approach to persuasion is difficult to define; it may have been encouraged both by Honorius's apparent willingness to negotiate, and by attitudes like that expressed in *Miranda tuis,* which emphatically deny the legitimacy of any partisan challenge to the "official" reading of events. *Miranda tuis* marks a kind of boundary; henceforth at least one thread of the papal-imperial correspondence will be focused on the significance of specific historical events. The papal rejection of debate does not silence the imperial chancery; on the contrary, it drives the chancellors to take more aggressive stands regarding recent history in letters like *Inter ceteris,* addressed to the King of England in December 1227, in which a distinctly anticlerical proposition is made in relation to several secular princes who had recently surrendered their autonomy to the Roman See.[18]

The distrust and dissension that emerged by the middle of the 1220s make traditional persuasive modes inadequate. One of the reasons for the development of the new approach to persuasion must have been to galvanize public opinion in situations of serious conflict. The imperial chancery's assault on the vision of history promoted by the church is inseparable from the development of a competing persuasive strategy that relies to a greater extent on "evident motives, supported by reason," to cite Matthew Paris.[19] Honorius is regarded as too compromising by historians, but his essential willingness to seek common ground to persuade the increasingly alienated emperor may have played some part in the genesis of the new paradigm.

Honorius's successor, Pope Gregory IX, will take the argument of ingratitude and the inadequacies of imperial rhetoric much further. In *Si memoriam* he proposes that ingratitude born of pride has rendered the emperor irrational, and he offers recent imperial letters as proof. In *Ascendit,* Gregory argues that Frederican letters distort reality because the emperor is a heretic who has alienated himself from the Logos, and the potential for verbal persuasion to bring about accommodation and accord is essentially extinguished at that point.

NOTES

1. Schaller, Hans Martin, "Die Kanzlei Kaiser Friedrichs II., ihr Personal und ihr Sprachstil 2," *Archiv für Diplomatik* 4 (1958): 278-79.

2. As Innocent writes in *Quia major,* issued from the Curia in April 1213 at the time of the summons to the Fourth Lateran Council: "Si enim rex aliquis temporalis a suis hostibus ejiceretur de regno, nisi vassalli eius pro eo non solum res exponerent, sed personas, nonne cum regnum recuperaret amissum, eos velut infideles damnaret, et excogitaret in eos inexcogitata tormenta, quibus perderet male malos? Sic Rex regnum, Dominus Jesus Christus, qui corpus et animam et cetera vobis contulit bona, de ingratitudinis vitio et infidelitatis crimine vos damnabit, si ei quasi ejecto de regno, quod pretio sui sanguinis comparavit, neglexeritis subvenire" (J.-P. Migne, Ed., *Patrologie cursus completus,* Series Latina 216 [Paris: Garnier, 1890] cols. 817-21). In *Post miserabile* Innocent pleads: "Ecce enim hereditas nostra versa est ad alienos, domus nostre ad extraneos devenerunt . . ." (Othmar Hageneder and Anton Haidacher, Eds., *Die Register Innocenz' III* 1. Publikationen der Abteilung für historische Studien des Österreichischen Kulturinstituts in Rom, 2nd ser., sect. 1 [Graz: Hermann Bohlaus, 1964] 498-505).

3. *Justus Dominus* is printed in J.-L. A. Huillard-Bréholles, *Historia diplomatica Friderici Secundi* 3.1 (Paris: H. Plon, 1852-1861) 376. The version of the letter included Huillard-Bréholles is addressed to King Philip of France.

4. The figure "post . . . post . . . post . . . ," to deepen the pain of a defeat is not original. See, for example, Innocent's *Post miserabile,* Hageneder and Haidacher, 1, 498-505.

5. The chief official in Honorius's chancery was Thomas of Capua, author of the first successful thirteenth-century ecclesiastical *Ars Dictandi*—as well as a *Summa* of traditional persuasion that included both instructions and a large collection of letters. See Chapter 1, note 3, and Chapter 2, note 7 of this book.

6. *Celestis altitudo* is edited in Huillard-Bréholles, 2.2, 710.

7. *Non dubitat* is edited in Huillard-Bréholles, 2.2, 708-10.

8. The passage to which I refer reads, "quod jam insultant nobis inimici nostri dicentes: 'Ubi est Deus vester, qui nec se potest nec vos de nostris manibus liberare? Ecce jam prophanavimus sancta vestra, ecce iam ad desiderabilia vestra manum extendimus et ea loca impetu primo violenter invasimus et vobis tenemus invitis, in quibus superstitionem vestram principium fingitis suscepisse. Jam infirmavimus et confregimus astas Gallorum, Anglorum conatus elisimus, Teutonicorum vires compressimus nunc secundo, Hispanos domuimus animosos. Et cum omnes virtutes vestras in nos duxeritis concitandas, vix adhuc in aliquo profecistis. Ubi ergo est Deus vester? Exurgat nunc et adiuvet vos et fiat vobis et sibi protector. Teutonici siquidem, qui se presumebant inauditum de nobis reportare triumphum, ad nos vehementi spiritu transfretarunt: et cum solum castrum Baruth nullo defendente cepissent, nisi eos sicut et alios principes vestros fuge beneficium liberasset, in se potentiam nostram graviter fuissent experti et eorum stragem ipsorum soboles perpetuo deploraret. Reges enim et principes vestri, quos dudum de terra fugavimus Orientis, ut timorem suum audendo dissimulent, ad suas latebras, ne dicamus regna, reversi, malunt se invicem expugnare quam denuo vires nostras et potentiam experiri. Quid igitur superest, nisi ut—hiis, quos fugientes in excusationem vestram ad terre custodiam dimisistis, gladio ultore peremptis— in terram vestram impetum faciamus, nomen vestrum et memoriam perdituri?'" Hageneder and Haidacher, 1, 500.

9. Thomas Curtis Van Cleve, *The Emperor Frederick II of Hohenstaufen, Immutator Mundi* (Oxford: Clarendon Press, 1972) 189.

10. Van Cleve 171. An example of a humble exordium is found in *Exhibitam nobis,* addressed to Honorius in 1220, on the eve of Frederick's Roman coronation. The document is discussed in Chapter 7 of this book.

11. We know this from the papal letter of response, *Miranda tuis. Miranda tuis* is in Huillard-Bréholles, 2.2, 589-99. All that we know of Frederick's letter comes from the passages cited by Honorius, for example, "Adjecisti preterea quod post reditum tuum in regunum Sicilie, reintegratis juribus tuis pro temporum varietate dispersis et exclusis rebellibus, dicis ecclesiam contra matris officium suspectos filios receptasse."

12. The text reads, "Tue quidem tenor epistole continebat, quod preter omnium opinionem et consilia principum, ut tuis verbis utamur, te invenerimus ad nostra beneplacita paratum, ita ut nullus predecessorum tuorum nullis retroactis temporibus recolatur adeo Ecclesie fuisse devotus ut tu. Sed de principibus tuis non aliter ex hiis verbis informabimus animum quam probabilis credulitas habeat facti experimento probata. De quibus Apostolice Sedis constantia recte opinionis judicium sinistre suggestionis instancia non mutabit,

cum facta preferenda sint dictis et certa prejudicent positivis. Ecce de archivo ecclesie publica monimenta prodeunt, que singulorum pene omnium principum munita sigillis opinionem repudiant quam forte videris ingerere contra illos, eo quod verisimilitudo non tales et tantos viros patitur excellentie tue dedisse consilium contrarium scripto tui et ipsorum signato signaculis" [Your letter implied that, contrary to everyone's expectations and the advice of princes, if we may use your words, you devoted yourself to our interests, so that not one of your predecessors in past years may be recalled to mind who was as dedicated to the Church as you. But regarding your princes, probable arguments will not change our opinion which is based on the proof of fact. For these reasons the constancy of the Apostolic See will not alter a correct judgment to an incorrect one because of your insistence, for facts must be preferred to declarations and facts that are certain demolish your arbitrary arguments. Here are the public documents from the ecclesiastic archives which, furnished with the seal of each and every prince, disprove the notion that you assert. Plausibility does not allow that so many and such great men offered advice to your imperial highness that is the opposite of their officially marked opinion].

13. David Abulafia, *Frederick II: A Medieval Emperor* (New York: Penguin, 1988) 161-62.

14. Lomax (John Phillip Lomax, *"Ingratus" or "Indignus": Canonistic Argument in the Conflict between Pope Gregory IX and Emperor Frederick II*, Diss., University of Kansas, 1987), explains the legal meaning of *evidentia facti* as the "widespread public knowledge of crime" (18) and more generally as the "evidence of the fact" (20).

15. Again the waning of Thomas of Capua comes to mind (See Chapter 1, note 36.)

16. The translation of this passage is borrowed from Van Cleve 174-75.

17. Van Cleve adds that "it is an extraordinary feature of this letter that Honorius pretends to be entirely oblivious of the role of his predecessor in attempting to force the election of Otto IV" Van Cleve 174.

18. See Chapter 2, note 21 in this book.

19. See Chapter 2, page 47 in this book.

CHAPTER 6

Limits of Persuasion at the Chancery of Gregory IX

Pope Gregory IX had been personally implicated in Frederick's failure to lead a Christian army into the Holy Land since the emperor delegated responsibility for the organization of the undertaking to him in 1221. Long before his ascension to the papal cathedra in 1227, Hugolinus Conti di Segni must have concluded that the *evidentia facti* proved Frederick's unworthiness of imperial honors, and as pope he seized the first available opportunity to act on his conviction.[1] In *In maris,* the Gregorian encyclical of excommunication dated October 1227, the pope endeavors not only to prove Frederick's guilt with respect to the specific excommunication charges, but more generally to persuade Christendom of the validity of his judgment of Frederick. Written nine years later, *Si memoriam,* the other letter discussed in this chapter, issues a clear warning to Frederick that a second excommunication is imminent. The rhetorical appeals as well as the legal arguments of *In maris* are intended for church and royal officials throughout Christendom. In *Si memoriam* the only public is the emperor and his court, yet again the pope operates on several levels: he provides requisite legal evidence and warning of charges that will result in excommunication if the emperor does not respond appropriately, and conflates them with powerful rhetorical appeals to persuade the imperial court of the gravity of the situation. Gregory's angry words are not balanced by intermittent professions of love for the sinner, as in Honorius's *Miranda tuis.* Lomax argues that Gregory sought not only the excommunication of Frederick in the 1227 encyclical *In maris,* but his deposition.[2] Three crimes could lead to deposition: ingratitude, heresy, and simony, and all three charges are made against the emperor in 1239. Although the charges that could lead to deposition are not included in the excommunication of 1227, papal disappointment and disgust with the emperor's ingratitude is a prominent theme.

The language of Pope Gregory's letters has been praised as the apex of medieval Christian style. It is interwoven with Biblical phrases and punctuated with emotional imagery and exclamations, but the verbal ornamentation is less elaborate than in the letters of his predecessors.[3] Schaller has shown that Gregory's chancellors, Dominican monks traditionally hostile to the liberal arts, resisted the verbal patterning associated with the Cistercians and the literary experimentation of the Loire schools.[4] Another way to understand the vigor of Gregory's correspondence concerning the emperor is that, unlike his predecessors, Gregory viewed Frederick as his enemy, and himself in the vanguard of a battle for the preservation of Christendom. That battle assumes Apocalyptic proportions at various points in his fourteen-year pontificate. The synthetic expression of power and love that characterized Innocent's letters is replaced by urgency and drama. Like Pope Honorius, Gregory demonstrates his awareness of the danger of rhetorical persuasion: he condemns imperial acts and he is equally aggressive in his censure of imperial words and arguments that exceed the confines imposed on Frederick as Christian emperor. Unlike Honorius, Gregory is less interested in responding to imperial communications than in censoring them, thereby limiting the harm he perceives they are causing in the courts of Europe and even in the streets of Rome.[5]

In maris devotes more energy and space to arousing a sense of indignation at Frederick's iniquity, and to moving church and royal officials to support the excommunication on an emotional level, than to the presentation of evidence pertinent to the legal charges levied against Frederick, which are placed at the very end of the long and highly dramatic piece of oratory.[6] The letter carries the Christian public from the depths of despair at the loss of Damietta to hope, and Frederick's ingratitude and immorality, signs of his unworthiness and the reason for Christian failure in the Holy Land, provide the principal theme. The turning point of the letter is Jeremiah's prophecy: Israel shall be restored! Christians will be redeemed from their disgrace! The upsurge from sin and despair to hope dominates the structure of the encyclical.

It opens with a traditional metaphor of an imperiled state: the ship of Peter is endangered and every prosperous breeze is beaten back by unfavorable winds. As the ship is about to capsize, the Lord, wakened by the clamor of His crew, calms the winds and waters. In language that extends the metaphor, the forces that threaten the church are enumerated.

Quatuor quidem procelle precipue quatiunt navim istam; nam perfidia paganorum terram inclytam Christi sanguine consecratam impie detinere contendit; rabies tyrannorum temporalia rapiens exterminat justitiam et conculcat ecclesiasticam libertatem; hereticorum insania Christi tunicam scindere nititur et subvertere fidei fundmentum; falsorum fratrum et filiorum dolosa perversitas concutit viscera et latus dilacerat matris sue.[7]

Four storms in particular rattle this ship; the treachery of the pagans who impiously grapple to hold on to the glorious land consecrated by the blood of Christ; the madness of tyrants who seize temporalia— banishing justice and trampling ecclesiastical liberty; the insanity of heretics who struggle to tear the tunic of Christ and subvert the foundation of faith, and the deceitful perversity of false brothers and sons who violate the womb and lacerates the flanks of the church.

The Bible is invoked ornamentally to express the peril of the church— "Sicque foris pugne, intus timores" (thus outwardly strong, within fearful) [2 Cor. 7:5]. An account of the church's long suffering, and the pains it has taken to nurture the emperor, follows. Frederick,

quem quasi a matris utero excepit genibus, lactavit uberibus, humeris bajulavit, de manibus querentium animam eius frequenter eripuit, educare studuit multis laboribus et expensis, usque ad virum perfectum deduxit . . . credens ipsum fore defensionis virgam et sue baculum senectutis.

whom almost from his mother's womb she took upon her lap, nursed at her breasts, bore on her shoulders, often snatched from grasping hands, labored to educate at great expense, until she had brought him to full manhood . . . believing that he would be her defending staff and cane in old age.

The mother's many sacrifices, her deception, and finally her fear are not included in *In maris* to be analyzed, but to shock the public into sympathy and to move lay and church officials to actively support the excommunication. The language also carried legal weight.[8]

The lament is not over: despite her great labors, the church has been cruelly deceived: "dum alere credit filios, nutrit in sinu ignem, serpentes et regulos, qui flatu, morsu, incendio cuncta vastare nituntur" (for when she thought she was nourishing a son, she nourished fire in her breast, serpents and dragons, who desired to devastate everything with breath and biting and fire). A recitation of the emperor's specific crimes follows, which serves as evidence to support accusations made against him at the conclusion of the letter. Frederick had voluntarily vowed to lead a crusade within a fixed period of time at the German coronation, and had been exuberantly praised and thanked by the church, but then he had sought to postpone the crusade.

> Nam sponte, non monitus, Sede apostolica ignorante, crucem suis humeris affixit, vovens solemniter se in terre sancte subsidium profecturum. Deinde se ac alios crucesignatos excommunicari obtinuit, nisi certo proficiscerentur tempore; sed incidenter absolutionem petiit et accepit, de parendo super hoc mandatis Ecclesie prius prestito juramento.

> In fact, spontaneously, unexhorted, unbeknownst to the Apostolic See, he affixed the cross to his shoulder, solemnly vowing to serve personally in the Holy Land. Then, he held that other crusaders and he be excommunicated if they did not serve within a specified time, but briefly he petitioned and was granted absolution, seeking the opinion of the church before swearing the oath.

The pope includes an account of the Roman vow that followed Aachen, remembered and described with a solemnity that reestablishes its sacral nature and inseparability from Frederick's imperial honor.

> Tandem cum de manibus felicis recordationis Honorii pape, predecessoris nostri, in beati Petri basilica recepisset imperii diadema, de manibus nostri, tunc in minori officio constitutis, crucem resumpsit, votum publice innovavit, plures de spe sui subsidii ad crucem suscipiendam induxit, certum recepit terminum transfretandi.

Finally when he [Frederick] received the imperial diadem from the hands of our predecessor, Pope Honorius of blessed memory, in the sacred basilica of Peter, he again took the cross from our hands, [we being] then appointed to a lesser office. He renewed the vow and inspired many to take up the cross in the hope of his assistance. He was told to make the crossing within a certain period of time.

The passage reminds Christians that the imperial crown (as well as the privilege to lead a crusade) depends entirely on the disposition of the papacy. It also conveys a sense of Gregory's personal involvement, a sense that Frederick's failure to honor his vow implicates Gregory, who had presided over the sacred swearing of the oath. The terms of the vow at San Germano, in the presence of many prelates and German princes, are also recounted.[9] The date by which the crusade was to have been undertaken, the number of soldiers, the number of ships, and the sum of money to be committed by the emperor all stand to condemn Frederick. Then the letter immediately takes an ironic turn. "But be advised how he fulfilled his vow":

Nam cum ad eius frequentem instantiam multa crucesignatorum millia per excommunicationis sententiam coarctata in termino destinato ad portum Brundussii properassent . . . ipse omnium promissorum que apostolice Sedi et crucesignatis per letteras suas fecerat de sponsione passagii, necessariorum et victus, et sue salutis immemor, tamdiu in estivi fervoris incendio in regione mortis et aeris corruptela detinuit exercitum christianum, quod non solum magna pars plebis, verum etiam non modica multitudo nobilium et magnatum pestilentia, sitis ariditate et multis incommoditatibus expiravit.

In fact, at his frequent urging, many thousands of crusaders hastened to the port of Brindisi within the designated term, pressed by the sentence of excommunication, . . . he, unmindful of his promise of passage, of necessities and victuals, and of his own salvation, detained the army of Christians so long in the deadly region and corrupt air, that not only a large number of the common people but indeed not a few of the multitude of nobles and lords expired from the pestilence, thirst, and many aggravating circumstances.

Among the dead is the Landgrave of Thuringia. Others fled to the cooler hills and forests to die. As for the emperor himself:

> Idem vero evacuatis promissionibus, ruptis vinculis quibus tenebatur astrictus, calcato timore divino, contempta reverentia Jesu Christi, censura ecclesiastica vilipensa, derelicto exercitu christiano, exposita infidelibus terra sancta, devotione populi christiani abjecta, in suum et totius christianitatis opprobrium retrorsum abiit, attractus et illectus ad consuetas delicias regni sui, abjectionem sui cordis frivolis excusationibus, ut dicitur, gestiens palliare.

> The same [Frederick] with empty promises, breaking the vows by which he was strictly held, trampling divine love, disdaining reverence for Jesus Christ, despising ecclesiastic censure, abandoning the Christian army, exposing the Holy Land to the infidel and denigrating the devotion of the Christian people, turned his back and went away, bringing shame upon himself and all his kingdom, attracted and enticed to the customary pleasures of his kingdom, masking with excuses the abjection of his frivolous heart, as they say.

Frederick is responsible for the disease and death in the Christian camp. In order to return to his habitual pleasures, Frederick has violated his pact with God and the Christian people. The relentless accumulation of details, each condensed into a brief clause, builds to an emotional peak. The emperor's illness, in fact a valid reason for postponing a crusade, is dismissed as the spiritual illness of a sinner.

But the jeremiad of the church is not over. "Attendite et videte, si est dolor sicut dolor apostolice Sedis matris vestre, sic crudeliter et toties decepte a filio. . . ." [Heed and see if there is sorrow like the sorrow of the Apostolic See, your mother, thus cruelly and so often deceived by her son . . .]. Not the phonic and figural complexity of Innocent and Honorius, but the echo of a Biblical lament structures the prose: the church weeps for the part of the crusading army that, without a leader, is lost at sea. The church moans for the destruction of the Holy Land that it had hoped to reclaim from pagan hands. All men groan with despair at the state of Christendom, just as the inconsolable Rachel wept at the massacre of her innocent sons.

Cum ergo vox eius jam in Rama insonuerit, et Rachel non solum filios, sed hec omnia irremediabili lamentatione deploret, quis fidelium se a gemitibus et suspiriis continebit? quis filiorum cernens acquarum profluvia matris oculis prodeuntia lacrymas non effundet? quis matris non compatietur angustiis, nec immensis eius doloribus condolebit? quis fidelium propter hoc non ardentius inflammabitur ad subsidium terre sancte, ne christiana juventus ex insperato casu prostrata penitus videatur et ignominiose animo consternata?

So when his voice has sounded in Rama, and Rachel weeps not only for her sons but for all those that are lost, who among the faithful will contain his groans and sighs? Who among the sons, seeing tears flow from the eyes of the mother, will not shed tears? Which mother will not suffer from this distress, not feel great sympathy? Who among the faithful will not burn more ardently to go to the assistance of the Holy Land, lest Christian youth be deeply abased and ignobly devastated by this unfortunate situation?

The climactic accumulation of rhetorical questions joined by anaphora (quis fidelium . . . quis filiorum . . . quis matris . . . quis fidelium) lead to but one possible conclusion.

Failure in the Holy Land is explained as the expression of God's anger at the immorality of the secular leader of Christendom, the emperor Frederick. And yet there is hope. From despair and ignominy, Christians will rise up and be saved—if they are willing to repudiate Frederick.

Etsi enim Dominus populo suo modicum ostenderit se iratum, de illius manu hoc tempore sacrificium non acceptans. . . . Speramus namque in misericordia Dei nostri quod viam nobis ostendet per quam in hoc negotio prospere gradiamur, et viros secundum cor suum Ecclesie designabit qui precedant in cordis puritate ac manuum munditia exercitum christianum.

And so indeed God has shown His people that He is angered, not accepting at this time the sacrifice from his [Frederick's] hand. . . . And indeed we place our hope in the mercy of our God, that He will show to us the way by which we may move prosperously in this enterprise, and will designate men of the church according to His

will, who will lead the army of Christians with purity of heart and
cleanliness of hand.

Frederick is not the pious son and defender of the church but an abject
sinner who brings shame and opprobrium to all.

The letter ends with a repetition of the legal grounds on which the
emperor is excommunicate. Even these charges are presented in a
package bound by anaphora, suggesting the inevitable condemnation of
the emperor.

> Porro ne tanquam canes muti, non valentes latrare [Isaiah 56:10],
> videamur deferre homini contra Deum, non sumentes ultionem de illo
> qui tantam ruinam in Dei populo procuravit, imperatorem Fridericum
> qui nec transfretavit in termino, nec illuc . . . prescriptam pecuniam
> destinavit, nec duxit mille milites per biennium tenendos ibidem ad
> suum pro subsidio terre sancte, sed in his tribus articulis manifeste
> deficiens in excommunicationis descripte laqueum ultroneus se
> ingessit. . . .

> But on the other hand, lest like dumb dogs without the strength to
> bark, we seem to defer to a man against God, not taking vengeance
> on him who has brought about such great ruin among the people of
> God, the emperor Frederick who did not sail in time, nor send money
> to that place . . . , nor lead a thousand soldiers, maintaining them
> there for two years for the assistance of the Holy Land, but in these
> three articles obviously deficient, stepped freely into the snare of
> excommunication. . . .

Frederick has not fulfilled his vow to lead an army of soldiers into the
Holy Land within a prescribed time, and to send money and ships.
Abulafia neatly sums up the last part of the papal accusation in a
parenthesis, "(Actually, he had: but Gregory's rhetoric took charge of
the facts.)"[10] The subtext to the outrage, as Lomax has shown, is the
pope's conviction that the emperor is *indignus,* unworthy of his high
office. Although the persuasive tension of the letter is centered on
Frederick's ingratitude and immortality and its disastrous consequences
for Christendom, the pope does not make the charge of unworthiness
explicit. He sticks to the more concrete accusation of the broken vow,
probably because it represents his best case.

In maris points both to the role of law in focusing persuasion in the thirteenth century, and to the perceived importance of rhetorical persuasion in the execution of the law. The underlying legal complaint that the emperor is unworthy of imperial honors, and that God will not accept the sacrifice and reparation offered by His people from Frederick's hand, dictates the tone of moral outrage, although it is not one of the specific charges listed at the end of the letter. On the other hand, there is no reason to investigate the reason for the failure of the emperor to lead the crusade beyond "ut dicitur," and such an investigation would, in all probability, have weakened Gregory's case. Notwithstanding the law, excommunication will be successful only if the pope is able to persuade powerful secular and ecclesiastical officials to recognize its validity, and to support the separation of Frederick from the body of Christ. Christians are invited not to understand the evidence but to join in a common sense of outrage and sorrow. The facts are not data to be reckoned in a rational manner; the account of Frederick's behavior functions to create a highly emotional—even eschatological— plot line.

The second letter from the Gregorian chancery, *Si memoriam,* is addressed to the emperor himself in October 1236. It warns Frederick, as required by law, that a second excommunication is impending. I will limit the discussion of this very complex document to the passages of *Si memoriam* that are strictly pertinent to the question of the impact of canon law on rhetorical persuasion, and specifically to Gregory's brandishing of the law to preclude discussion of events. Honorius had denounced imperial *novella opinio* in *Miranda tuis,* and in *Si memoriam* Gregory uses logical, legal and spiritual arguments to condemn recent imperial endeavors to defend its interests, and to prove that Frederick's reasoning, perverted by pride, has become irrational. The same argument is taken a step further in *Ascendit,* where Gregory claims that imperial rhetoric is irrational and dangerous because Frederick is a heretic alienated from the Word.[11]

Si memoriam is partially motivated by Gregory's wrath against the emperor who, in a recent missive, has dared to judge him and make inferences regarding his reasons for naming the Bishop of Palestrina as papal legate in Lombardy. Frederick, in his questioning of papal motives, invalidates his identity as Christian and the defender of the church. The exordium promises a sweeping clarification of the truth. Ornamented with Biblical and liturgical language, it coalesces in the words of the Psalms: "[the wicked] set their mouth against the heavens, and their tongue walketh through the earth," and they shall be brought down.

> Si memoriam beneficiorum Conditoris eterni que per ministerium sponse sue in sublimes personas et humiles largiter emanarunt, humane ingratudinis oblivio deleret, si Dominus noster Jesus Christus, judex vivorum et mortuorum, judicaturus apertis libris conscientie, revelatis tenebrarum operibus, universos, ut Dominus timeretur, origo virtutum fides inconcussa persisteret, opera statera justitie ponderaret, verba sub veritatis signaculo clauderentur et os contra Deum non poneretur in celum [Psalm 72:9], unde tonitrua prodeunt et fulgura contra persecutores suos sepe mittit Deus et Dominus ultionum.[12]

> If the memory of the favors of the Eternal Founder, which emanate broadly through the ministry of His Bride to both sublime and humble, is not to be destroyed by the oblivion of human ingratitude, if our Lord Jesus Christ, Judge of the living and dead, Who will judge all deeds with the open book of consciences, all darkness being destroyed, is to be feared as Lord, then the faith, origin of virtues, ought to remain unshattered and acts ought to be weighed on the scales of justice: "Words ought to falter under the sign of truth and the mouth should not be set up against Heaven" whence the thunder comes and God, Lord of vengeance, often sends lightning against His persecutors.[13]

Words are interpreted as symbolic acts—like the wicked raising their mouths against the heavens, like Uzzah daring to right the ark of God, Frederick has violated his covenant.

Faith and the promise of salvation are born and nurtured of humble gratitude, and destroyed by the willful oblivion of pride, expressed in the irascible style of recent imperial letters. The spiritual well-being of the emperor, and the words and arguments he chooses to advance his cause are inseparable.

> Sane ex pluribus litteris ad nos et fratres nostros nuper ab imperiali excellentia destinatis plura collegimus que si stilus mitigasset humilior et amaritudinem pagine dulcorasset affectus reverentie

filialis, virtus discretionis sub manna dulcedinis irascibilem spiritum temperasset, et imago Dei que resultat in speculo rationis ac similitudo eius que per affectum bonum et zelum rectitudinis in potentiis anime naturalibus invenitur, non fuissent sic scribendo forsitan deformate.

Clearly, we have collected many of the numerous letters sent to us and our brothers from the imperial excellency, in which letters, if a more humble style had mitigated and a sentiment of filial piety had sweetened the bitter page, if the power of discrimination had been tempered by the manna of reason, the anger of the spirit by sweetness, then also the image of God that reflects in the mirror of the intellect, and his likeness which is found in the natural powers of the soul through good feeling and the zeal for righteousness, would perhaps not have been so deformed by writing in this way.

In flagrant disregard for the facts, Frederick has asserted that James, bishop of Palestrina, is detestable and heinous. The pope does not defend James's record as papal legate in Lombardy, for who could raise a wrinkle of suspicion regarding the sincerity of that man, who could darken the purity of snow with duplicitous argument [Quis illius sinceritati rugam suspicionis objicere, quis illius puritatem nevo duplicitatis opposito poterit offuscare]? In the following year the imperial chancery will counter the papal defense of the purity of the bishop by arguing that a man must be judged by the consequences of his actions, not his reputation, and that despite his sanctity, James's actions bear witness to an implacable enmity towards the empire.[14]

Gregory refutes what he regards as specious and tendentious arguments raised by the imperial chancery and some attention is given to refuting each point that the imperial chancery has made. The very act of examining papal motives for the selection of James of Palestrina is insane: "Nonne miserabilis insanie esse cognoscitur, si filius patrem, discipulus magistrum conetur arguere, a quibus non solum in terris, sed in celis sese ligari posse institutione divina docetur?" [Is it not known to be miserable insanity, if the son endeavors to blame the father, the students the master who not only on earth, but in heaven, is bound to be guided by divine institution?] The greater may not be subordinated to the lesser. Elsewhere the papal letter insists that even the novice can see the weakness of the imperial position: "Erubescere igitur poterit novus logicus de nobis mali alicuius initium vel participium paralogismo concludere, cuius falsitatem etiam imperiti de longe speculantes possunt luce clarius improbare. . . ." [Therefore the novice logician will blush to conclude that we initiated or participated in some kind of wrongdoing, the falsehood of which, even the inexperienced can condemn (when it is presented) in a clearer light . . .]. Gregory points out the logical inconsistencies of the imperial response to recent papal admonitions regarding the treatment of the church in the Kingdom of Sicily: the imperial chancery seeks to obfuscate what is obvious to all by jumbling specific historical circumstances with general principles.

> Sed ecce super facto ecclesiarum regni quod tibi in litteris nostris primo directis sub genere indefinite proponitur, quod ad hoc non tenearis quasi dubia respondere, a te reali responsione preterita vocali commentario incongrue respondetur, tum quia frustra requiritur ut singularia speciei vel specialia fidem faciant generi, cum genus et species manifestam ex se prebent notitiam veritati, et cum individuorum scientia quasi ex infinitate confunditur, ad doctrinam universalium supervacue singularia colliguntur.

> But look, as for what is proposed to you generally and indefinitely in our initial letter, about what was done to the churches in the kingdom, although you are not bound to make, as it were, dubious responses, it is inconsistent of you to reply with a word by word commentary, and not with a response to our point: both because it is futile to demand that singulars or specifics should confirm something generic inasmuch as genus and species of themselves provide public knowledge of the truth, and since the knowledge of individual things is almost infinitely confused, it is useless to collect single facts in order to confirm a universal proposition.

However, the pope does not limit his condemnation to the logic of the emperor. It is the act of questioning papal premises rather than submitting obediently to them, the act of defending himself that inculpates Frederick. Several pages into *Si memoriam* Gregory thunders:

> Et ideo si prudenter adverteres quod lignum vite est in paradisi medio positum, sic in centro tuorum finium prudenter persisteres, quod

nequaquam incaute ad judicanda secreta conscientie nostre cuius
judex in celo est conscius in excelsis, proprie ruinam conscientie
metuens evolasses, cum regum colla et principum submitti videas
genibus sacerdotum, et christiani imperatores subdere debeant
excecutiones suas non solum Romano pontifici, quin etiam aliis
presulibus non preferre, necnon Dominus Sedem Apostolicam, cuius
judicio orbem terrarum subjicit in occultis et manifestis, a nemine
judicandam soli suo judicio reservarit.

If you would prudently note, the tree of life is placed in the center of
paradise, so in the center of your kingdom should you prudently
remain. By no means should you, fearing the ruin of your soul,
foolishly rush forth to judge the secrets of our conscience, whose
judge in heaven is knowledgeable of all things, when you see the
necks of kings and princes lowered before the knees of priests, and
Christian emperors subservient not merely to the Roman pontiff, who
is not preferred to other prelates. The Lord, to whom all are subject in
secret and open things, reserved for himself—and no other being—
the judgment of the Apostolic See.

Gregory's assertion is inspired by the "sweeter" and "fair" logic of the
spirit of the letter. The reified metaphor that betokens divine
proscription of the emperor's right to judge is dazzling, but given the
political polarization of the time, its effectiveness at the Frederican
court is dubious.[15]

Frederick has questioned papal authority, to which he owes
everything, and according to Gregory the emperor rants with the
distorted words of the proud, the first enemies of God. The pope
interprets the emperor's infraction symbolically and spiritually: like
Uzzah, Frederick has exceeded the limits imposed on him by his office.

At fortassis ignoras quod Oza morte percutitur eo quod arcam Domini
inclinatam manu temeraria sustinere conabatur, et tribus Chaath qua
vasa tabernaculi propriis involuta portabat humeris, paribus addicitur
detrimentis, si tabernaculum solius Aaron dispositioni commissum
ingredi vel vasa sanctuarii priusquam involuta fuerint ulla curiositate
audeat intueri?

> And perhaps you do not know that Uzzah was struck down because
> he tried with bold hand to right the ark of God, and the tribe of
> Kohath, that carried the vessels of the tabernacles wrapped on their
> shoulders, are condemned with the same penalty if they dare to enter
> or gaze upon the tabernacles of the temple, protected from the
> inquisitive, the care of which fell only to Aaron.

Gregory does not respond to Frederick; he censors him. He seeks no
response; he seeks obedience.

Si memoriam concludes with what Gregory invokes as indisputable
proof from history that the pope is overlord and judge of all things
secular and sacred. A recitation of the deeds of previous pious
emperors, from Constantine on, demonstrates the validity of his claim
of absolute dominance in the secular sphere as well as the
ecclesiastical.

> Sed vade ad tuorum memoriam predecessorum et inspice, transi ad
> felicis recordationis Constantini, Caroli magni, Arcadii et
> Valentiniani imperatorum exempla, et ea diligentius speculare ubi
> infaillibilis solutionis conclusio sine instantia super premissis
> accipitur, ubi reprobanda false opinionis assumptio confutatur. Illud
> autem minime preterimus toti mundo publice manifestum quod
> predictus Constantinus quis singularem super universa mundi climata
> monarchiam obtinebat, una cum toto senatu et populo non solum
> Urbis, sed in toto Romano imperio consituto, unanimi omnium
> accedente consensu, dignum esse decernens ut sicut principis
> Apostolorum vicarius in toto orbe sacerdotii et animarum regebat
> imperium, et existimans illum terrena debere sub habena justitie
> regere cui Dominum noverat in terris celestium regimen commisisse,
> Romano pontificis signa et sceptra imperialia. . . .

> Go back to the memory of your predecessors, pass to the examples of
> the Emperors of happy memory Constantine, Charlemagne, Arcadius
> and Valentinian and examine more carefully those things in which the
> conclusion of an infallible solution is accepted without contradiction
> and where the reprobate assumptions of a false opinion is refuted. For
> we by no means overlook that it that it is publicly obvious to the
> whole world that the aforesaid Constantine, who had received the
> exclusive monarchy over all parts of the world, decided as just—with

the unanimity of all and with the full consent of the whole Senate and
people, established not only in the City of Rome but in the whole
Roman Empire—that as the vicar of the Prince of Apostles governed
the empire of priesthood and of souls in the whole world so he should
reign over things and bodies throughout the whole world; and
considering that he should rule over earthly matter by the reins of
justice to whom—as it is known—God had committed on earth the
charge over spiritual things, the Emperor Constantine humbled
himself by his own vow and handed over the Empire to the perpetual
care of the Roman Pontiff with the Imperial insignia and scepters and
the City and Duchy of Rome. . . .

This is infallible proof, according to Gregory, that imperial authority is
entirely dependent upon the will of the pope: "you should therefore
realize that you will clearly stand convicted of infringing the rights of
the Apostolic See and your own faith and honor as long as you do not
recognize your own creator [the Apostolic See]." Imperial words,
policies, or laws that impinge on canon law, or challenge the supreme
pontiff in any way, assail providential history.

Si memoriam closes with a reiteration of the idea that the
emperor's exercise of logic and judgment does not reflect or respect
providential order on earth because he has been corrupted by pride. To
argue is to display his arrogance and to prove his unworthiness. The
emperor has no valid argument on the matter of James, the churches of
Sicily, or anything else—his prerogatives are logically, legally, and
spiritually subject to papal judgment, as the lesser is subordinate to the
greater. Divine punishment, at the hand of the pope, looms before him.
The presentation of evidence is required by law, and the pope follows
the prescription, but Gregory is less interested in quibbling over the
facts than in delivering Christendom from the arrogant, wicked, and
corrupt sinner who is emperor.

In maris and *Si memoriam* show the tremendous mastery of
political persuasion at the Gregorian chancery. The letters are logically
and dramatically structured and employ a vast array of strategies to
bring about a desired end. The dangers that Gregory's pontificate faced,
not only of imperial aggression, but of imperial words and modes of
interpreting evidence, push the elderly defender of the faith to
vehemently preclude and censure the emperor. By daring to question
papal motives, Frederick demonstrates his unworthiness, inveterate

arrogance, and ingratitude born of his alienation from the Word. The imperial version of the facts lacks credibility and legitimacy, and moreover, it is dangerous to the well-being of Christendom. Gregory combats the imperial challenge by girding papal interests with the protection offered by canon law, by censoring the emperor for the very act of raising objections to papal policy, and by seeking the support of the other Christian princes and priests. *Si memoriam* is at once a grandiloquent articulation of papal plenitude of power, and a testimony to the urgency and intensity of verbal persuasion in the third decade of the thirteenth century. None of its arguments is gratuitous—each was perceived as potentially persuasive in the extremely fluid and vital intellectual climate of the period. I will propose in the third part of this book that Gregory's aggressive stance is one of the factors that motivates the Frederican chancery to develop a new mode of epistolary persuasion which seeks to justify interpretations of events that stand in direct contradiction with those of Rome.

NOTES

1. Abulafia refers to the grounds for the excommunication as a "technical breach." (David Abulafia, *Frederick II: A Medieval Emperor* [New York: Penguin, 1988] 167), and Van Cleve reports that when Frederick attempted to explain the circumstances of his failure to fulfill his vow in the summer of 1227 to Rome, Gregory "was in no mood to receive valid excuses. . . ." (Thomas Curtis Van Cleve, *The Emperor Frederick II of Hohenstaufen, Immutator Mundi* [Oxford: Clarendon Press, 1972] 196).

2. This is the point demonstrated most conclusively by John Phillip Lomax, *"Ingratus" or "Indignus": Canonistic Argument in the Conflict between Pope Gregory IX and Emperor Frederick II*, Diss., University of Kansas, 1987, 355-57. In a letter to the imperial court announcing the first excommunication, Gregory insists on charges other than the broken crusade vow that is stated in the encyclical, and he especially protests the treatment of church in Sicily. Abulafia also interprets Gregory's message as the first step to depose Frederick as regent of the Kingdom of Sicily: "Sicily was under the suzerainty of the Roman Church itself. What Gregory required, clearly, was recognition of this authority, and the separation of Sicily from the rest of Frederick's empire. The issue of Frederick's continued rule over Sicily, latent under Honorius III, had now become a public source of disagreement" (166-67). Gregory's invasion of

the Kingdom of Sicily during Frederick's absence in the Holy Land supports this interpretation of Gregory's intentions.

3. Martin Grabmann praises Gregory's language in *I divieti ecclesiastici di Aristotele sotto Innocenzo III e Gregorio IX* (Rome: Saler, 1941) 70.

4. Hans Martin Schaller, "Die Kanzlei Kaiser Friedrichs II. Ihr Personal und ihr Sprachstil 2," *Archiv für Diplomatik* 4 (1958): 288. A typical example of the Gregorian exordium, richly laden with Biblical citations, is the following letter, addressed to King Louis IX in 1230: "Ecclesiam suam Dominus continua pietate custodiens, quam in multis sibi miserationibus desponsatam tanta caritate complectitur, ut ipsa levam eius sub capite suo sentiens et dexteram in amplexu, (Cant. 2:6) letabunda dicat: 'Dilectus meus inter ubera mea commorabitur; ne dimittam illum, donec me introducat in sue cubiculum genitricis (Cant. 3:4)!' sepe ipsam temptari permittit, ne sibi forsan innoxia videatur, sed erudita potius ad salutem terrena despiciat ?t celestia concupiscat, et ad supernam patriam ardenter aspirans, defleat ıncolatum suum cum habitantibus Cedar esse diutius prolongatum (Ps. 119:?)." *Epistolae Saeculi XIII e Registis Pontificum Romanorum Selectae per G. H. Pertz* 1, Ed. C. Rodenberg, Monumenta Germaniae Historica (Berlin: Weidmann, 1883) 338.

5. Abulafia explains that Gregory's turbulent relationship with the citizens of Rome was exacerbated by the conflict with Frederick. "Gregory attempted on Easter Day to preach against Frederick in St Peter's, and was rewarded with a riot. He was chased out of the Church and down the streets of Rome; he escaped northwards to Viterbo. Mob violence in Rome only strengthened his resolve to bring Frederick to heel: the humiliation was acute" (169-70).

6. Perelman and Olberchts-Tyteca argue that "conviction is merely the first stage in progression toward action. . . . On the other hand, to someone concerned with the rational character of adherence to an argument, convincing is more crucial than persuading." Chaim Perelman and Lucie Olbrechts-Tyteca, *The New Rhetoric: A Treatise on Argumentation,* Trans. John Wilkinson and Purcell Weaver (Notre Dame: University of Notre Dame Press, 1971) 27.

7. The text of *In maris* is in J.-L. A. Huillard-Bréholles, *Historia diplomatica Friderici Secundi* 3 (Paris: H. Plon, 1852-1861) 23-30.

8. See Chapter 4, note 8.

9. The text is very detailed: "Apostolica vero Sedes ne tantis laboribus exsufflatis et inutiliter sic exhaustis totum dissolveretur negotium, quod humeris huius principis post Romanam Ecclesiam principalius incumbebat, habito plurium episcoporum et aliorum proborum virorum consilio, de contingentibus nil omittens, venerabilem fratrem nostrum P. Albanensem episcopum, et bone memorie G. tituli Sancti Martini presbyterum cardinalem ad

firmanda ea que imperator pro Crucis obsequio spontaneus promittebat, transmisit. Cumque apud sanctum Germanum, cum pluribus Alemannie principibus pariter convenissent, imperator propria manu juravit, quod inde ad biennium, id est in passagio augusti proximo nunc transacti, omni excusatione ac dilatione cessantibus, transfretaret, mille milites ibidem per biennium teneret ad suum in obsequiis terre sancte, centum millia unciarum auri in quinque passagiis proximo tunc futuris illuc destinaret certis assignanda personis; et tunc cardinales predicti de imperatoris assensu in eius conspectu, principum ac populi circumstantis, sententiam excommunicationis publice auctoritate Sedis apostolice protulerunt in quam incideret imperator, si forsan in aliquo deficeret predictorum. Obligavit se insuper imperator ad centum calendras et quinquaginta galeas ducendas et tendendas biennio ultra mare, ac quod insuper duobus millibus militum passagium certis terminis largiretur, in animan suam jurari faciens se ista que prediximus impleturum, et sponte consentiens in ipsum et regnum suum ferri sententiam, si hec non fuerint observata."

10. Abulafia 167.

11. *Ascendit* is discussed in Chapter 9.

12. *Si memoriam* is in Huillard-Bréholles, 4.2, 914-23.

13. This translation and the final two passages that I cite from *Si memoriam* are from Sidney Z. Ehler and John B. Morrall, Trans., *Church and State through the Centuries: Collection of Historic Documents with Commentaries* (Westminster: Newman Press, 1954) 76-77.

14. *Evidentium clara,* the imperial response to *Si memoriam,* is dated March 1237. It opens as follows: "Evidentium clara cognitio certum plerumque facit hominibus quadam ratione probabili judicium de occultis nec casus eventibus ascribi patitur quod procuratum consiliis hominum et curiosa subtilitas intrinseca colligens manifeste convincit. Illud tamen inficiari nolumus quin absit rerum veritas a conjectis, quin a factis interdum intentio sit remota. Tamdiu certitudinis locum probabiliter obtinet violentia conjecture, tamdiu conscientie lumen siderationis umbra vel dissimulationis obducit, quamdiu dilucida probatione contrarii veritas clareat in utroque. In verbo verumtamen patris justissime miratus est filius dum id quod per industriam hominis, si tamen cardinalis est homo, in detrimentum imperii provenisse non conjectura, sed veritas manifeste testatur, serenitatem nostram impinxisse descripsit Ecclesie puritati." Huillard-Bréholles, 5.1, 33.

15. Smalley speaks of the "sweeter" and the "fair morality" of spiritual exegesis. Her description of Langton's exegetical method may be applied to the passage. It reflects a prelate "still living in an Augustinian world of mirrors and reflections," where "Scripture, like the visible world, is a great mirror,

reflecting God, and therefore all and every kind of truth" (Beryl Smalley, *The Study of the Bible in the Middle Ages,* 3rd ed. [Oxford: Blackwell, 1984] 262).

PART 3

Persuasion and Resistance at the Imperial Chancery

CHAPTER 7

Emergence of a New Paradigm of Persuasion

i

The subtext to papal-imperial coexistence in the first half of the thirteenth century is the new theoretical alignment of power, the "conflict of laws" at the core of the papal-imperial relationship.[1] The conflict is expressed in a series of epistolary exchanges as the emperor and popes grappled to interpret, enforce, or resist the restructuring of power. The failure to launch a vowed crusade, the launch of a crusade without papal blessings, the treatment of the churches in the Kingdom of Sicily, the activities of a papal legate in Lombardy, and imperial pretensions to jurisdiction in northern Italy and Sardinia emerge as issues of bitter controversy, and at the heart of each is the relative authority of the pope and emperor. The Frederican chancery was continually rewriting its history in relation to the Roman church. Its purpose in doing so was not to define a unified and coherent chronicle for posterity; on the contrary, the distance between propaganda and historical narrative collapses in elaborations of past events designed exclusively to persuade a specific public of a particular interpretation of an event. According to the pontifical chancery, however, there was only one version of providential history, and Honorius roared with outrage when Frederick questioned Innocent's support for Philip and Otto, competing contenders for imperial honors: "Unde tam contraria istis, tam novella processit opinio?" Opinions have no validity, and similarly the questioning of papal motives is absolutely inappropriate. In this chapter and the next I will trace the evolution of the Frederican chancery's treatment of the narration, the "minor premise" of the epistolary argument, where the evidence supporting the *novella opinio* is introduced, and becomes detailed and systematic enough to make the imperial letter a serious, prestigious model for opposition to papal authority.

ii

The demands that Frederick placed on his chancery continued to evolve during his thirty-year imperial career. The chancery was Frederick's principal instrument for asserting his political power; it established law and composed official edicts and propaganda. Under Frederick, chancery history can be divided into three periods.[2] In the first two periods, churchmen dominated. From 1198 to 1220, control was in the hands of prelates and Norman-Sicilian magistrates. Walter of Palear, the most important official, was Archbishop of Troia and a trusted agent of the papacy; he had served under Henry VI and Constance and led the Norman-Sicilian opposition to the German nobles and Markwald of Anweiler. In the second period, 1220 to 1227, the chancery was reorganized and the powerful Walter of Palear definitively exiled. Rainald, Archbishop of Capua and nephew of Walter, served as pronotarius or head of the chancery. But many chancellors remained in place. In 1227 Frederick restructured the chancery into a hierarchical and extremely responsive political unit. A meritocracy of bureaucrats, almost all trained jurists, was established, thereby displacing the traditionally dominant partnership of landed aristocrats and ecclesiastical officials. Thirty-six new notaries entered into the service of the imperial chancery. The majority of the chancellors no longer composed important documents; they merely carried out the instructions of the cohort of trusted advisors that accompanied the restless emperor. This organization remained in effect for the remainder of Frederick's rule. A letter written by one notary to another describes the new chancery as modeled on the plan of the divine hierarchy: the will of the earthly majesty corresponded to that of God, the organization of chancellors mirrored the angelic orders in heaven.

The question of Frederick's direct participation in the production of imperial documents is not easily resolved. Abulafia writes that in the one imperial register that survived intact until the destruction of

Neapolitan archives during World War II, the voice that resounded from the faded pages was, at certain points, that of the emperor.

> Rarely, but powerfully, Frederick expresses his pained fury at the conduct of the papacy. . . . No doubt the routine varied: when the emperor was heavily involved . . . he had to trust the good sense of his civil servants; but when enforced leisure . . . left him free to think about Sicilian affairs he was happy to provide very detailed answers to question about the minutiae of government.[3]

The actual composition of documents was, naturally, the duty of the chancellors.

Scholars do not distinguish the magniloquent language of the imperial chancery from the elevated prose style championed by the pontifical chancery. Descriptions of Frederican rhetoric tend to focus on the linguistic virtuosity of Pier della Vigna, faintly praised in his own day for writing "obscurely and in the grand manner."[4] The Florentine Guelf Brunetto Latini, writing several decades after Pier's death, commemorates the imperial official as the exemplary master orator, and as such, master of Frederick and of the empire.[5] Pier was a high court justice, and in 1247 he became logothete of Sicily, an office he held until his arrest for treason in 1249. As logothete Pier drafted the laws, concessions, privileges, and speeches of the emperor. Van Cleve goes almost as far as Brunetto when he explains that "in these offices he was, in fact, head of the chancery, adviser and trusted agent to the Emperor in matters diplomatic, fiscal and political, as well as judicial. . . . Next to Frederick himself . . . the most powerful official of the Sicilian court."[6] Pier della Vigna had been assigned the most stylistically taxing letters since his engagement in imperial service in 1221. But his formation at Capua, Bologna, and with the Cistercian Giovanni of Casamari accounts only in part for the rhetorical distinction associated with his name. The formulation and defense of a comprehensive and autonomous ideology of imperial office, spurred by the challenge of protecting secular juridical and political prerogatives in a period when Rome, fortified by canon law, was aggressively redefining and limiting them, had a significant effect on the epistolographic practices of the chancery and its chief official. After 1225 the focus of the epistolary arguments shifts in some of Pier's letters from an enthymemic model, in which persuasion resides in the praise and affection that the writer lavishes on the addressee and the strength of the exordium, to a new epistolary paradigm in which persuasion is posited in a dialectical relationship between the major and the minor premises, the exordium and the narration. Exordia feature statements of imperial ideology of office, and the evidence is presented in the narrations, in order to affirm the necessity of imperial rule, win the adherence of other secular leaders, and counter the aspirations and arguments of the papal chancery.

iii

Imperial letters of the early 1220s embrace the vision of Christendom formulated so eloquently by Frederick's tutor, Pope Innocent III. Word play similar to that found in the letters of Innocent and Honorius provides a gracious and ceremonious tone to *Exhibitam nobis,* to take one example, addressed to Honorius in 1220 on the eve of Frederick's Roman coronation.[7] A humble exordium, typical of those prescribed by the *artes dictandi,* opens the letter.

> Exhibitam nobis in nostris negotiis, petitionibus et necessitatibus universis vestre gratie plenitudinem devote recognoscimus et recognoscentes apostolice sanctitatis pedibus humiliter inclinamus, utpote qui per Romane ecclesie et vestre paternitatis grata subsidia et favorem reminiscimur nos adeptos quidquid honoris et glorie possidemus.

> We devotedly recognize your extending to us the fullness of your grace in all our concerns, petitions, and necessities, and recognizing this we humbly prostrate ourselves at the feet of the holy father, as is natural for those who do not forget that what we possess in honor and glory is because of the gracious assistance and favor of the Roman church and your paternal benevolence.

The exordium is solemnly paced, redolent with humility and gratitude, ornamented with alliteration and assonance (nobis in nostris negotiis ... necessitatibus), and chiastically structured around a figure of polyptoton (... recognoscimus et recognoscentes ...), as if the sentence were folded upon itself in a humble pose of gratitude.

The letter petitions the pope for a concession: soon to be crowned emperor, Frederick had abdicated his title of King of Sicily to his son

Henry. In *Exhibitam nobis* the emperor requests the right to rule there in place of his son, and to inherit the kingdom should Henry predecease him without heirs. In the meantime, he maneuvered to have Henry elected King of the Romans in Germany. To the great consternation of the pope, Frederick was seeking exactly what he had promised to renounce, that is, a *Regnum Italicum* that included Sicily and surrounded papal territories in Italy. The imperial letter continues in a tone of fervent obedience, insisting on the unity of will between the greater and lesser powers:

> Quis enim devotior inde erit Ecclesie quam qui Ecclesie ubera suxisse recolit et in eius gremio suscepisse inde custodiam et etatis ac salutis et honoris augmentum? Quis fidelior, quis accepti beneficii magis memor? Quis de gratitudine commendabilior existimari potest quam is in quo crescit cum fide devotio? Acceptorum beneficiorum tenax memoria perseverat, et sue devotionis debitum, se cognoscens videlicet debitorem, solvere nititur juxta benefactoris arbitrium et mandatum.

> Who, in fact, will be more devoted to the church than the man who recalls having been nourished at her breast and clasped to her bosom, from whence came protection of life and limb and an increase of honor? Who more faithful, who has a greater memory of benefits received? Who can be reckoned more grateful than he who was raised in faithful devotion? The steadfast memory of accrued benefits endures, and clearly the debtor consciously strives to discharge his debt of devotion according to the will and command of the benefactor.

Anaphora gives form to the lesson of the relationship between papal father and imperial child. The only natural conclusion is that papal nurturing and honors and the profound gratitude of the child make the latter the perfect secular advocate of the church, and therefore to increase his power is advantageous to the church.

There follows an update on a Diet at Nürnberg, convened by Frederick to forward the crusade, which was a project as dear to Honorius's heart as Frederick's petition to rule in Sicily was inimical. The chancery evidently hoped that Honorius would move to satisfy both parties, as indeed he did. The underlying assumption of the imperial appeal was formulated by Rome: Frederick is the Christian emperor who, in response to papal commands, serves as the devoted advocate and defender of the church.

Another letter exhibiting the same stylistic and ideological inclination is addressed to the Abbot of San Sepolcro in November 1220, a month before the Roman coronation. The exordium proclaims the emperor's role as *defensor ecclesiae*.[8]

> Imperialem decet sollertiam ecclesiam et religiosos et loca specialiter imperio pertinentia in sua justitia manutenere ac defendere eisque bona ipsorum ac possessiones que a ducibus, imperatoribus et regibus predecessoribus nostris sive a quibuslibet aliis personis eis tradite et confirmate fuere et liberaliter augmentare ac privilegia firmare perpetuo ac corroborare. Hoc enim ad presentis vite cursum feliciorem et ad eterne vite retributionem nobis profuturum non dubitamus.

> It is fitting that within its justice, imperial expertise maintains the church, clergy, and monasteries, which is its particular responsibility, and defend grants and possessions made and confirmed by our predecessors, the dukes, emperors, kings, and whomever else, and liberally increase and perpetually affirm and protect those privileges. We do not doubt that this is truly the course to happiness in the present life and to the reward of eternal life in the future.

This exordium reminds the abbot of the emperor-elect's largesse, as well as his long line of noble, illustrious, and liberal ancestors, all of which served to bolster Frederick's legitimacy. Grammatical control is very deliberate here. Solemnity marks the opening phrase, composed of substantives and adjectives in the accusative (imperialem decet solertiam ecclesiam), followed by a rhymed list of Frederick's predecessors of various noble ranks (a ducibus, imperatoribus et regibus predecessoribus nostris), a list that portrays Frederick in a most flattering light, and finally, the new privileges are expressed with three verbs and two adverbs that convey action, power, and largesse (liberaliter augmentare ac privilegia firmare perpetuo ac corroborare). The divinely sanctioned coordination of emperor and church celebrated in the exordium, a relationship that can only lead to a flourishing church and to salvation, is followed by a straightforward narration in which the renewed privileges are spelled out in detail. Within the year, however, Frederick would revoke all privileges, including those he himself had granted, in the Edicts of Capua. The Edicts state that the royal seal had fallen into the hands of Frederick's enemies after his parents' deaths, and been abused by them. The reason for the move was obviously to consolidate control of the Kingdom of Sicily, and it was bitterly denounced by the church.

Many letters from the early 1220s celebrate the harmony between church and empire and the prospects of the emperor. Frederick's felicitous ascent to imperial honors offers proof of the divine favor with which he is blessed. The event is communicated ornamentally, and the public invited to joyfully acquiesce to the good news, not to analyze the events leading to it. A 1221 letter announcing the imperial crusade and addressed to his father and friend, Hugolinus, Cardinal Bishop of Ostia (later to become the hostile Pope Gregory IX), opens with an exordium proclaiming universal joy. The statement is both phonically and semantically chiastic.[9] "Jocunde fame felicitas et felicis rumoris jocunditas . . . " (Happiness in the joyful report and joy in the happy news . . .). Preparations for the crusade by the supreme pontiff Honorius are announced. A celebratory tone, underlined by anaphora, continues.

> Gaudeat igitur Romana ecclesia, quia . . .
> Gaudeamus et nos, quia . . .
> Gaudere debet et totus populus christianus, quia . . .

All the orders must rejoice, the church because a project so zealously initiated must surely succeed, the emperor because Hugolinus, "a man of perfect reputation, untainted in his faith, pure in his life, very eloquent, and attentive to moral rectitude and scholarly achievement" (vir fama integer, religione perspicuus, vita purus, facundia eloquentissimus et claris virtutum et scientie titulis circumspectus), will inspire other Christians to follow his lead so the sins of Christendom may be expiated, and all Christians must rejoice because to the land where Christ shed his blood to save mankind, so long suffering under pagan superstition (not because of its power but as a consequence of our sins), the True Cult will be restored. Furthermore, the devoted submission of the empire to the church insures the success of the enterprise. These fervent affirmations are reinforced with Biblical verses.

> Et quidem licet ea simus devotione subjecti Sancte Romane ecclesie matri nostre ut credamus quemlibet missum de latere summi pontificis patris nostri facere dignum fructum [Matt. 3:8], tamen sicut stelle in firmamento a se invicem differentius lumen habent et alia magis alia minus lucet [1. Cor. 15:41-42], sic salva reverentia aliorum firmam spem gerimus et indubitatam dante Domino fiduciam obtinemus, quod pre cunctis, qui huic essent ministerio deputati, vestrum verbum igne caritatis accensum gratum fructum afferet nomini sancto Dei et toti populo Christi caractere insignatio.

> Truly it is granted that we be that for our devotion to the subjects of the Holy Roman Church our mother, since we believe that whatever comes forth from the office of the highest pope, our father, will produce worthy fruit, just as the stars in the firmament have different light from one another and one shines more, one less, so with holy reverence we bear the firm hope of others and, offering unquestioning faith to God, we will obtain the desired end, because more than others charged with this responsibility, your word ignited by love's fire will convey the desired results in the holy name of God and the Christian people.

Again the chancery reiterates that Frederick's past blessings are a guarantee of his future success. "Nam ex retroactis infallibilem de futuris elicimus coniecturam" [For from past infallibility we elicit the knowledge of the future]. In the brief narration, responsibility i s conceded to Hugolinus for the organization of the crusade.

The letter presents an elegant example of the style of the Frederican chancery before it broke from the Roman model of epistolary rhetoric. It celebrates the status quo that guarantees salvation and the recuperation of the Holy Land. Persuasion is posited in references to Frederick's present felicity, interpreted as divinely ordained in the person of Hugolinus, and in the concord of church and empire, and these auspicious signs are communicated in a language ornamented by parallelism, accumulation, alliteration, and Biblical citations. Analysis of detail has no place here: the letter is an expression of the joy of the *societas christianorum.*

Letters like Innocent's *Apostolica sedes* show how the popes, because they dominated the legal pyramid of Christendom, could maintain an attitude of paternal benevolence, coaxing and cajoling a sinner back into the fold, attributing sin to the influence of pernicious advisors. On the other hand, a defense of imperial interests, where they conflicted with those of the church, translated into an attack against the church, and the offense was heightened by the forfeiture of the formulas of gratitude and humble obedience prescribed by the papacy. In the act of championing his own cause, the emperor had little choice but to publish conflict.

The transformation of imperial rhetoric began before the dramatic outbreak of hostility provoked by the first excommunication. I do not intend to suggest that Frederick became, with the first excommunication or for over a decade thereafter, an implacable enemy of the papacy. I agree with Abulafia when he writes that "Frederick was . . . aware . . . that papal claims to primacy must be confronted not by searching out grounds for dispute. . . ; pope and emperor must try to find a *modus vivendi*. . . ."[10] Nevertheless, there is a breach of confidence between pope and emperor in the middle of the 1220s. The principal mode of imperial epistolary persuasion gradually evolves from a celebration of the status quo fortified by eternal principles, and a tendency to justify imperial actions by evoking events as indices of divine intention, to a type of argument in which events are interpreted in the light of the requirements of the state or justified by specific circumstances. Abulafia notes that in the second half of the 1220s, Frederick's letters "to France and England show a close awareness of the recent history of the papacy, particularly of the pontificate of Innocent III."[11] The enthymemic structure of the earlier letters gives way to an active dialog between the major and minor premises. The chancery reexamines events in a temporal context, and singles out human history, the *varietas temporis,* as the force that has diminished the imperial estate and determined its response. For example, the chancery opens the encyclical announcing the Diet at Cremona with the pronouncement "jura imperii pro varietate temporis precedentis conculcata jaceant et depressa" [the laws of the empire lie trampled and beaten down as a result of past vicissitudes of time].[12] The same point is made in the fundamental ideological statement of the imperial chancery, the *Prooemium* to the Constitutions of Melfi.[13] Honorius has taken Frederick to task in *Miranda tuis* for precisely this kind of sinful presumption: it is the major premise of universal salvation that is important, not the minor premise from historical contingency.[14]

The October 1227 papal encyclical of excommunication, *In maris* (discussed in Chapter 6), repeatedly invokes the emperor's immorality as evidence of his unworthiness for imperial honors. Like falling dominos, Frederick's sensuality is blamed for Christian humiliation at Damietta and the failure of the crusade that was supposed to be launched at Brindisi in the summer of 1227. The facts of Frederick's imperial career are important only insofar as they incite indignation against him. *In admirationem,* the letter circulated by Frederick in December 1227 to protest the excommunication, aims to bolster Frederick in the court of public opinion by discrediting the papal letter. Gregory is not judged in terms of his moral character (as in *Iocunde fame* cited above); he is condemned for his inaccurate portrayal of the emperor. The imperial letter of defense shifts the debate from Frederick's morality to the crusade itself; it includes a straightforward and detailed account of the crusade negotiations from the time of the coronation at Aachen to the present. *In admirationem* attempts to convince Christendom that the emperor has consistently fulfilled his duty and that Gregory has not judged him fairly.

The imperial encyclical opens with a wholly traditional expression of indignation at the treatment Frederick has received from Pope Gregory, which threatens the well-being of Christendom.

> In admirationem vertimur vehementem quod unde pro multis beneficiis prestolabamur gratiam, inde tam offensionis quam etiam contumelie diversa genera reportamus.[15]

> Our admiration has turned to anger, for where we expected favor in exchange for many services, there we encounter hostility and all sorts of abuses.

Imperial words do not issue forth by choice, but by necessity: Gregory's insinuations in *In maris* make it so. "Inviti loquimur, sed tacere nequivimus" [We are reluctant to speak but cannot remain silent], and the motive for the letter follows, ornamented with polyptoton, "ne in eo quod diu tacuimus spes que multos decipit nos forte dicipiat" [lest hope in the man who has deceived us so, for which reason we were long silent, deceive others]. The delinquency of Rome and the description of the chaos that has resulted from Gregory's rule are traditional, the language and images generic, borrowed from the Old and New Testaments. The structures are simple and accessible.

> Non enim solum gens contra gentem insurgit nec regnum regno minatur, non pestis et fames tantummodo corda viventium premisso terrore conturbant, sed ipsa caritas qua celum et terra regitur non tantum in rivulis, sed videtur in fonte turbari, ac Romanum imperium ad fidei christiane defensionem divinis provisionibus deputatem non a quibuslibet infimis, sed ab ipsis quos honorarat et sibi proposuit patribus graviter infestatur.

> Indeed, not only do peoples rise up against peoples, not only does kingdom menace kingdom, not only do plagues and famines move the hearts of the living with premonitions of terror, but charity itself, by which heaven and earth is ruled, is fouled not only in its streams, but, it seems, at its source, and in fact the Roman empire, providentially ordered for the defense of the Christian faith, is seriously menaced by those whom it had honored and proposed for itself as fathers.

Verbal and phonic repetition abound (gens . . . gentem; regnum regno; terra regitur . . . rivulis turbari; defensionem divinis . . . deputatem; proposuit patribus). God ordained the empire to preserve peace among men but the Roman empire is seriously threatened by the Holy Father himself.

> Sed cum universalis ille pater Christi vicarius et beati Petri successor in quo locavimus fiduciam spei nostre contra personam nostram indigne et acute moveatur et ad conflandum in nos odium totus videatur intendere.

> But what can we do when the vicar of Christ, the successor of the blessed Peter, in whom we placed our trust, viciously and unworthily attacks our person, and seems totally devoted to exciting hatred against us?

Frederick would humbly submit to papal judgment "non nisi urgens necessitas nos invitos cogeret obviare" [if urgent necessity did not compel us to oppose (the pope's injustice), unwilling as we are]. The implication is that the welfare of all Christendom depends on the emperor's opposition to Gregory's injustice.

In admirationem goes on to propose two arguments in an effort to persuade the Christian public of the emperor's innocence. First, Frederick's nearly incredible ascension to the imperial throne is offered as proof of God's blessings on him and his ambitions. Two metaphors from Gregory's *In maris,* the troubled ship of state tossed in a stormy sea and the serpents that describe an ill-defined sense of revulsion inspired by Frederick's conduct, are appropriated by the imperial chancery to convey the period of papal tutelage in the Kingdom of Sicily. The serpents are transformed, in the imperial letter, to suggest the voracious aristocrats and prelates who rioted for control of the Kingdom of Sicily during Frederick's minority:

> Et sicut navis in tempestate sine remige, sic absque gubernatoris regimine pupillaris hereditas indefensa in partes divisa fuit et ab inimicorum morsibus quasi penitus dissipata.

> And like a ship without oars, likewise without the guidance of a tutor, the inheritance of the minor was unprotected, divided into portions, and almost totally consumed by the teeth of the enemies.

It is the immediate need to restore peace and justice to the empire that has prevented Frederick from undertaking an overseas crusade: "quod libentissime fecissemus nisi voluntas principum et evidens necessitas, quia nondum fuerat plene imperii pacata turbatio . . . " [because very gladly we would have done so were it not for the will of the prince and evident necessity, because the upheaval of the empire was not fully controlled]. Eventually the situation is rectified, for man's intentions are not those of God: "aliter homo, aliter videt Deus." The greater good of providential design prevails and Frederick takes command of the derelict and storm-tossed ship.

The second argument, which is the subject of the remainder of the letter, focuses on the issue of the crusade, and figurative language essentially disappears. Frederick defends his actions on the basis of his gratitude to God and the necessities of state. Christian failure in Damietta, interpreted as God's anger at Frederick's immorality in the papal encyclical, is ascribed not to imperial negligence or impiety, but to inept leadership: "incaute ductus populus incidit in lacum, immo laqueum, improvisum" [the men, imprudently led, fell into a pit, or actually an unforeseen trap]. If the emperor were not truly dedicated to leading the Christians in the Holy Land, then why had he gone to such great lengths to expedite the crusade? Readiness for the crusade is described in detail including the number and types of ships that the emperor had prepared, the troops he had equipped, the armies that were sent overseas, the money Frederick had forwarded to the Holy Land, the emperor's departure in spite of the disease that weakened his body, and finally the thwarted attempts by imperial representatives to communicate Frederick's circumstances to Pope Gregory.[16]

In admirationem concludes with a reminder that the imperial chancery has set the facts out *seriatim,*[17] with a call for renewed zeal for the crusade, and the assurance that God would restore Gregory to his senses. The letter was enthusiastically received, at least in Rome where Gregory was unpopular, and at the behest of the Roman Senate and people, a public reading was held on the Campidoglio.[18]

In keeping with traditional medieval epistolary modes, the first part of *In admirationem* argues on the basis of divine intention and approbation. Figurative language invites the public to grasp the danger that an unjust man like Gregory poses to the well-being of Christendom. In contrast, the second part offers a detailed accounting of Frederick's crusade preparations, and a discussion of the facts pertaining to the charges leveled against him by Gregory. The evidence is intended to render the papal accusations of *In maris* implausible, inflammatory, and unworthy of attention. The narration implicitly portrays Gregory as a dangerous meddler in the realm of secular power, and princes may have nodded their heads in assent as they listened, because of their own dealings with Rome.

In other letters Frederick articulates his concerns about the papal appropriation of secular power more explicitly. Events of the recent past are interpreted as the direct consequences of papal greed. *Inter ceteros,* addressed to the King of England and also written in December 1227, seeks to persuade Henry III of the danger that the church, under the guidance of Gregory, represents to his sovereignty. The letter evokes the memory of Henry's cousin, the disinherited Count of Toulouse, "and many other princes" including Henry's own father, John, whose divine inheritances have been diminished by papal interference.[19]

> Revolvant hec inclyti barones Anglie quos papa Innocentius bullatis
> litteris communitos animavit ut in regem Johannem quasi ecclesie
> inimicum insurgerent obstinatum, sed postquam enormiter
> memoratus rex est incurvatus, et se suumque regnum ecclesie romane
> velut effeminatus mancipavit.

> Recall the illustrious English barons whom Innocent incited with
> papal bulls, so that they rose against John as if he were an obstinate
> enemy of the church, and afterwards the noble king was greatly
> compromised and he and his kingdom were, so to speak, made
> subject to the Roman church.

Papal intervention is painted with a broad stroke: the focus is on the detrimental consequences of papal interference, not the causes. Frederick does not mention that he himself is excommunicate and the Kingdom of Sicily a papal fief. The letter is rife with Biblical imagery, centering on the lesson of 1 Timothy 6:10, "For the love of money is the root of all evil: which while some coveted after, they have erred from the faith, and pierced themselves with many sorrows." The church is guilty of simony, excessive taxation, hypocrisy, and open and covert usury, but its corrupt state will be known by the fruit it bears: "excognitis fructibus suis certum faciens argumentum."

The imperial chancery roots its attack on papal policy in one of the most powerful ideas sweeping Europe in the period: that the material wealth of the church has corrupted the apostolic message and mission. The church, founded in a spirit of poverty and simplicity, had been blessed with many miracles. But the reign of miracles passed when the church fell into the hands of greedy and avaricious priests. The desire to return to the apostolic poverty of the early church animated the Spiritual Franciscans and various heretical sects, and became increasingly attractive to Ghibelline propagandists in the course of the thirteenth century. *Inter ceteros* concludes with a reference to Matthew 7:15—wolves lurk in the midst of the flock—for papal legates have been dispatched to excommunicate and otherwise punish secular potentates. The words may have still been fresh in the minds of English courtiers and church officials when, a year later, Gregory dissolved the oath of loyalty in the Kingdom of Sicily and placed a heavy tax on England and other European kingdoms to pay for an invasion of Frederick's lands.

The persuasive approach of imperial letters always depended on the public it was addressing, and secondarily on the subject matter of the document. The most exultant document of the years between 1220 and 1230 announces the "victory" negotiated by Frederick in the Holy Land. Reminding the public of the bleak picture of Christendom painted by the imperial chancery since the excommunication, the encyclical letter opens with an invocation modeled on Psalm 49: "Letentur omnes in Domino et exultent recti corde quoniam beneplacitum est ei super populo suo ut exaltet mansuetos in salute" [May men rejoice in the Lord and those righteous in heart exalt because it pleases Him that the meek be exalted].[20] God has not forgotten his ancient mercy, and "He renews in our day the miracles that He is said to have performed in ancient days." For, He

> nunc dedit sibi gloriam in paucitate virorum ut cognoscant et intelligant omnes gentes quod ipse sit terribilis in magnificentia, gloriosus in majestate et mirabilis in consiliis super filios hominum.

> now has given glory to Himself by means of a small group of men, so that all people may know and understand that He is awful in His magnificence, glorious in His majesty, and marvelous in His design for the sons of men.

He has shown his magnificence to the humble: Frederick and an elite company of soldiers have been permitted the success in the Holy Land which for so many years eluded other Christian princes and armies. An anaphorically structured exaltation (O quam laudanda . . . quam metuenda . . . O quam glorificanda) follows:

> O quam laudanda est clementia Creatoris [Psalms 50:19] et quam metuenda semper potentia virtutis ipsius, quia cum in humilitate mentis et devotione cordis semper processerimus ad servitium sanctum eius, nobis ab ipso principio consilio et auxilio sue non defuit pietatis. O quam glorificanda est ineffabilis misericordia Redemptoris qui super devotum populum suum peccatis nostris facientibus tamdiu derelictum nunc ex alto respiciens, ipsum secundum miserationum suarum multitudinem visitavit.

Oh how the clemency of the Creator must be praised and how the strength of His power must be feared, for when from the beginning of His holy service, we moved with humble mind and devoted heart, His counsel, help and pity were not denied us. Oh how the unspeakable mercy of the Redeemer must be glorified, [the Redeemer] who, looking from on high upon his devoted people, so long neglected owing to our sins, visited them in his mercy.

The encomium of the excommunicate emperor is followed by a description of the hardships endured by his small band of soldiers, and the efforts of the papal agents in Jerusalem to sabotage the negotiations.

In the 1220s the rhetoric of the Frederican chancery begins to assume its mature characteristics. At the time of Frederick's Roman coronation, the structure, themes, and style of imperial documents resemble those of the Roman chancery. The appeal of these letters resides in the expression of goodwill toward the recipient, the reiteration of shared ideals that guarantee the desired end, and celebratory language. The reorganization of the chancery in 1227 and the replacement of ecclesiastical officials by jurists made the transformation of imperial epistolary persuasion possible. The political conflict of the period, and in particular Pope Gregory's excommunication of the emperor in 1227, made it necessary. In the course of the third decade of the thirteenth century, imperial political persuasion is gradually transformed from one that attempts to resolve differences by reiterating and celebrating the status quo, to a more finely articulated polemical instrument. The chancery becomes an alembic where the accidents of time are distilled into a persuasive and productive discourse. As far as epistolary persuasion is concerned, there is a shift of gravity from the exordium, the "major" premise, to a balance between the exordium and a detailed and nuanced narration recounting the *varietas temporis* and imperial responses to it.

Nevertheless, it is important to keep in mind that the persuasive approach of a letter ultimately depends on its content and intended public: *Letentur omnes,* a celebration of the imperial "victory" in the Holy Land, exhibits persuasive techniques reminiscent of the chancery of Honorius III and the pronouncements that date from the period of Frederick's coronation in Rome in 1220, ornamental language being the most appropriate expression of Frederick's invitation to participate in the universal joy of Christendom. *In admirationem* reflects a different goal. When papal ire over the treatment of the Sicilian church, the humiliating failure to arrange a "summit meeting" with the Lombard communes in Cremona, and excommunication by Gregory IX cloud the horizons of Frederick's political ambitions, the imperial chancery defends the emperor with a detailed account of his policies.

Finally, it is clear that the public had changed. The reasons for this are numerous, but the renewed vitality of law, especially canon law in the early thirteenth century, was one factor, and the political pressure of the papacy on secular and ecclesiastical leaders throughout Europe another. Rhetorical persuasion evolved because of an awareness that new ideas and a new intellectual elite were transforming the culture of the ruling class.

NOTES

1. James A. Brundage, *Medieval Canon Law* (New York: Longman, 1995) 177.

2. My discussion of the imperial chancery is based on Hans Martin Schaller, "Die Kanzlei Kaiser Friedrichs II. Ihr Personal und ihr Sprachstil 1," *Archiv für Diplomatik* 3 (1957): 209-49.

3. David Abulafia, *Frederick II: A Medieval Emperor* (New York: Penguin, 1988) 326-27. In this volume, see Chapter 2, note 4 on the papal registers, and the discussion of the preservation and transmission of the imperial registers in Chapter 2, note 7.

4. The Bolognese jurist Odofredus wrote of Pier, "Volentes obscure loqui et in supremo stilo ut facium summi doctores et sicut faciebat Petrus de Vinea." Hélène Wieruszowski, "Rhetoric and the Classics in Italian Education in the Thirteenth Century," *Politics and Culture in Medieval Spain and Italy,* Storia e letteratura 121 (Rome: 1971) 606. For descriptions of the imperial elevated prose style see Emily Heller, "Zur Frage des kurialen Stileinflusses in der sizilischen Kanzlei Friedrichs II.," *Deutsches Archiv für die Erforschung des Mittelalters* 19. 2 (1963): 434-50; Hans Niese, *Zur Geschichte des geistigen Lebens am Hofe Kaiser Friedrichs II.* (Darmstadt: Wissenschaftliche Buchgellschaft, 1967): 48-9; Ettore Paratore, "Alcuni caratteri dello stile della cancelleria federiciana," *Atti del Convegno Internazionale di Studi Federiciani, 10-18 December, 1950. VII Centenario della morte di Federico II, Imperatore e*

re di Sicilia (Palermo: A. Renna, 1952) 300-04; Aurelio Roncaglia, "Le corti medievali," *Il letterato e le istituzioni,* Letteratura italiana 1 (Roma: Einaudi, 1982) 139-40, and most important, Hans Martin Schaller, "Die Kanzlei Kaiser Friedrichs II. Ihr Personal und ihr Sprachstil 2," *Archiv für Diplomatik* 4 (1958): 264-325.

5. Brunetto Latini, *La Rettorica,* Ed. Francesco Maggini (Firenze: Le Monnier, 1968) 5. "Orator è colui che poi che elli àe bene appresa l'arte, sì ll'usa in dire et in dittare sopra le quistioni apposte, sì come fue maestro Piero dalle Vigne, il quale perciò fue agozetto di Federigo secondo imperadore di Roma e sire di lui e dello 'mperio" [An orator is he who, when he has learned the art well, uses it in speech and in writing to respond to appropriate questions, as did Maestro Piero dalle Vigne, who was for this reason "agozetto" (logothete) of Frederick the Second, Emperor of Rome, and lord of him and of the empire].

6. Thomas Curtis Van Cleve, *The Emperor Frederick II of Hohenstaufen, Immutator Mundi* (Oxford: Clarendon Press, 1972) 520.

7. *Exhibitam nobis* is in J.-L. A. Huillard-Bréholles, *Historia diplomatica Friderici Secundi* 1. 2 (Paris: H. Plon, 1852-1861) 741-44.

8. *Imperialem decet* is in Huillard-Bréholles, 2.1, 14-7.

9. *Jocunde fame* is edited in Ludwig Weiland, Ed. *Legum Sectio IV: Constitutiones et Acta Publica Imperatorem et Regum* 2, Monumenta Germaniae Historica (Hannover: Hahn, 1893-1927) 114-15. The document is dated February 1221.

10. Abulafia 189.

11. Abulafia 169.

12. *Qualiter jura* is in Huillard-Bréholles, 2, 548-49.

13. See the discussion of the *Prooemium* to the Constitutions of Melfi in Chapter 8 of this book.

14. *Miranda tuis* and the content of the lost letter that provoked it are discussed in this book in Chapter 5.

15. *In admirationem* is in Huillard-Bréholles, 3, 37-48.

16. Copiam vero navium tantam habuimus quod pro defectu peregrinorum multa in portu navigia remanserunt. De corruptela vero aeris que nocuit peregrinis, per quam divina Providentia que previderi non potest ab homine diversas mundi partes et regni nostri specialiter occulto judicio flagellavit, nulli magis quam nobis molestum extitit et dampnosum. . . . Commisimus insuper dilecto principi et consanguineo nostro duci de Limburch interim usque ad felicem transitum nostrum curam totius exercitus christiani, et quinquaginta galeas que pro transfretatione nostra erant armate in portu, assignari precepimus

venerabili patri ... patriarche Ierosolymitano, ... magistro domus
Theotonicorum et aliis magnatibus transituris, de quibus non nisi XX pro eorum
itinere recipere voluerunt. Nos autem ad succursum eorum quos premisimus et
ad terre sancte subsidium intendentes, competentiorem in vasellis et chelandris
aliis fieri fecimus apparatum, proponentes in estate futura circa medietatem
futuri mensis maii, quando tempus est aptius et magis offert se mare
navigantibus opportunum, in majori potentia transfretare.... Quin potius ad
postulationem eorumdem nuntiorum nostrorum cognitores et judices non
concedens, infirmitatis nostre casu inevitabili non inspecto, solutione non
considerata pecunie pretaxate nec militibus ad nostra stipendia jam missis
animo revolutis, quod non absque cordis anxietate proferimus, denuntiavit in
nos pro eisdem tribus capitulis in quibus, cum defectus non sit, defectum, quia
sic placet, allegat. Videlicet quod personaliter non transfretavimus, quod non
miserimus centum millia unciarum, quod non direxerimus M milites tenendos
ad biennium ad stipendia nostra pro subsidio terre sancte. Qui cum ad
deliberandum super hoc provinciale concilium quorumdam prelatorum totius
Italie convocasset, solempnes nuntios ad Sedem apostolicam replicavimus,
videlicet Reginum et Barensem archiepiscopos, ducem Spoleti et comitem
Henricum, familiares et fideles nostros et procuratores in eadem causa statutos
a nobis ad proponendum in presentia omnium qualiter persone nostre
transfretationem infirmitas que in promptu est, cuius adhuc manent vestigia,
prepedivit, et quod in presentiarum ultra mille milites nostros in transmarinis
partibus ad stipendia nostra pro Dei servitio teneamus, videlicet septingentos
milites transalpinos per manus magistri domus Theotonicorum ad nostra
stipendia solidatos, CC et L milites regni quos anno preterito de pecunia
ecclesie quietatos sequenti anno ad solidos nostros ibi fecimus retineri; quod
inter familiam nostram et alios regni milites, qui ad expensas nostras transacto
passagio transierunt, fuerunt ultra centum, et insuper quadringentos milites
nobis a Lombardis ecclesia mediante promissos, ultra quam ex promissione
tenebamur, deputavimus pro eodem servitio transmittendos, nisi dilationi et
more eorum ecclesia, per quam accelerari debuerant, consensisset. Quin etiam
de centum millibus unciarum satisfecimus, mittentes primo in tribus terminis
sexaginta millia unciarum; in quarto vero termino magister domus
Theotonicorum qui est unus de statutis ad ipsam pecuniam reservandam, petiit
assignari sibi siclam nostram Brundusii pro quarta solutione viginti millium
unciarum, et ipsam recepit et uncias habuit pro solutis. Si quidem dominus
apostolicus in presentia fratrum et omnium prelatorum, presentibus quoque
nuntiis nostris, sicut per eos recepimus, in vigilia beati Martini fuit recordatus
quod dictus magister pro nobis absolutionem habuit; residua vero viginti millia

unciarum que tenebamur in transfretatione nostra deferre, cum camera nostra premisimus, et parati erant iidem nuncii nostri et procuratores facere plenam fidem: qui cum, priusquam prelati consulerentur, audiri debuerint, eos, ordine postposito in quo nostrum fuit gravatum propositum, vix admisit; quia primo consultatis semotim per se singulis prelatorum et communi consilio per cedulam assignato, premonitis, ut dicitur, universis ne a deliberatione qualitercumque prehabita dissentirent, eidem nuntiis et procuratoribus nostris audientiam prestitit; non deliberans postmodum cum prelatis et nuntios nostros ulterius non admittens, justis excusationibus et causis rationabilibus non receptis et clauso eisdem procuratoribus et nuntiis nostris ostio justicie que apud Sedem apostolicam pro omnibus in omni debetur, denunciationem prout voluit replicavit.

17. Que omnia supradicta cupimus ad universalem noticiam pervenire, in veritate pura talem fuisse rei seriem et processum, et nos penitus inculpabiles coram celo et orbe terrarum ineffabiliter protestantes ut universi et singuli seriatim plenius cognoscatis manifestam injuriam et gravamen que pro tot predictis obsequiis et expensis ab illis perferre conquerimur a quibus nos et universus orbis optata pro crucifixi negotio suffragia sperabamus.

18. Ernst Kantorowicz, *Frederick the Second, 1194-1250*, Trans. E. O. Lorimer (NewYork: Frederick Ungar Publishing Co., 1957) 175.

19. *Inter ceteros* is in Huillard-Bréholles, 3, 48-50.

20. *Letentur omnes* is in Huillard-Bréholles, 3, 93-9.

CHAPTER 8

Persuasion and the Science of Nature at the Court of Frederick II

Epistolary rhetoric was a porous discipline: intellectual developments like spiritual exegesis and the new legal science influenced traditional practice, as did external factors like politics. In this chapter I will argue that the Aristotelian science of nature promoted the development of new inductive modes of argument, particularly at the imperial chancery.[1]

The recovery of the *Posterior Analytics* in the second half of the twelfth century opened an epistemological fault line in Latin Europe: what man could know rationally and experientially was distinguished from revealed Truth. The *Posterior Analytics* defines scientific demonstration as the establishment "in precise language not only that things are so . . . , but also why they are . . . , and why they have to be that way."[2] A half century later, Aristotle's "biological" studies were translated from Arabic into Latin, and the logical and systematic approach to living creatures exemplified by the texts had a profound impact on thirteenth-century man's modes of perceiving and interpreting his environment. Aristotelian biology confirmed the ability of the mind to comprehend creation, and ultimately human motivation, without reference to the transcendent and spiritual.

The Aristotelian texts endow observed data with an epistemic status. In created nature, the first cause, the "for the sake of which," is the definition of the creature, and it is comprehended through direct observation. Knowledge of the created world is pursued from the starting point of perceptible phenomena, not from the abstractions of the Christian mystical-symbolic conception of nature, nor from the widely held opinions (*endoxa*) that serve as premises for dialectical argument.[3]

Time and resources were spent on the unveiling of nature's mysteries and the exploration of the laws by which nature functioned at the imperial court. Frederick wrote a work of ornithology, *De Arte Venandi cum Avibus,* which was outstanding in the early thirteenth century for its empiricism.[4] Michael Scot, chief scientist and astrologer at the imperial court, provided the method. When he arrived there, sometime after 1225, he brought with him the first Latin translations of three of Aristotle's zoological works, the *Liber Animalium,* the *De Partibus Animalium,* and the *De Generatione Animalium,* translations he had made from the Arabic a decade earlier at Toledo. The Aristotelian *Physics* had been translated into Latin in the previous century and also provided methodological instruction for investigation in the science of nature, and more broadly, natural philosophy.[5] Michael Scot remained at the court until his death sometime before 1236. He is credited with the translation from Arabic into Latin of numerous Aristotelian texts and accompanying commentaries by Averroes.[6] Averroes's commentaries, disseminated in the Latin West in large part because of the patronage of the Frederican court, emphasize the autonomy of nature and its laws.

Of course the Aristotelian texts were in the cultural avant-garde, and Aristotelian terminology spiced intellectual jargon in the period. Contrary to Haskins's assertions that the scientific activity of the court leaves no discernible trace in the production of the chancery, official documents do contain occasional elaborations of Aristotelian science.[7] For example, a 1232 letter announcing an imperial assault on heresy borrows a proof from *De Caelo* to demonstrate that Peter's two swords are only one in substance.[8] The church is the single sheath for both swords, "ex quo invincibiliter assumitur et necessario comprobatur quod gladiorum istorum una sit substantia, cum sit impossibile de natura unum et eumdem locum duas posse substantias continere" (from which it is irrefutably derived and necessarily proven that the substance of these swords is one, since it is impossible in nature that one and the same place can contain two substances). The attraction of the new science was also felt at the papal court, as Smalley has shown.[9] In a letter of admonition addressed by Pope Gregory to Frederick soon after the former ascended to the Roman cathedra, the pontiff alludes to Avicenna's *De Anima* when he praises the emperor's innate intelligence. Smalley comments that Gregory's prohibition of the study of the new scientific texts, sent to the masters of theology at Paris in the following year, was clearly "not intended to preclude private study" of those texts.

But was Aristotelian science valued at the imperial court merely as a prestigious intellectual ornament—was it dissipated there as a sprinkling of technical terminology or an occasional novel argument? Did the Aristotelian science of nature actually influence the *forma mentis,* the essential mode of interpreting experiential data, of arguing a cause, at the imperial chancery? Frederick's own empirical bias is most often illustrated by his *De Arte Venandi cum Avibus,* in which even Aristotle's authority is rejected when it runs counter to the experimental method the ancient philosopher had established for the determination of the axioms of the science of nature.

> Inter alia, we discovered by hard-won experience that the deductions of Aristotle, whom we followed when they appealed to our reason, were not entirely to be relied upon, more particularly in his descriptions of the characters of certain birds. There is another reason why we do not follow implicitly the Prince of Philosophers: he was ignorant of the practice of falconry—an art which to us has ever been a pleasing occupation, and with the details of which we are well acquainted.[10]

And,

> In his book, the *Liber Animalium,* we find many quotations from other authors whose statements he did not verify and who, in their turn, were not speaking from experience. Entire conviction of the truth never follows mere hearsay. The whole subject of falconry falls within the realm of natural science, for it deals with the nature of bird life. It will be apparent, however, that certain theories derived from written sources are modified by the experiences set forth in this book.

The axioms of the science of nature are discovered through inductive reasoning from the evidence of perceptible phenomena, from experimentation. Hearsay and commonly held opinions are not admissible to establish the premises of a scientific discipline.[11] Passages like these indicate that the Aristotelian texts were studied for their methodological implications at the court, and not merely assimilated as another authoritative trove of *naturalia.*

In his 1239 encyclical *Ascendit,* Pope Gregory accuses the emperor of professing naturalistic determinism associated with Aristotelian science at the expense of the articles of faith.

> He, moreover, presumed plainly to affirm (or rather to lie), that all are foolish who believe that God, who created nature, and could do all things, was born of a virgin. This heresy he confirms by the false doctrine that no one can be born whose conception has not been preceded by union of man and woman and no man ought to believe anything beyond what can be proved by the force and reason of nature.[12]

The imperial chancery, of course, denied the accusation, and affirmed that the emperor believed in a God "non de potentia ordinata, sed de potentia ordinante."[13] Naturalistic determinism was taken seriously by the ecclesiastical establishment and condemned at Paris in 1277.

The influence of the Aristotelian science of nature may well have been far more profound than any of these well known passages indicate. It introduced new methods of investigation and new categories of demonstration, and offered new tools for rationalization. The most significant of these tools for the imperial court was, I believe, the concept of contingent necessity. Aristotle defines necessity in the sublunary world as hypothetical and contingent, based on the principle of cause and effect, and conceived in terms of what will come to be. Michael Scot translates *necessitas* in the first book of *De Partibus Animalium,* the methodological introduction to the biological sciences, as "that which is, is not, unless because of something."[14] Only in the sublunary world of coming-to-be and passing-away does Aristotle treat "hypothetical necessity as a philosophically important special *kind* of necessity."[15] Aristotelian contingent necessity challenged the Christian concept of a nexus between Creator and creation—which, if broken by Adam's sin, had been restored by Jesus's sacrifice. In Aristotle's nature what is, is not accounted for by some higher imperative.

The impact of the new mode of understanding and interpreting inevitably influenced the rhetorical. Whereas lessons of the Scriptures, as well as medieval moralized nature and human history, were shrouded in figurative language, the Aristotelian texts promised that nature's order and meaning could be directly investigated, demonstrated, and logically expressed.[16] Honorius's interpretation of famine as a divine lesson on charity, in *Celestis altitudo,* and Gregory's time-honored exegesis of Christian failure in the Holy Land as God's refusal to accept the sacrifice of His children as long as they were led by the immoral Frederick, in *In maris,* were rebutted with new explanations of famine and failure that were accessible to all rational men. However, traditional, allegorical readings of events and ornamental techniques of persuasion were not abandoned: the new persuasion is found only in letters in which it was perceived as potentially effective.

While it is difficult to prove that Aristotelian science had a direct effect on modes of persuasion (there is no smoking gun), the culture and persuasive paradigm characteristic of the Frederican court suggest that the chancery is an appropriate milieu, and 1231 an appropriate date, to tackle the issue. The new epistemic status of observed phenomena, the inductive arguments that led to the formulation of principles in Aristotelian biology, and the very specific understanding of contingent necessity in the Aristotelian texts were, I believe, as influential a subtext to the new epistolary persuasion as developments associated with canon law. I will explore these ideas in three different types of documents authored at the imperial chancery in the 1230s. The first establishes principles of governing, the second is a political letter addressed to King Louis of France, and the third a series of letters celebrating the imperial victory at Cortenova.

The *Constitutiones Regni Siciliae or Liber Augustalis,* were published at Melfi in 1231, a code of 253 articles asserting the absolute and unlimited authority of the prince in his kingdom. Although the code was composed in consultation with the elders of the Kingdom of Sicily, and recognized the validity of existing feudal and ecclesiastical law in Sicily, Frederick was defining himself as a new kind of tyrant.[17] The following discussion will focus on the *Prooemium* to the new legal code.

The *Prooemium* to the Constitutions offers a parallel recounting of God's history and man's, and develops a running analogy between God and the prince. Retelling the creation of mankind and the evils that befell the human race after the original act of disobedience, the need for a prince to preserve peace and restore justice among men is justified inductively. The necessity of the new constitution in the Kingdom of Sicily is also demonstrated from the evidence provided by the *varietas temporis,* and in particular the chaotic state of the kingdom during Frederick's minority. Berman observes that the Sicilian legal code was "intended to be—and was—rooted in the historical circumstances of the Sicilian kingdom and designed to meet its practical needs of government."[18] Significantly, not only the code, but the justification for the code, or in other words, the demonstration of the code's necessity in view of the prince's divine mandate, is "rooted in the historical circumstances of the Sicilian kingdom."

The chancery's concept of "necessity" is not absolute or predestined; it is determined and conditioned by circumstances, and it explains, in conjunction with divine providence, the creation of princes as well as the promulgation of the new law code. In the imperial letters of the 1230s, the *necessitas rerum* becomes the most defensible rationale for action in a prince's world that is constantly changing, and it characterizes the prince's actions with respect to his mandate.[19]

The *Prooemium* to the *Constitutiones* opens with a cosmology and an account of the divine designation of temporal power. The language is richly ornamented and cadenced. Biblical, patristic, legal and Aristotelian phrases resound, suggesting the universality of imperial rule.[20]

> Post mundi machinam providentia divina firmatam et primordialem materiam naturae melioris [conditionis] officio in rerum effigies distributam qui facienda providerat facta considerans [et] considerata commendans a globo circuli lunaris inferius hominem, creaturarum dignissimam, ad imaginem propriam effigiemque formatam, quem paulo minus minuerat ab angelis, consilio perpenso disposuit praeponere ceteris creaturis.[21]

> After Divine Providence had formed the universe and had distributed primordial matter by favor of a better nature into images of things, He, who had foreseen what should be done, looked at what He had done and was satisfied with what He saw. He made man in His own image and likeness, the worthiest creature of the creatures below the globe of the lunar circle. He made him a little less than the angels, and, after deliberate counsel, He decided to put him in charge of the other creatures.[22]

The passage condenses the creation in Genesis, in which God "saw everything that he had made, and behold, it was very good" [I:31]; "So God created man in his own image" [I:27], and "And God blessed them, and God said unto them, . . . have dominion over the fish of the sea, and over the fowl of the air, and over every living thing that moveth upon the earth" [I:28]. Phrases like *primordialis materia* and *officio naturae melioris conditionis* have, on the other hand, distinct Aristotelian overtones. The description of man as *creaturam dignissimam* is Aristotelian. The omission of the creation of primordial material *ex nihilo,* in keeping with the Aristotelian concept of the eternity of matter, seems almost meant to bait theologians.

The text continues with an explanation of the creation of princes. Fallen man, unable to rule himself, learns hatred and divides what should, according to natural law, be shared:

> Inter se odium conceperunt, rerum dominia inter se jure naturali communia distinxerunt, et homo, quem Deus rectum ac simplicem procreaverat, immiscere se quaestionibus non ambegit.

> They conceived hatred among themselves for one another. They divided up the common ownership of property by natural law. Thus man, whom God created virtuous and simple, did not hesitate to involve himself in disputes.

Again key phrases may be traced to Biblical sources, Ecclesiastes and Job; to classical sources, in this case Cicero's *De Officiis,* to the patristic *De Civitate Dei,* and to natural law—as the text makes explicit.

The *varietas temporis* and the multiple acts of disobedience of the creatures threaten all that the clement Creator has done. These contingencies become the direct causes, in conjunction with divine providence, for the designation of a prince. Presented with the iniquity of his creation, God responds by placing his steward among men to rule: He "created princes to rule over fallen man."

> Sique ipsa rerum necessitate cogente nec minus divinae provisionis instinctu principes gentium sunt procreati, per quos possit licentia scelerum coerceri; qui vitae necisque arbitri gentibus, qualem quisque fortunam, sortem statumque haberet, velut executores quodammodo divinae sententiae, stabilirent.

Therefore, by this compelling necessity of things and not less by the inspiration of Divine Providence, princes of nations were created through whom the license of crimes might be corrected. And these arbiters of life and death for mankind might decide, as executors in some way of Divine judgments, how each man should have fortune, estate and status.

The prince maintains peace and justice among men. He is called upon by God to render a complete account of the condition of mankind and of the church. The prince guarantees the salvation of mankind.

The *Prooemium* shifts, at its conclusion, from universal history to a brief but telling historical reference to the chaos in the Kingdom of Sicily during Frederick's minority and absence from the realm.

Cum igitur regnum Siciliae, Nostrae maiestatis hereditas pretiosa, plerumque propter imbecillitatem aetatis Nostrae, plerumque etiam propter absentiam Nostram, praeteritarum turbationum incursibus exstiterit hactenus lacessitum, dignum fore decrevimus ipsius quieti atque iustitiae summo opere providere. . . .

Therefore, since the Kingdom of Sicily, a precious inheritance of our majesty, has until the present been harassed quite often because of the weakness of our youth and because of our absence by the assaults of past disturbances, we have decreed that it would be worthy to provide by the highest work for its peace and justice. . . .

The authority of the prince is thus justified not only by the Biblical account of the state of mankind following his transgression of divine law (in essence, Augustine's theory of the necessity of the state), but also by the experience in Frederick's own kingdom during the lawless period of his minority. The analogy between God, who foresees all through the eternal prism of divine providence, and the prince, who operates with his human intellect and relies on his human optical lens, a lens that is impaired by time and limited by space, is unavoidable. The former has chosen the latter as his agent in the world of contingency. Frederick is not the servant of the church; he is the steward of God in the society of men and in a kingdom; he has been called upon to act with intelligence and agility, not meek obedience.

God of the *Prooemium* differs from God of Genesis; in the latter an almost mechanical creation is suggested by the paratactic sentences. In the *Prooemium,* on the other hand, God not only "vidit quod esset bonum," as in Genesis, but "qui facienda providerat facta considerans [et] considerata commendans. . . ." The emphasis is not on the perfect and complete but on the ongoing process expressed with gerunds and present participles (facienda . . . considerans . . . commendans). He places man above the animals with "deliberate counsel" (consilio perpenso). The process of divine reasoning is elaborated in the explanation of the punishment of man:

> Ne tamen in totum, quod ante formaverat tam ruinose, tam subito divina clementia deformaret, et ne, hominis forma destructa, sequeretur per consequens destructio ceterorum, dum carerent sujecta praeposito et ipsorum commoditas ullius usibus non serviret, ex amborum semine terram mortalibus fecundavit ipsamque subjecit eisdem. . . .

> But in order that divine clemency might not so totally and suddenly despoil what He had formed earlier with such disastrous results, and so that destruction of other creatures might not result from the fall of man insofar as they might then lack a purpose and their value might not serve the needs of another creature, He made the earth abound with mortals from the seed of those two, and He subjected it to them. . . .

The Creator is depicted as a pensive, clement, unwavering ruler who acts as each contingency presents itself in view of the good of mankind and the lower creatures, in much the same way that Frederick does, or seeks to portray himself doing, in the imperial documents of the 1230s.

Three fundamental ideological formulations emerge from the *Prooemium:* the emperor is the divine steward on Earth who receives his authority directly from God; the emperor is the agent of peace and justice among men, the *lex animata* charged to alter the law as well as the course of human events to the end of the preservation of peace and the implementation of justice, and the justice of the emperor, like that of his divine Mentor, is determined according to the necessity of things (rerum necessitate cogente), as it defines itself in the world of mutability. It is the duty of the prince to "preserve peace, and after the people have been pacified, justice, which embrace each other like two sisters." Peace, according to Title 1.8 of the document, "is the concept of public order guaranteed by royal authority." Throughout the document the church is portrayed as the protected client of the temporal power.

In contrast to the pope, who as God's vicar on earth discerns and acts not as pure man but as true God (according to Innocent's argument in *Quanto personam*), the emperor relies on his human acumen to determine the course of justice and to preserve peace. While Innocent glosses over the details of conflict, and recasts it in spiritual terms in his attempts to persuade a sinner, the narrations of imperial political letters from the 1230s offer systematic elaborations of the contingent circumstances of events. A structural innovation of great importance is the inclusion of a statement of the imperial mandate (sometimes reinforced by an Old Testament incantation of divine justice) at the opening of letters intended to advance imperial political ambitions. The mandate-exordium serves to create a frame of reference by which events, recounted in the narration, as well as the imperial response to them, are to be judged by the intended public. In other words, persuasion is posited in an understanding of the dialectic between exordium and narration. The events of time are not mere accidents, nor are they indices of the ways of the Divine Mind; events justify action in imperial documents. They "acquire their functional character"[23] in a different way than they do in papal letters and in the traditional persuasion based on harmony.

This does not imply that the chancery entirely abandoned figurative and allegorical interpretations of events or the musicality of the elevated prose style. The manner in which events were interpreted depended first and foremost on the perceived culture of the public. Traditional ornament and Biblical language continued to be employed in all imperial polemical documents, but these figures usually did not provide the structure for the amplification of the material as they had in the documents of the previous decade. In many documents their persuasive function became secondary.

In the decade following the promulgation of the *Constitutiones,* the intransigence of the Lombard communes and the pope's inability to reestablish order there in his role of arbiter are constantly lamented as impediments to the realization of the imperial mandate. *Inviti loquimur,* a letter of 1236, warns the French King Louis IX of the threat to established order posed by rebellious Lombards, and of Frederick's intention to intervene militarily to enforce imperial law. In the letter, arguments based on causality discernible to the human mind provide a counterpoint to traditional strategies of persuasion: the secret machinations of the Lombard rebels are denounced with indignant exclamations while imperial actions are explained "tam plane quam plene" (clearly and completely) so that Louis might judge and affirm the rationality and justice of Frederick's cause. Louis is called upon to understand that imperial actions have been dictated by necessity in order to resolve the tension between the imperial mandate and the contingencies of reality, a reality of a "continually disturbed state of affairs." This is the principal argument that the imperial chancery makes in order to gain Louis's support.

> Juri prefertur injuria et voluntas justitie dominatur, dum quidam Italie populi sceptrum contemnere conantur imperii, ac etiam proprie commoditatis immemores, libertatis cuiusdam vage luxuriam quieti pacis imponunt et equitati justitieque pretulerunt.

> Lawlessness is preferred to law and individual will overwhelms justice, when certain Italian peoples struggle to defy the imperial scepter, and, oblivious to their own benefits, impose the riotousness of an uncertain liberty, which they have preferred to equity and justice, to the quiet of peace.[24]

The letter also informs the zealous crusader Louis that Frederick cannot undertake a new crusade, his dearest wish, before Lombardy is pacified. Before that has taken place, imperial resources cannot be fully dedicated to the service of the Holy Land. The third argument that the imperial chancery makes to Louis is that all secular princes face the same threat from rebellious subjects.

> Vos igitur cum ceteris regibus orbis terre interest plene perspicuas aures et oculos aperire et diligenter attendere quanta contradictionis fiducia omnibus a jugo dominii subtrahere se volentibus prebeatur, si Romanum imperium jacturam huiusmodi rebellionis pateretur.

> Therefore it is important that you and the other princes of earth fully perceive, and open your ears and eyes, and carefully heed how great

the boldness of contradiction exhibited by all those wishing to withdraw themselves from the yoke of their lord, if the Roman empire were to suffer any kind of loss from such revolts.

Louis and other secular princes to whom the chancery appealed were, apparently, persuaded either by self-interest or by one of the other arguments, because the imperial armies that marched against Lombardy included royal and mercenary soldiers from England, France, Greece, Hungary, and Spain.

A concentration of the verbal virtuosity that characterizes the elevated prose style is found in the exordium of *Inviti loquimur*. The opening is familiar, the regrettable subject of the letter introduced by the formula "inviti loquimur, sed tacere non possumus" [we are reluctant to speak but cannot be silent]. Citing Luke 3:9, the emperor tells how great is his grief because of the present situation, and he sounds a battle cry. "Jam enim securis ad radicem arboris posita et gladius fere usque ad animam transiens labia dissolverunt . . ." [And now the ax, laid unto the root of the trees, passing almost to the soul, releases our lips . . .]. The ruthless implications of the remainder of Luke's pronouncement— "every tree therefore that bringeth not forth good fruit is hewn down, and cast into the fire"—though not stated, must have echoed at the French court.

The struggle to renew and reinvigorate the empire will be pursued to its conclusion. Luke's words become a declaration of war against the Lombard rebels—the emperor's sword is the instrument of justice. Political fulfillment of imperial ambition is described with the same inevitability as physical maturity.

Quamprimum enim in nobis pubescentibus annis ac mentis et corporis calescente virtute, ad Romani culmen imperii preter spem hominum nutu solummodo Providentie divine conscendimus ac regnum Sicilie, preclara materne successionis hereditas, ad jura nostra pervenit, aciem mentis nostre continuo direximus ad predicta.

For as soon as we had grown to manhood, and the virtues of mind and body glowed within us, we were raised to imperial dignity beyond all human hope by the will of divine providence alone. And with the kingdom of Sicily, the precious inheritance of our mother coming into our possession, we directed the eyes of our mind to the aforesaid matters.

The offense of rebellion confronts Frederick as it did his ancestors. Since early manhood, Frederick has constantly directed his intelligence to the reform of the pernicious rebels. The emperor's goal and purpose have been steadfast, but he would like Louis to understand that given the *varietas temporis,* he has been moved to respond in different ways. He is the clement and wise ruler who acts according to each new circumstance, yet holds fast to his purpose.

Quo proposito et volubilitate consilii et motu rerum continuo presentium immutato, nos a tanto bono recedere non volentes, Ferentini denuo cum papa predicto collatione habita, curiam apud Cremonam indiximus. . . .

This design was, however, changed, owing to the fickleness of counsel and the continual disturbed state of affairs at the time; but we, not wishing to abandon such a good intention, after again holding a conference with the pope at Ferentino, appointed a court to be held at Cremona. . . .

Unfortunately the upheaval brought about by rebellious Lombards continually interferes with Frederick's ability to fulfill his mandate.

Ad exaggerationem dein nequitatie adhuc occulte ac perfidie, malitiam manifestam insolentiamque adjecerunt, quod contra nos et imperium conspirantes, nobis presentibus et contemptis conjurationes nefarias contraxerunt. Et sic desiderata filii nostri visione fraudati in Apuliam redeuntes, quia preparatio passagii transmarini ad quod tenebamur ex voto, tunc temporis nos arctabat, causam ipsam de satisfactione nobis et imperio facienda arbitrio summi pontificis commisimus terminandam, per quem in quingentis militibus pro negotio Terre Sancte sub eorum sumptibus per biennium exhibendis fuerunt nobis arbitrali sententia condemnati. Quos nedum quod nobis transeuntibus ad nostrum obsequium transmisissent, immo inimico pacis Ecclesiam inter et imperiam discordiam seminante, ipsos contra nos in Apuliam transmiserunt, et sic per contrarie satisfactionis modum precedentes injurias geminarunt.

> To increase their as yet concealed wickedness and perfidy, they
> added malice to open insolence, for in their plots against us and the
> empire, they, in spite of our being present among them, formed
> nefarious conspiracies. Being prevented in our expectation of seeing
> our son, upon returning into Apulia, and pressed for time to make our
> preparations for the passage over the sea to which we were bound by
> our vow, we entrusted this matter, with respect to satisfaction made to
> us and to the empire, to be determined by the decision of the supreme
> pontiff, by whose award they [the Lombards] were condemned to
> supply us, at their own expense, five hundred soldiers for the service
> of the Holy Land. In submission to us who were in transport [to the
> Holy Land], they were to send them, [but] they sent [them] into
> Apulia against us, sowing discord between the church and the empire,
> and thus, by a perverse mode of satisfaction, they redoubled their
> former injuries.

If the motives of the emperor in his struggle with the Lombards are
articulated in a clear and rational way, those of the Lombards are
obscured by the insinuation that the rebels are in league with diabolic
forces. In fact, the portrait of the enemy as the evil and cowardly sons
of Belial who seek to control by stealthy deceit, occurs in appeals
throughout the decade. For example, the imperial chancery writes that
the Lombards induced Frederick's own son to rebel against his father,
thereby offending God and natural law.

> Hiis omnibus non contenti, velut in profundum miseriarum immersi
> et ad omnis iniquitatis extrema deducti, in ipsius Dei injuriam et juris
> naturalis offensam, predicto compromisso pendente, per nuntios
> usque in Theutoniam destinatos contra nos cum filio nostro
> conjurationis federa contraxerunt.

> These men, not content withal, as if immersed in profound abjectness
> and led to the extreme point of every iniquity, in injury to God and
> offense to natural law, sent messengers to Germany and contracted a
> bond of conspiracy with our son against us.

The Lombards are traitors, enemies of peace and agents of discord
between the church and the empire. The assignment of guilt to the
Lombards deflects blame from the two principals, a strategy

reminiscent of Innocent which may have played well in the French court.

Frederick has announced that in order to preserve his imperial rights, he will invade Lombardy. But Gregory, as arbiter and guarantor of those rights, opposes Frederick's plans and chooses instead to accuse him of engaging in *guerre,* or wanton territorial warfare. The pope also views the invasion as a delaying tactic that prevents the empire from carrying out his true mission in defense of the church in the Holy Land. To label imperial forays into northern Italy as private wars and a distraction from the emperor's commitment in the Holy Land is a perverse misinterpretation of imperial intention, and the emperor protests vigorously—although no modern historian has ever taken his explanation of events seriously.

> Sed ut firmiter confiteamur, licet evidens sit nostri processus intentio quem ad nichil aliud direximus nisi ut Crucifixi negotium assumamus, quod provocari directius non valeret quam vigore justitie pacatis undique populis et imperii nostri viribus quod est in tam nobili regione dissitum et de cuius manu terra potissimum prestolatur auxilium, in integrum restitutis, non guerre nomine debuit tam salubre propositum denotari, sed juris executio potius, a qua omnis abest injuria, nuncupari.

> But we insistently confess, if the evidence of our intention is permissible, that we have directed ourselves towards no goal other than the undertaking of the crusade, which could not be achieved more directly than by means of a vigorous implementation of justice, so that our people and soldiers could lend assistance, and our empire, which covers so vast a space, could be restored to its former condition. Such a proposal should not be called by the name of private war, but rather as the execution of law, by which injustice is removed.

Although papal support of the emperor is underlined in the first half of the letter, the pope himself is portrayed as partial and unreliable in the second half of the letter. "Nunquam enim intentionem pape talem esse credimus quod occasione transmarini negotii deberet justicie gladius hebetari" [To be sure we never believed the intention of the pope to be such that the occasion of the crusade should blunt the sword of justice].

The imperial chancery claims to set forth every detail of papal-imperial relations so that Louis may judge intelligently and independently the merits of the imperial case as well as recent papal missives accusing Frederick of neglect of the crusade. The chancery implies that the facts speak for themselves and present their own imperatives.

> Hec igitur omnia vobis tam plane quam plene satiataque relatione transcripsimus ut ad scientiam et conscientiam vestram ex toto corde perveniant cum nostra justitia, apud vos locum non habeat aliquis contrarius aut malignus interpres, qui quod nos pro recuperatione nostrorum jurium facimus, hoc cum aliorum injuria nos facere forte describat, aut incrementum negotii Terre Sancte, que velut Cunradi karissimi filii nostri materna successo, pre ceteris terre principibus specialius nos contingit, pretermittere, cuius, ut diximus licet nos astringat ad presens instantia necessitatis, tamen periculum non astringit, utpote treugis inter nos et soldanum initis adhuc per triennium duraturis, quas in fidei nostre rupturam infringi nullo modo, quantum salubriter possemus resistere, medio tempore permittemus.

> Therefore we transcribed all these things for you clearly and completely, so that knowledge and wisdom may reach you together with the justice of our heart, and no opponent or malicious interpreter may find favor with you, that what we do for the recuperation of our laws he perhaps represents as our injuring others, or overlooking the conquest of the crusade (which, as the maternal succession of our dearest son Conrad whose [inheritance] it is, pertains to us most especially, before other princes of the earth); as we have said, it is possible that for now we hold to present immediate necessity, for danger [in the Holy Land] does not press inasmuch as there is a truce between us and the sultan which should last another three years, and which, as long as we can safely resist breaking our faith with any kind of infringement, permits us some time.

The letter concludes with the suggestion that whatever threatens Frederick's autonomy also endangers lesser princes, along with the admonition that Louis be aware of the forces that might limit his freedom to respond to rebellion within his kingdom.[25] Although

Gregory is not mentioned, the trusted impartial arbiter of the first half of the letter is clearly implicated, here and elsewhere, of obstructing the implementation of justice.

From the point of view of rhetoric, the persuasive force of the document lies in the recounting of contingent events, the historical record. The *varietas temporis* and *rerum necessitate cogente* have determined the emperor's actions, in view of his steadfast resolve to restore peace and justice to the state in Lombardy, and ultimately to reinforce the gains of Christians made during his previous sojourn to the Holy Land. Perhaps as a reflection of the chancery's ambivalence about the type of argument that would be effective at the French court, the letter reflects both the traditional and the new appeal: the corollary to the emperor's insistence on presenting his actions in the light of reason is that the enemy operates in secret and in darkness.

The most celebrated victory in the four imperial campaigns against Lombardy was at Cortenova in November 1237. Frederick dispatched a series of letters announcing the imperial military victory at Cortenova, which will be the focus of the remainder of this chapter.[26] They are interesting as examples of the contrasting persuasive approaches adopted by the chancery when addressing its allies, client states, and enemies. The letters show the chancery's awareness of the diversity of the cultures of its public, and illustrate the profound difference between the traditional, moralistic persuasion of the period and the "mature" persuasion of the chancery that presents the facts with a minimum of embellishment and encourages the intended public to judge the credibility of the evidence on the basis of its own experience. The victory at Cortenova, essentially won by a vanguard of German knights, is variously transformed into a triumph of the forces of light against darkness, a testament to the ascendancy of the spirit of the Caesars, a celebration of courage over pusillanimity, and a purely fortuitous military encounter. The letter to the German princes is rich in Biblical imagery and verbal figures, reflecting the chancery's recognition of the ecclesiastical culture of the German princes and prelates; that addressed to the Romans is distinguished by its use of the lexicon and ideology established in the *Prooemium* to the Constitutions of Melfi.

In the letter to the German princes and prelates, the battle at Cortenova is described as a struggle of light against darkness. The Lombards are a cowardly lot, morally and physically corrupt: they are the sons of Belial, Satanic offspring who rose in revolt against the

Davidic line of kings.[27] They dare not show their faces to the light but sow tares in the fields by night. Their end is recorded in Matthew's parable.[28] The description of the enemy armies is operatic in its drama and musicality. It is the awful voice of the ancient prophets.[29]

> O quanta erat multitudo militum! quanta numerositas et universitas bellatorum! Ibi superbia pulsavit tympanum, voluptas tuba concinit, resonat cythara, plaudit lyra: et sic voluptatis ager cum pudendi decoris insignibus pullulavit.

> Oh how great were the ranks of soldiers, how great the multitude of warriors! Here pride beat the drum, passion sounded the horn, struck the zithers, plucked the lyre: and thus the field of passion was bristling with bright banners of shame.

Frederick, the new Solomon, comes to Lombardy to bring peace. But the sons of the Devil will not be subdued. Finally the emperor, whose victory is guaranteed by the heavens, dons his cuirass, arms himself, and, accompanied by the angelic army of the Lord, enters into the fray like a giant.

> . . . et audita est vox tonitrui et stuporis: "Euge! euge! ad Mediolanenses impiger advola Friderice." Quo audito, Mediolanensis protervitas statim fuit perterrita: compagnie projiciunt cimbala, sumunt arma: et dum a trementi cuiuslibet dextera retineri vix poterat gladius, quilibet mutus in suo pectore tacitos vertit questus: "Heu! heu! anime nostre: quid sic torques nos acriter atrox et immisericorditer immisericors Friderice?" Fit clamor ad sydera: "Ve! ve! tibi misera Lombardia." Quid plura? mactatur senex, puer diripitur, juvenis ut vitulus immolatur, campi madescunt sanguine, ac interfectorum exuberant ubertate.

> . . . and the voice of thunder and stupor was heard, "Euge! Euge! the swift-footed Frederick flies towards the Milanese." Hearing this, the rash Milanese were frozen by fear. The cymbals of the assembly sounded, arms were donned, and with great trepidation anyone who could, took up a sword in his right hand. Each man implored silently in his breast, "Heu! Heu! my soul, why do you torture me so terribly and unmercifully with the cruel and ruthless Frederick?" And the

instruments sounded: "Alas! Alas! for you, wretched Lombardy!"
What more? the old man was slaughtered, the child torn to pieces, the
youth sacrificed like calf, the fields drenched in blood and strewn
with the wealth of the vanquished.

Frederick, the patient and omnipotent peacemaker, wields a sword that
thirsts for blood and devours flesh. The letter concludes in the same
hyperbolic tone: a description of the defeated sinners is juxtaposed to
the portrait of the German princes, luminous in mind, noble in reason,
rich in virtue. The emperor, the almighty soldier of Christ, invites the
princes to share the glory of the magnificent victory.

If God ensured imperial victory in the letter to the Germans, the
straightforward and chronological account of events in the letter sent to
Richard, Earl of Cornwall, exemplifies the new persuasive strategy.
There is no attendant figurative reading of the events. Each act is
explained as the consequence of well or poorly laid plans or pure
chance. The foolhardy and wicked temerity of the Lombards who have
long defied imperial rule in Italy is condemned. That the situation has
caused suffering in the region is known far and wide. Other remedies
having proved inadequate, the emperor is finally moved by necessity to
resort to arms in order to curb the criminal conduct of the adversary.

Quante audacie quanteque temeritatis sint Ligurum excellentie nostre
rebellium factiones, . . . nec latere vos credimus, nec mundus ignorat
tam longe nostre dissimulationis constantiam circa eos, ut tolerantia
nostra verum patientie nomen amitteret et vitiose notam
pusillanimitatis incurreret pro decore virtutis. Animadvertentes
postmodum quod ferro secanda sunt vulnera, que fomentorum non
sentiunt medicinam, necessario nos ad arma convertimus. . . .

How audacious and rash have been the proceedings of the Ligurians
. . . in rebelling against our royal person. . . . And we think that you
are not unaware of what the world knows, namely that our constantly
passing over their offenses has continued so long, that, if we were to
continue to do so, our tolerance would lose the name of true patience,
and would incur the stigma of vile pusillanimity, instead of the
honorable name of virtue. Considering, after some little time, that
wounds which do not feel any effect from the application of

fomentations, ought to be cut with the knife, we of necessity resorted to arms. . . .[30]

The analogy between medical intervention and the emperor's necessary recourse to arms (necessity defined by the historical situation) is traditional but in keeping with the tone of the letter. The concept of necessity is that which is conditioned by the situation in view of a positive good; that is, the establishment of imperial peace and justice in the region.

The battle between the imperial and Lombard forces is neither divinely ordained nor divinely monitored. It is by chance, "casualiter tamen feliciter," that a small imperial advance guard sets up camp on the shore of the Oglio River opposite the Milanese. Sight of the imperial band puts the Milanese to flight. At this point the main corps of the imperial army, apparently including the emperor, makes haste to join the advance guard, but its way is impeded by the debris of the Milanese army—unmanned battle horses and corpses of enemy knights—abandoned by the vanquished.

Et sic cum in cavernis morari diutius ultra flumen, rerum ipsos arcente penuria, non valerent, Mediolanenses et socii per pontes et vada fluminis Olei transeuntes, in apertam planiciem exiverunt, credentes se nobis per subsidium occulte fuge subripere, dum nos adeo prope consistere forsitan non putarent. Sed cum de adventu nostro terror et fremitus tanquam de celo tonitruum ipsis intonuit, ad premissas nostre celsitudinis acies . . . in fugam sic subito a facie nostra contriti se converterunt. . . . Et dum auxiliares acies, et post eas nos cum nostrorum agminum robore, gressibus festinatis, hiis qui in levi manu precesserant necessario cursu succurrere crederemus, . . . ad carrochium tandem quod juxta muros municipii Curtis Nove fossatorum vallis circumdatum et immensa militum copia et suorum omnium peditum mira defensione pugnantium munitum invenimus applicantes. . . . Supervenientis autem noctis umbrosa caligine, quam nostrorum vota longissimam suspirabant, tentatum aggressum tantisper obmisimus usque mane sequenti. . . . Et ut multa sub compendio concludamus, tum capti tum mortui, inter quos multi Mediolanensis factionis primates et principes corruerunt, decem milia fere numero computantur.

The Milanese and their allies, not being able to stay any longer in their hiding-places, owing to the scarcity of necessaries, crossed the river Oglio by the fords and bridges, and came into the open plain, thinking to escape from us by a secret flight, and perhaps not imagining that we were so near. When, however, they knew of our proximity, fear and terror fell on them like a clap of thunder from heaven, and at sight of the advance guard of our imperial army . . . they turned to flight before us . . . and, as we believed that it was necessary for us to hasten to the assistance of the auxiliary troops, who had proceeded in advance in a small body, we marched after them with all speed with the strength of our army. . . . At length we discovered their carrocio [cart that carries the standard], near the walls of Cortenova, surrounded by trenches, and protected by an immense body of knights and all their foot soldiers, who fought wonderfully in its defense. . . . The shades of night, however, coming on, which our men ardently wished for, we desisted from the attack till the following morning early. . . . To make a short account of the matter, almost ten thousand men were said to have been taken or slain; among whom a great many nobles and chiefs of the Milanese faction fell.

The dissimilarity between the two letters could not be more striking. In the letter to Richard, moral interpretations do not provide the key to explain the success or failure of human endeavors. The battle is recounted and its outcome explained on the basis of a knowledge of human nature and the particular attendant circumstances. For example, the Milanese are forced to leave their hideouts due to scarce supplies, unaware of the proximity of the imperial advance guard. The few rhetorical flourishes do not distract from an essentially sober account of the battle, which includes praise for the courage of the enemy infantry. There is no indication that the emperor ever engaged in combat. The melodramatic and moralistic fervor of the letter to the Germans leads to flagrant distortions, the most obvious being the transformation of the emperor into a battlefield titan and Old Testament hero. There is a timeless, epic, inevitable quality to the first letter that is absent in the second, in which events are presented chronologically and dictated by diurnal rhythms as well as by physiological needs; in the second, the emperor's military adventurism is introduced as a necessary remedy for a destabilizing situation, and not as a preordained encounter.

The letter sent to the imperial subjects in the Kingdom of Sicily resembles the exhortations to join the crusade of the previous decades. It employs the persuasion of joyful celebration. The power and glory of Frederick's imperial reign have been proven to all at the battle of Cortenova. The letter opens with two phonically resonant antithetical proclamations:

> Exultet jam romani imperii culmen, et pro tanti victoria principis mundus gaudeat universus. Erubescat illicita Lombardorum societas, confundatur rebellis insania, et pro tante stragis exitio, inimici populi contremiscant.

> Exult now the majesty of the Roman Empire; may all the world rejoice in the victory of such a prince. May the illegal league of Lombards, confounded with the insanity of the rebels, blush for shame, and the enemy tremble at these massacres.

More than all others, conquered Milan must lament. "Infelix Mediolanum ingemiscat et doleat, et amare prorumpat in lachrymas de tantis occisorum catervis militum et civium captivorum, et modo mundi obedire domino assuescat" [unhappy Milan may groan and lament and bitterly weep, for the soldiers of such great armies are dead and the cities are captured, and they must become accustomed to obeying a lord as others do]. Magnanimous and astute, Frederick pursues the cowardly army of the Milanese. Since the enemy will not meet him in open battle, he tricks them into combat. Like the letter to the German princes, this one paints Caesar's army and the devastated enemy fighting amidst rivers of blood. But the battle is not portrayed in the atemporal manner of the letter to the German princes; it marks a portentous and glorious day of Frederick's reign on earth, among men.

> Et ita imperatoris militia se preparavit ad prelium expedite, tanquam leones, quos fames stimulat, ad stabula cursitant armentorum: nec ulterius mora protracta, die vigesimo-septimo mensis novembris undecime indictionis . . . bellum terribile inceperunt. . . .

> And thus the militia of the emperor promptly prepared itself for battle; they raced to the armory like lions, spurred on by hunger, and without further delay, on the twenty-seventh of the month of

> November, in the eleventh indiction . . . they entered into the terrible battle.

A series of rhetorical questions introduced by anaphora follows:

> Sed quis posset illius diei narrare pericula? Quis valeret hostium acervos cadaverum scribere? Quis captivorum multitudinem numerare?

> But who could tell of the dangers of the day? Who would be capable of describing the mounds of enemy corpses? Who of numbering the multitude of captives?

Quite obviously, "Deus justus judex jura respexit imperii" [God, the just judge, has turned his attention back to the empire]. Frederick, who conquered Jerusalem for the Christians without shedding a drop of blood, is here portrayed as a great and awful warrior. The details issue forth to the sound of the military drum: *tunc . . . tunc . . . tunc.*

> Tunc Cesar pre omnibus suis militibus sue virtutis potentiam est expertus. Ipse enim inimicorum cuneos manu propria feriebat. Tunc Theutonici suos gladios rubenti sanguine rubricaverunt: tunc felices fidelesque Apulie milites collaterales principis mirabiliter pugnaverunt. Tunc miranda Papie militia se de Mediolanensibus militibus vindicavit . . . nullus eorum de manibus Cesaris evasisset.

> Then Caesar, before all of his soldiers, proved the strength of his virtue. He, in fact, struck at the ranks of the enemy with his own hands. Then the Germans reddened their swords in the ruby blood, then the fortunate and loyal army of Apulians fought valiantly at the side of the prince, and the astonishing Roman troops avenged themselves on the Milanese army, . . . none of whom escaped the hands of Caesar.

The celebration of imperial might concludes with a prophecy of the fullness of time, "Vere de throno Dei sententia prodiit inferens judicium ultionis" [Truly from the throne of God came forth the judgment of vengeance].

The letter sent to the pope and the cardinals resembles that sent to Richard, Earl of Cornwall, except for the heavy dose of irony in the chancery's call for Gregory to celebrate the Milanese defeat. (Gregory is reported to have wept at the news.) It opens with a proclamation of "the common joy of all the princes of the earth and of the mother church especially." The frequent and flagrant offenses of the Lombards have finally provoked the long-suffering emperor to act, to operate with his sword what could not be effected with medicines. The emperor, sleeping too long, has been spurred to action. In the letter to the pope, a straightforward passage recounts the capture of the castle of Montechiaro which preceded the battle of Cortenova. Frederick, the humble son and defender of the church, is portrayed at prayer in the company of priests before embarking on the day's campaign. He is not the great Caesar of Antiquity, nor is he the all-conquering hero. In fact it is again only by good fortune that the imperial army happens to trap the Milanese by the side of the Oglio River and challenge them to battle.

The narration proceeds chronologically and gives the impression of a factual recounting, with only minimal recourse to embellishment. It tells of the slaughter, the discovery of the abandoned carrocio which carried the battle standard at Cortenova, and the cross left behind by the retreating Milanese. The letter closes with the quasi-apocalyptic vision of the dangerous monster of communal autonomy, and devout prayer for divine favor when in the Holy Land. "Domino Jesu Christo filiali devotione rogamus, qui suum prosequendo negocium, sacrum imperium victoriose sublimat et extollit" [In filial devotion to Jesus Christ, we beg that in the next crusade, He victoriously elevate and exalt the sacred empire].

To accompany the carrocio, Frederick's gift to the city of Rome, the imperial chancery writes a letter that is constructed on three themes: the dictates of all-powerful reason (*ratio prepotens*) must be observed in a universe where the adversary is irrational; the evocation of the greatness of Rome in Antiquity, and the assurance that in this great imperial victory, Rome has again found her Caesar, her conqueror who will renew the ancient greatness of the city. An exaltation of the city opens the letter and the verb *extollere* occurs three times in a figure of polyptoton.

Ad extollendum imperii nostri temporibus decus Urbis, quod per gloriam triumphorum futurum excelsius extimavere majores, et ratio prepotens que regibus imperat et natura nos obligat et civiliter obligatos voce dignissima profitemur. Ecce enim cum ad sue cause naturam triumphus necessario redicatur, quod extollere decus imperiale non possimus quin interim Urbis honorem quam causam imperii fuisse cognoscimus, extollamus.

Both ascendant reason, whose commands kings must obey, and nature oblige that the present-day emperor exalt the fame of the city which our forefathers elevated with glorious triumphs to an ever-loftier future, and we offer homage urbanely and with solemn words. Behold, truly, since the triumph must necessarily be traced back to its cause, so we could not exalt our imperial glory without exalting first the honor of the city which we of old recognized as the origin of our power. [31]

Rome is the cause and the origin of the empire and in her name the emperor has triumphed. Although Frederick establishes the law according to his perception of the *varietas temporis,* he must obey the dictates of all-powerful reason, the mother of law.

Rome sent her untried child to conquer imperial glory in Germany, and the son now begs the city to receive her conquering hero, as in Antiquity. To the city he offers the Milanese caroccio, the *opima spoglia,* in the manner of the ancient Caesars. The carrocio is a pledge by the emperor to reestablish peace in Italy. It is a tribute to the ancient traditions and a symbol of the forthcoming renewal of the city, a frequently recurring topic in the imperial rhetoric of the 1230s.

Imperatoris igitur vestri victoriam, quirites, gratanter accipite; spes ex hoc vos pulcherrima foveat quia quum libenter antiqua solemnia sequimur, ad reformationem antique nobilitatis in urbe libentius aspiramus.

Receive therefore with gratitude, O citizens, the victory of your emperor! The fairest hope may smile on you, for dearly as we love to follow the old ceremonies, more eagerly do we aim at renewing the ancient nobility of the city.

The letter ends with a denunciation of the detractors of the empire and their symbol. They are the enemies of light, of reason, of glory, and of the authority of the people and senate of Rome. The emperor's appeal had profound resonance in Rome. By order of the Senate, the caroccio was mounted on five marble columns in the Capitol.

In the Cortenova letters we see the full range of imperial persuasive appeals: from the letter to Richard of Cornwall where the assumption that men are able to interpret the experience of their world rationally prevails, and actions are explained in terms of physiological and political necessity, and the letter to the Romans, in which the celebration of human reason and nature becomes the persuasive dynamic for Romans to turn to Frederick as their new Caesar, to the self-acclaim of the letter to the Sicilians, to the portrait of Frederick as the colossal champion who commands a divinely ordained victory over the cowardly sons of the devil in the letter to the German princes and prelates. The versatility and virtuosity of the imperial chancery is evident—rhetorical choices depend on the subject matter of the epistle, but the perceived culture of the public is as important a consideration in the determination of which argument or modes of interpretation will be effective in a given situation.

The persuasive techniques that emerged in the 1220s continued to develop, especially after the publication of the *Constitutiones* in 1231. Imperial political letters show an active dialectic between the major and minor premise: events justify and are justified by the statement of imperial ideology in the exordium. The letters offer deductive and inductive arguments for the justice of imperial acts, proof that the emperor is acting in accordance with his mandate, and that the mandate is necessary. In keeping with the staking out of a sphere of knowledge that could be grasped rationally, imperial justice is described as human justice, and it is defended with reasons that are accessible to the human intellect. The accidents of time "acquire their functional character" in a different way, and become an integral part of the argument to persuade the public of the justice of imperial actions. While it is not true that "secret" intentions and moral explanations are entirely eliminated in the characterizations of human behavior, a new emphasis is placed on reasons for actions—by allies and enemies alike—that are discernible to all, reasons like self-interest and self-preservation in the face of political, legal, and physiological pressure.

The new rhetoric was motivated by several factors, including the immense challenge that canon law posed to secular leaders and cultural developments like the rediscovery of the Aristotelian science of nature. It responded to the powerful and alluring language issuing from the pontifical chancery, a language that implicitly defined dissent as disobedience and pride. The most important consequence of the new rhetoric is that it justifies partisan argument, which had been denounced as *novella opinio* by Honorius.

NOTES

1. I have already broached this argument in two articles, "Rhetoric and Aristotelian Natural Philosophy," *Imagining New Worlds: Essays on Factual and Figural Discovery During the Middle Ages,* Ed. Scott D. Westrem (New York: Garland Publishing, 1991) 142-56, and "Rhetoric and Science at the Court of Frederick II of Hohenstaufen," *Studi di filologia e letteratura italiana in onore di M. Picchio Simonelli,* Ed. Pietro Frassica (Alessandria: Edizioni dell' Orso, 1991) 289-300. Parts of the present chapter draw from and elaborate on those two articles. Some of the broader implications of the introduction of the Aristotelian science of nature are the fruit of conversations with Cristiana Fordyce, a doctoral candidate in Romance Languages and Literatures at Boston College.

2. John Herman Randall Jr. *Aristotle.* (New York: Columbia University Press, 1960) 33-34.

3. For example, of reproduction among bees, Aristotle writes, "But the facts have not been adequately ascertained and if they ever are to be, credence must be given more to perception than to reasoned arguments, and to reasoned arguments only if what they show is in agreement with the *phainomena.*" *Generation of Animals* 760b27-33. Quoted by Robert Bolton, "The Epistemological Basis of Aristotelian Dialectic," *Biologie, Logique et Métaphysique chez Aristote. Actes du Seminaire C.N.R.S.-N.S.F. Oléron June 28-July 3, 1987,* Eds. Daniel Devereux and Pierre Pellegrin (Paris: Éditions du Centre Nationale de la Recherche Scientifique, 1990) 192.

4. *De Arte Venandi cum Avibus* has been edited by Carl Arnold Willemsen, *Friderici Romanorum Imperatoris Secundi "De Arte Venandi cum Avibus,"* 2 vols. (Leipzig: Insula, 1952). It was edited and translated into English by Casey A. Wood and Marjorie G. Fyfe, *The Art of Falconry Being the "De Arte Venandi cum Avibus" of Frederick II of Hohenstaufen* (Palo Alto: Stanford University Press, 1943). In Edward Grant, *A Source Book in Medieval Science*

(Cambridge, MA: Harvard University Press, 1974), the work is described as "one of the great scientific treatises of the Middle Ages" (657).

5. I am defining the science of nature as the study of that which "comes into being and passes away," (Randall 164). This includes Aristotle's investigation of nature in the *Physics* and his works on biology, especially *De Partibus Animalium, De Generatione Animalium,* and *Historia Animalium,* as well as some brief monographs. The *De Anima* pertains in part to the science of nature, as do some of the studies of the heavens.

6. Lynn Thorndike, *Michael Scot* (London: Nelson, 1965) 22-31. Although there is disagreement among scholars on whether or not Michael Scot was the first to translate all of the following works into Latin, the Aristotelian texts that are generally credited to him include *De Caelo et Mundo,* completed after 1217 and accompanied by the "great commentary" by Averroes, *De Partibus Animalium, De Generatione Animalium,* and *Historia Animalium,* all three translated at Toledo before 1220, and the *Physics* with a commentary by Averroes. Scot composed a Latin Compendia of *Parva Naturalia;* he translated *De Anima* and the accompanying commentary by Averroes, and parts of the *Metaphysics* with an Averroes commentary. He dedicated another work, Avicenna's *Abbreviatio de Animalibus,* based on the Aristotelian *Liber de Animalibus,* to Frederick II. According to Thorndike, Scot "has been held largely responsible for the introduction of Averroism into western Christian Europe. . ." (24).

7. Haskins wrote, in an article dedicated to the scientific activity at the Frederican court, "The more literary members of the Magna Curia, such as Piero della Vigna, are silent respecting their scientific associates." Charles Homer Haskins, *Studies in the History of Medieval Science* (1924. New York: Frederick Ungar Publishing Co., 1960) 248.

8. *Languentis orbis* is in J.-L. A. Huillard-Bréholles, *Historia diplomatica Friderici Secundi* 4.1 (Paris: H. Plon, 1852-1861) 409. The basic intent of the letter, which follows the proof that the two swords of Peter are really one, is stated in the sentence, "Igitur, beatissime pater, nos duo qui unum dicimur et idem pro certo sentimus, salutem communis fidei unanimiter procuremus, relevemus ecclesiasticam libertatem oppressam, et tam ecclesie jura quam imperii restaurantes, commissos nobis gladios in perversores fidei et rebelles imperii acuamus."

9. Beryl Smalley, *Studies in Medieval Thought and Learning* (London: Hambledon Press, 1981) 117-20.

10. This quotation and the next are from Wood and Fyfe 4.

11. See note 3 above.

12. J. A. Giles, Trans. *Matthew Paris's English History. From the Year 1235 to 1273* 1 (London: Harry G. Bohn, 1852) 228. The passage is discussed in this book in Chapter 9.

13. Huillard-Bréholles, 5, 349. The letter is *In exordio,* 348-51.

14. According to the Gonville and Caius MS 109/178, "Et necessitas significat quod hoc quod est non est nisi propter quid." The thirteenth-century manuscript contains a copy of Michael Scot's translation of the Aristotelian work from the Arabic. Cambridge University, Gonville and Caius College, MS 109/178, fol. 60v. Contingent necessity is also described in *Physics* 2.9.
In Aristotle "necessity" is defined in various ways. The necessity of the heavens, like logical necessity, is and cannot be otherwise. But contingent, hypothetical necessity, a term used to demonstrate in physics and nature, is neither ontologically nor logically determined. Randall explains that according to Aristotle, "in physics, if the end or goal is to be attained, then the conditions are necessary; if the conditions are not present, then the end will not be attained" (185). "Aristotle understands by a goal (*hou heneka*), whether natural or not, something good (from some point of view) that something else causes or makes possible, where this other thing exists or happens (at least in part) because of that good." John M. Cooper, "Hypothetical Necessity and Natural Teleology," *Philosophical Issues in Aristotle's Biology,* Eds. Allen Gotthelf and James G. Lennox (New York: Cambridge University Press, 1987) 245. For discussions of the term *necessitas* in the imperial documents see Thea Buyken, "Über das *Prooeium* der *Constitutionen von Melfi*," *Revista Portuguesa de História* 14 (1941): 169; Ernst Kantorowicz, *Frederick the Second, 1194-1250,* Trans. E. O. Lorimer (New York: Frederick Ungar Publishing Co., 1957) 261, and Wolfgang Stürner, "*Rerum Necessitas* und *Divina Provisio:* Zur Interpretation des *Prooemiums* der *Konstitutionen von Melfi* (1231)," *Deutsches Archiv für die Erforschung des Mittelalters* 39 (1983): 506-11.

15. Cooper 243, note 1.

16. Dante, at the beginning of the fourteenth century, makes an explicit connection between Aristotle's method in the *Physics* and the correct mode of interpretation of the canzoni in the *Convivio.* Dante insists on the absolute priority of the literal sense of a text for understanding because the literal contains within it the other levels of meaning. To proceed otherwise, according to Dante, would be irrational. He explains in *Convivio* 2.1.13: "Onde, sì come dice lo Filosofo nel primo de la Fisica, la natura vuole che ordinatamente si proceda ne la nostra conoscenza, cioè procedendo da quello che conoscemo meglio in quello che conoscemo non così bene; dico che la natura vuole, in quanto questa via di conoscere è in noi naturalmente innata" [Whence, as the

Philosopher says in the first book of the *Physics,* nature desires that one proceed in an orderly manner in our knowledge, that is proceeding from that which we know better to that which we don't know so well; I say that nature wants this, in that this way of knowing is by nature innate in us]. Dante is not, of course, discounting the verity of the allegorical interpretation of the text, which he takes pains to elucidate in the exegesis of his poems that follows. But he is emphatically insisting on the authority of the literal reading of the text. The literal sense of the text, like material reality, is not merely a medium through which the truth might be attained. The literal, non-figurative reading of the text, like the created world, is the starting point of human reason ["E in dimostrar questo, sempre lo litterale dee andare innanzi, sì come quello ne la cui sentenza li altri sono inchiusi..." (2.1.8)]. And to argue his case Dante alludes to the methodological instruction of the *Physics.* Dante Alighieri, *Il Convivio,* Ed. Maria Simonelli (Bologna: Patron, 1966).

17. Berman notes the important influence of the *Assizes* of Ariano, issued by Frederick's grandfather, King Roger, founder of the "first absolute monarchy in Western Europe." Harold J. Berman, *Law and Revolution: The Formation of the Western Legal Tradition* (Cambridge, MA: Harvard University Press, 1983) 419. For a discussion of Roger's influence see Berman 417-26, and Francesco Brandileone, *Il Diritto romano nelle leggi normanne e sveve del regno di Sicilia* (Rome: Fratelli Bocca, 1884). Berman points to Article 22 of the *Assizes* as evidence of the pervasive influence of canonical procedures: "'A diligent inquisition should examine arguments, witnesses, written evidence, and other indicators of truth,' and . . . the judge should respect not only the evidence presented by the prosecutor but also 'should be in the middle between each person, so that he will only render judgment according to all competent evidence carefully sought out.' This is a very early example of the introduction of a system of rational proof in the royal courts of Europe. In Carolingian times, to be sure, proof by inquest or inquisition had been used, but in a much more primitive form and for proof of facts in a much narrower circle of cases, and only in the court of the king himself or the courts of ecclesiastical or noble dignitaries specially designated" (423-24). Also see James M. Powell, Ed. and Trans., *The "Liber Augustalis" or "Constitutions of Melfi," Promulgated by the Emperor Frederick II for the Kingdom of Sicily in 1231* (Syracuse: Syracuse University Press, 1971).

18. Berman 425.

19. The term came to be considered "so characteristic that forged letters and exercises in style that sought to catch the note of the Hohenstaufen chancery rarely forgot to drag in the *necessitas rerum.*" Kantorowicz, *Frederick* 247.

20. Most helpful in identifying sources for the language of the *Prooemium* is Buyken, "Über" 161-76. Also useful is Stürner 467-554.

21. The text of the *Prooemium* is from Hermann Conrad, Thea von der Lieck-Buyken, and Wolfgang Wagner, *Die Konstitutionen Friedrichs II. von Hohenstaufen für sein Königreich Sizilien* (Cologne: Bohlau Verlag, 1973) 2.

22. The translation is from Powell 3-4.

23. The phrase is borrowed from Nancy Streuver, "The Study of Language and the Study of History," *The Journal of Interdisciplinary History* 4.3 (1974): 404.

24. *Inviti loquimur* is in Huillard-Bréholles, 4.2, 873-80. The letter is partially translated by Giles, 1, 191-93, but I have modified Giles's translation to give a more precise rendering of the Latin.

25. The entire passage reads, "Vos igitur cum ceteris regibus orbis terre interest plene perspicuas aures et oculos aperire et diligenter attendere quanta contradictionis fiducia omnibus a jugo dominii subtrahere se volentibus prebeatur, si Romanum imperium jacturam huiusmodi rebellionis pateretur; ac oculo cernite perspicaci si vobis expedit quod, cum ad edomandam interdum protervam audaciam subditorum intenditis, vestris negotiis extrinsecus aliquis [se] interponat, causamque aliquam aut occasionem afferat per quam vestra precidat proposita vel retardet."

26. The letters are in Huillard-Bréholles, 5. The first, *Quia vestre,* addressed to the German princes (147-49); the second, *Quante audacie,* to Richard of Cornwell (132-34); the third, *Exultet jam,* to Frederick's loyal subjects (137-39); the fourth, *Communem omnium,* to the pope and cardinals (142-45) and the final letter, *Ad extollendum,* to the Romans (161-63). I discussed these letters in my dissertation, "Rhetorical Innovation in the Chancery of Frederick II of Hohenstaufen and its Reception by Vernacular Poets of the Thirteenth Century," Diss., Boston College, 1985, as well as the two articles mentioned above in note 1.

27. My thanks to Scott Westrem for pointing out the political importance of the epithet. See 2 Chronicles 13:6-17.

28. Matthew 13:24-30.

29. Joel 2. Again, my thanks to Scott Westrem.

30. The translation is by Giles, 1, 93-95.

31. The translation is partially based on Kantorowicz, *Frederick* 448-49.

CHAPTER 9

The Failure of Persuasion

Gregory excommunicated Frederick for the second time on Palm Sunday, March 29, 1239. The charges, stated in *Excommunicamus,* were sent to prelates and secular lords of Europe in two different documents, both dated April 7, 1239. *Cum nuper* announces the excommunication and procedures for its observation, while *Sedes apostolica* is "a full-scale encyclical that also elaborately justified the sentence and provided a digest of charges contained in *Excommunicamus.*"[1] Lomax argues that Gregory's intention was not merely to excommunicate the emperor, but to set in motion a legal procedure that would lead to the emperor's deposition. The documents lists eight crimes (paucis de multis) of which the emperor is guilty: Frederick has incited disturbances against the pope in Rome, thereby violating his oath to defend the church; he has interfered with the missions of several prelates including James of Palestrina and Peter the Saracen; he has interfered with the election of church officials in Sicily, and he has overtaxed and reduced to ruin the Kingdom of Sicily, "which is the spiritual patrimony of St. Peter, and for which he is bound by an oath of fealty of the Apostolic See, and is its vassal." As a result of the dilapidation of the Kingdom of Sicily, "Frederick impedes the cause of the Holy Land and the Roman empire." The emperor is guilty of seizing and devastating papal lands, against his oath. He detained the nephew of the King of Tunis, preventing the latter from receiving baptism at Rome. The pope emphasizes that Frederick has been previously admonished for the aforesaid crimes, as required by law, yet he "does not feel the remedy of correction, as the ulcers of his offenses are become hardened, and he daily presumes to commit worse crimes." Because of these crimes, Gregory, albeit unwillingly, sees fit to "promulgate the sentence of excommunication and anathema against the said emperor Frederick, consigning him to Satan, that by the death of his body on the day of the Lord, his soul may be saved." The prelates are warned, exhorted, and commanded to publish the excommunication.

A passage from a recent imperial letter, *Cum sit Christus,* is cited as evidence of Frederick's ingratitude. In the letter the emperor rants that the only appropriate response to the injustice that he has suffered at the hands of Gregory is the "ultiones cesareas" (the vengeance of the Caesars). Nevertheless, the emperor restrains himself because "we are compelled, in defending ourselves, to give greater offense by our resistance."[2] The pope, after citing the passage, editorializes,

> Wherefore, as the Lord, who lays open the hidden things of darkness, and reveals the secrets of all hearts, wished to disclose the hidden thoughts of his [Frederick's] heart, we gather from the purport of these letters what kind of devotion he feels towards the Roman church, his mother; what reverence or respect he has for the supreme pontiff and his brethren and the Apostolic See . . . for he seems to have conspired against us and them, from which it is sufficiently shown what kind of, and how great a crime he has committed.

Despite Gregory's familiarity with Frederick's hidden thoughts, he apparently did not anticipate the emperor's response to excommunication.

Levate, the imperial encyclical issued at Treviso on April 20, 1239, sets out a lengthy account of papal-imperial relations from the time of Frederick's minority. The imperial chancery's intention is to shore up support for Frederick—to persuade officials that Frederick is innocent of the charges leveled against him because he has always acted in accordance with his mandate, and to convince them that the sentence of excommunication itself is invalid since Gregory is not a worthy judge.[3] Furthermore, Gregory, in his blind defense of the Lombard cities' rebellion against imperial jurisdiction, is himself guilty of heresy and should therefore be subject to the judgment of a council of Christian prelates and potentates. The letter "calls on the cardinals of the holy Roman church . . . to summon a general council of the prelates and other faithful followers of Christ" to judge the misguided man who occupies the papal cathedra. Heresy was the only charge that exempted the pope from immunity from prosecution and subjected him to the judgment of men, and that was the charge that the imperial chancery attempted to pin on Gregory. The imperial letter opens with a warning that all men heed of the present danger.[4]

> Levate in circuitu oculos vestros, arrigite filii hominum aures vestras, videte generale orbis scandalum, dissidia gentium, generale justitie doleatis excidium.

> Cast your eyes around you, sons of men, prick up your ears and grieve over the scandal of the world, the quarrels of nations and the universal banishment of justice.

The princes and peoples are called upon to understand the cause which the emperor champions in the name of all secular princes. "Sedete, principes, et intelligite, populi, causam nostram; de vultu Domini judicium prodeat, et oculi vestri videant equitatem" [Be seated, princes; and understand, nations, our cause. Let the judgment come forth from God's presence and let your eyes contemplate Justice]. It is an exordium that urges the public to hear and learn more, resolved in a verse of Psalm 16, in which the innocent and just suppliant begs for God's help against a powerful enemy.

If, as Pennington states, "Innocent elevated the papacy beyond the confines of human understanding and law,"[5] then the imperial chancery sought to drag the man who occupied the papal cathedra back to the realm of human judgment. Gregory has behaved "like a merchant . . . making himself his own sealer, writer, and, perhaps, his own accountant."[6] From the papal cathedra one expects the greatest mercy, benevolence, and wisdom, but Gregory,

> quem speravimus ea solummodo que sursum sunt sapere, et visu celestia contemplantem mente credidimus in celestibus habitare, subito inventus est homo: quin immo per inhumanitatis opera, non solum a veritate sepositus, sed a qualibet humanitate desertus.

> whom we hoped savored only of things which are above, and whom we believed in contemplation of heavenly things, was found all at

once to be a man, not only void of truth by his deeds of cruelty, but even cut off from all feelings and humanity.

Not steadfast in his contemplation of the divine, like all men Gregory is mutable, "suam fidem cum tempore varians et mores cum dignitate commutans" (altering his faith with circumstances and his character with his dignity). In the course of the narration a hopeless breach is opened between the spiritual demands of the papal office and the man who occupies that office, between the sound and reasonable expectations of the son and the disturbing reality of the father, between the steadfast justice and measure of the emperor and the enormous, unrelenting enmity of Gregory. The narration consists of a long recitation of the struggle between pope and emperor from the time of Frederick's minority. The purpose is to provide evidence that the papal charges on which the excommunication is based are false, and to show that the accusation of imperial ingratitude is, in reality, an expression of Gregory's inveterate hostility toward Frederick. Because of his hatred for Frederick, Gregory has responded with malice to the most extravagant gestures of good faith on the part of the imperial party. The church has been a true mother, permitting Frederick to triumph and to reign benevolently; yet faith in the mother prevented the emperor from recognizing the abominations of the father.

> Adhuc tamen conscientie nostre fidelis integritas et pura devotio, quam ad matrem sacrosanctam Romanam Ecclesiam habebamus, novercalia deliramenta patris agnoscere filium non sinebant: quin quod erat justitie crimini imputantes. . . .

> In addition to this, since the uprightness of our conscience, and the sincere devotion which we felt towards the infinitely holy Roman Church, our mother, did not allow the son to notice the unnatural follies of his father, since we attributed to chance what belong to craft. . . .

The consequence of the son's devotion has been the deterioration of divinely ordained imperial rights. Gregory blocked Frederick's efforts to establish peace and justice in Italy, prescribed by divine mandate. He forbade the advance of the imperial army, and yet on the very day that the papal truce between the emperor and the Lombards was to go into effect, Gregory ordered the emperor to take up arms against rebellious Romans. "Ecce qualiter pater noster iste sanctissimus nos amabat!" [This is how our very holy father loved us!]. In his role of impartial arbiter on the question of imperial rights in Lombardy, Gregory nominated the Bishop of Palestrina as legate there, which led to a state of chaos:

Ad alias artes postmodum se convertit, mittens obvium in vestimentis albis lupum rapacem, episcopum Penestrinum, per quem apud nos litteris apostolicis de vita sanctissima commendatum, Placentia nobis subditam et nostris amicam ad Mediolanesis factionis perjuria revocavit; per ipsum firmiter estimans sic universaliter et in totum fideles nostros evertere, ut processus nostros in Italiam penitus enervaret. Qua spe faciente divina clementia, que suum tuetur imperium, omnino frustratus, clamantibus apud eum rebellium nostrorum incendiis, depopulationibus rerum et stragibus occisorum, qui ipsum de data eis rebellionis secura fiducia, necnon de fide mentita, eo quod contra nos et imperium ipsis assistere promisisset, publicis vocibus arguebant. . . .

He then had recourse to other devices, sending a rapacious wolf in sheep's clothing to meet us, namely the bishop of Palestrina, commended to us by the apostolic letters as a man of most holy life, by whose means he recalled to the perjuries of the Milanese faction the city of Piacenza, which was subject and friendly to us, firmly thinking, by his means, so generally to confuse his faithful subjects, and to such a degree that he might entirely enervate our purpose of proceeding into Italy. In this hope, however, by the mercy of God, who protects his empire, he was entirely deceived; and the fire spreading amongst our rebellious subjects, and the depopulation caused by the slaughter of the guilty, cried aloud upon him, reproaching him for having inspired them with confidence in their rebellion, and also for his breach of faith, because he had promised to assist them against us and the empire.

The passage illustrates the dangers posed by political rhetoric, a discussion of events rooted in the accidents of time and not in the sacred pageant of providential history that reveals itself only within the sanctuary of the papal court. The extended narration invites speculation on papal motives, and the prestige of the epistolary form contributes legitimacy to the act.

Levate questions whether, considering the corruption of Gregory, it is not right to be excommunicate. Only the emperor's sense of duty as defender of the church makes the state of excommunication grievous to him: "owing to the justice of our cause and the infamy of his proceedings, we ought justly to have preferred it . . . but we grieve in our heart, out of shame for the holy mother Church." Nevertheless, the sentence of excommunication is not valid. In word and deed Gregory is hostile and has promoted the enemies of the divinely mandated empire. Frederick does not recognize him as a legitimate judge.

The evidence presented to prove that the emperor is innocent, and that Gregory's enmity toward Frederick renders him unworthy to judge in this case, is then reinterpreted to show that Gregory is heretical, as Lomax has shown. The true cause of Gregory's heresy is the Lombard affair, "which pricked the heart of the pope and burnt within it." His crimes are explained by his allegiance to the Lombards against Frederick. Showing favor to the city of Milan, "which is, according to the testimony of a great many credible religious men [testimonio religiosorum et quamplurium fide dignorum] inhabited for the most part by heretics," Gregory is heretical by association. Other charges are listed against Gregory, including cupidity and simony. The heretic is unable to exercise his duty as the vicar of Christ on Earth.

The prince, who has been divinely appointed to protect the church, urges the cardinals to convene a council to sit in judgment of the shepherd who is leading the flock of the Lord astray.

> Et ut omnes primates nominis christiani sanctum intentionis nostre propositum et pie devotionis zelum in nobis agnoscant, et quod non ex odii fomite, set ex causa justissima vel necessaria Romanus princeps contra Romanum antistitem commovetur, dum metuit ne grex dominicus sub tali pastore per devia deducatur, ecce quod sacrosancte Romane ecclesie cardinales per sanguinem Jesu Christi et sub attestatione divini judicii per nuncios nostros et letteras attestamus, ut generale concilium prelatorum et aliorum Christi fidelium debeant evocare. . . .

> And let all nobles and princes bearing the name of Christians know our holy intention and the zeal of pious devotion that is in us, and that

it is not from the fuel of hatred but from a most just or necessary cause, that the Roman prince is provoked against the Roman high priest, since he fears that the Lord's flock, under such a shepherd, may be led through pathless places. Behold, we, by our letters and messengers, call on the cardinals of the holy Roman church, by the blood of Christ, and under attestation of the Divine judgment, to summon a general council of the prelates and other followers of Christ. . . .

Levate persuades with arguments that are similar to those used in the appeal to Louis discussed in the previous chapter: Frederick's acts are justified by circumstances in the light of the imperial mandate. The message to Christian lords is that the pope is actively pursing his own political agenda, and Frederick's conflicts with the all-too-human man who occupies the papal office, are, like their own, legitimate. *Levate* offers a model for rational, systematic political dissension, and shows how far the imperial chancery has moved from the letters of the early 1220s. The fears of Frederick's *opinio novella,* expressed by Honorius in *Miranda tuis,* are realized in *Levate.*

The letter returns, at its conclusion, to its original appeal to the Christian princes. The emperor's cause is their own, and the disgrace heaped on Frederick, the first son of the church, taints all the princes. Moreover, successful against Frederick, Gregory might as easily topple legitimate rulers in other kingdoms. "Ad domum vestram cum aqua currite, cum ignis accenditur in vicinis . . . " [hasten to your house with water when the fire is raging in the neighboring ones]. An admonition and a call for the support of the secular princes follows: "sed ut totus mundus agnoscat quod honor omnium tangitur, quicunque de corpore secularium principum offendatur" [for the humiliation of all other kings and princes is believed to be an easy matter, if the power of the Caesar of the Romans is overthrown; as his shield endures the initial shock of the darts of the enemy]. How serious is Frederick's call for a general council? According to Lomax,

the purpose of the appeal was to prevent the pope from being able to induce the princes to enforce the sentence [of excommunication]. The emperor hoped that his arguments, which were based on the law of the church, would win, if not the active support, at least the neutrality of those to whom the pope would turn for support. The call for a council to judge the alleged crimes of the pope was meant to reinforce this strategy by placing Gregory on the defensive. . . . Frederick hoped to direct the attention of Christendom away from himself and onto the political activities of the papacy. The emperor probably did not ever expect to get the pope before a council of the sort proposed in *Levate,* but he did intend to attack Gregory's standing as a disinterested defender of the faith and the Church.[7]

Matthew Paris, never particularly sympathetic to the papacy, prefaces the presentation of *Levate* in the *Chronica Maiora* with a description of the general astonishment and consternation among the princes and prelates upon learning how great was Gregory's abuse of the papal office.[8]

Levate appears to have infuriated Gregory. *Ascendit,* his encyclical in response issued at the Lateran on June 21, 1239, is even longer than *Levate,* and it betrays the threat perceived in *Levate. Ascendit* represents a radical attempt to preclude the possibility of a rational exchange with the Frederican chancery. The ad hominem attacks in *Levate* are described as the deceitful and despicable words of the heretic which corrupt the hearts of the innocent. Gregory will counter the contagion of imperial rhetoric by addressing the public with "argumento puritatis" (arguments of purity). Gregory's principal motive for writing *Ascendit* is stated near the beginning of the letter:

> Sed potius ut eius resistere aperte veritate mendaciis ac illius confutare fallacias puritatis argumento possitis, caput, medium et finem huius bestie Frederici dicti imperatoris inspicite diligenter, et in eius verbis abominationes duntaxat invenientes et scelera, contra ipsius dolos sinceros animos scuto veritatis armate. . . .[9]

> But, that you may be the better able to oppose his lies by open truth, and to confute his deceits by the arguments of purity, carefully examine the head, the middle, and the lower parts of this beast Frederick, the so-called emperor; and, as you find only abominations and wickedness in his words, arm you sincere hearts with the shield of truth. . . .

In *Levate* the imperial chancery asks princes and prelates to join in a judgment premised on Frederick's and their own experiences. *Ascendit* does not call for a judgment, but a clarification of the Truth that has been obfuscated. The emperor's denial of the word of God alienates him from the community of rational men. He has isolated himself from the Logos and the logos; he is a stranger to men whose minds, hearts, and words are enlightened by the love of God.

Ascendit opens with an apocalyptic vision: "Ascendit de mari bestia blasphemie plena nominibus, que pedibus ursi et leonis ore deseviens ac membris formata ceteris sicut pardus." [There has risen from the sea a beast, full of words of blasphemy, which, formed with the feet of a bear, the mouth of a raging lion, and, as it were, a panther in its other limbs]. Gregory assumes the same public forum that Frederick had in *Levate:* their polemic takes place before all of the Christian princes, prelates, and peoples.

> Igitur admirari desinite omnes ad quos ab hac bestia contra nos edita pervenerunt obloquia blasphemie. . . . Admirari desinite si injuriarum in nos mucronem exerit, quod ad perdendum de terra nomen Domini jam assurgit. . . .
>
> Cease, therefore, to wonder, all of you, to whose ears the slanders of blasphemy against us which have emanated from this beast have reached. . . . Cease to wonder if he draws a sword of injury against us, because he now aims at blotting out the name of the Lord from the earth. . . .

The beast is Frederick, "dictus imperator . . . figulus falsitatis, modestie nescius" (the so-called emperor . . . the worker of falsehoods, ignorant of all modesty). Frederick is the forerunner to the Antichrist, "a wolf in sheep's clothing," "Potiphar's wife," "Simon reincarnate," "staff of the impious," "hammer of the earth."

The pope describes his revelation of the truth as an act of salvation for souls tainted by the venom of imperial mendacity. Repeatedly the emperor is accused of lying. His words are "polluted"; they are "falsehoods"; Frederick "spreads lies against God"; he is a "son of lies, heaping falsehoods on falsehoods;" his letters contain "lying words"; he is a "false-speaking man" who acts "without regard to the truth"; he is not ashamed of his "lying pen"; there is "not the least atom of truth mixed up with (his) falsehoods." In the long narration, every charge made by the imperial letter is reviewed, and each is declared the perverse creation of a deceitful counterfeiter. The account of events in *Levate* is especially dangerous because it may have the effect of transforming the truth into lies in the minds of many men.

Licet autem hec figmenta publica notitia reprobat, quia tamen nonnunquam rectitudinis sedem velatum occupat in aure sincera mendacium, apud quam pro se veritas non invenit advocatum, ne in corda vestra falsitas quecunque possit fraude surripere, dignum est verum rei per nos geste modum et ordinem non latere. . . .

Although the general knowledge of facts disproves these falsehoods, yet sometimes a concealed lie takes possession of the seat of truth in the ear of sincerity, when truth finds in it no advocate for itself therein. And in order that falsehood may not by any deceitful means creep into your hearts, it is proper that you should not be left in ignorance of the true particulars and manner of our proceeding. . . .

Frederick's words of calumny must be welcomed by anyone who is pure at heart, "ex quo cum malorum opprobria laudem, laudes quoque opprobrium resonent" (wherefore as the insults of wicked men resound praise, and their praise insult). The emperor has excluded himself, or perhaps been excluded by God, from the Truth: "iste vero cui ne veritatem fateri aut enarrare possit, judicium a divina forsan est indignatione negatum" (this man, to whom was perhaps denied by divine judgment the power either to confess the truth or to pronounce justice).

Gregory accuses Frederick of having poisoned the Landgrave of Thuringia "sicut mundus clamat" (as the world reports) at Brindisi at the time of the aborted crusade. In the Holy Land, Frederick "was changed from a defender to an enemy," because he left "the Lord's temple to the company of the Saracens, who there sang the praises of Mohammed." A similar charge is leveled against Frederick regarding the Kingdom of Sicily. The invasion of Sicily by papal troops during Frederick's expedition to the Levant is justified by the imperial regent's incursion into papal territories. (No mention is made in this context of Gregory's dissolution of the oath of loyalty that bound imperial subjects to Frederick on July 31, 1228, the act that historians say triggered the foray.

) The assumptions of obedience that premise letters like Pope Innocent's *Apostolica sedes,* the spiritual interpretations of letters like Pope Honorius's *Celestis altitudo,* or even the emotionally charged language of an earlier Gregorian encyclical like *In maris,* are no longer perceived as adequate in 1239. Nor is it enough for Gregory to refer to his pious intentions. In *Ascendit,* the facts are laid out for the Christian leaders to judge for themselves.

Gregory appeals to his public to note the lack of plausibility in Frederick's account of "destructive consequences" of papal interference in Lombardy.

Quanquam autem his figmentis modica veritas intermixta aliquid coloris adjiciat, ut tamen apertius intelligatis quod tantam huius commenti seriem non modica falsitatis adjectio decolorat, scitote pro certo quod cum, sicut nunc ex temporum eventu cognoscitur, discrete menti verisimilie videretur ipsum de Lombardis suum potius consequi propositum potuisse, si se illis quos populorum numerositas profunditasque vallorum, armatorum copia ac murorum reddit alitudo munitos, pietatis parentem exhibuisset et clementie dominum quam si trementibus pro culpa imposita subditis ultionis exerto mulcrone terribilis occurret in cuneis armatorum. . . .

But although there is not the least atom of truth mixed up with these falsehoods, so as to give them a coloring, in order that you may more clearly understand that no slight mass of falsehoods discolors the whole of these statements, we wish you to know for certain that, although, as is now known by the course of events, it would appear probable, to the discreet mind, that he could better have gained his ends with the Lombards if he had shown himself as an affectionate parent and a merciful lord to them, as they were strong in the number of their people, the thickness of the ramparts, their large army, and the height of their walls, than if he were to draw the sword of vengeance on his subjects, who were trembling for the offense imputed to them, and to strike terror into them by coming upon them with his legions of soldiers. . . .

The emperor's argument that his problems in Lombardy are the consequence of papal meddling is false, dangerous, and also implausible to an orderly mind. The other implication, of course, is that papal success in thwarting imperial ambition in Lombardy is proof of Gregory's clemency and wisdom.

Gregory strengthens his outraged censure of Frederick with a careful rationale for each and every issue raised in *Levate*. The persuasive dynamic of this letter is not rooted in premises and assumptions, but in the particular details expounded in the narration of the letter. *Ascendit* reinterprets episodes in the imperial letter according the Roman chancery's version of history, and in the context of the interests of the church. To cite one example, in response to the imperial charge that the papacy had retained control of the Lombard city, Castellana, in spite of a pledge to deliver it into imperial hands, *Ascendit* states,[10]

Venimus autem ad Civitatem Castelle cuius cives se ille violato sacramento fidei Ecclesia ignorante prodentes, nullum jus per hoc in seipsis adquirere, nullum nobis circa possessionem cum jurisdictionem civitatis et civium quasi possideret Ecclesia, prodendo potuerunt prejudicium generare; quia illis a quibus alteri potius quam sibi possidentibus non requiritur, possessionis initium leges possessionum evertere et extraneis jura conferre nequivit possessorum; necnon qui de reddendis possessionibus Ecclesie [absque] ratione ad eum pertinentibus pluries juramentum prestiterat, satis improvide a nobis videbatur petere quod non poterat absque perjurio retinere.

We came to the city of Castellana, the citizens of which, violating their oath of fealty, and without the knowledge of the Church, betrayed that Church, and gave themselves up to him, but could not by this proceeding acquire any rights in themselves, nor could they bring any injury on us as to the possession of the city, inasmuch as it was as if we possessed the jurisdiction of the city and the citizens. For if men possess for the benefit of another and not of themselves, it is vain to make demands upon them; the beginning of possession cannot destroy the laws of possession, and confer on strangers the right of the true possessors. Also, as he [Frederick] had often given his oath to restore the possessions which belonged to him, by reason of the

Church, he seemed to act imprudently in asking from us what he could not retain possession of without being guilty of perjury.

Gregory goes to great lengths to undermine the very possibility of the promise of a transfer of jurisdiction claimed by the imperial chancery in *Levate,* an indication of the danger that the papal chancery perceived in the imperial letter. His outraged censure of Frederick and his cohorts is not left to stand on its own; it is coupled with a careful explanation for each and every issue raised in *Levate.*

In a passage that apparently responds to the satirical portrait of Gregory the "merchant . . . making himself his own sealer, writer, and, perhaps, his own accountant," the pope humbly confesses his inadequacy to serve as the vicar of Christ, but pleads that he has fulfilled his responsibilities as an overlord to men, with God's help, to the best of his abilities.

> Fatemur autem nos defectu meritorum nostrorum indigne Christi esse vicarium, fatemur nos oneri tanto insufficientes existere, quod humana conditio non potest absque divino suffragio supportare. Nihilominus tamen vices nobis commissas, prout melius nostra permittit fragilitas, exequentes, secundum quod locorum, temporum, personarum et negotiorum qualitas et natura requirunt, disponenda disponimus et cum excellentibus personis pure et secundum Deum, cum necessitas id exposcit, de notre potestatis plenitudo dispensamus.

> We confess that we are wanting in merit to be the vicar of Christ; we confess that we are inadequate to such a heavy burden, which no mortal of any condition can support without God's assistance; nevertheless, we perform the duties of the office entrusted to us as well as our frailty allows us, and endeavor to dispose matters as the quality and nature of places, times, persons, and circumstances require, and when necessity demand it, and grant dispensations to the full extent of our power, freely, and in accordance with our duty to God, to those deserving it.

The passage appears to signal that at least in the eyes of the Roman chancery, the symbolic supremacy of the papacy has sustained a serious blow. Gregory's words are motivated by the perception that humility will be more effective with the public than an evocation of his power, like that sent to the Frederican court in *Si memoriam,* or to the German bishops *Quanto personam.*

The most important proof of Frederick's alienation from Truth and the truth that streams from it is saved until the end of *Ascendit.* Gregory brands Frederick as heretical on the basis of two statements.

> Iste rex pestilentie a tribus baratoribus, ut eius verbis utamur, scilicet Cristo Jesu, Moyse et Mahometo, totum mundum fuisse deceptum, et duobus eorum in gloria mortuis, ipsum Jesum in ligno suspensum manifeste proponens.

> First, this king of pestilence openly asserts that the world was deceived by three (and we quote him), namely Christ Jesus, Moses, and Mohammed; that two of them having died in glory, the said Jesus was suspended on the Cross.[11]

Secondly, Frederick is reputed to have rejected the virgin birth on the basis of the laws of nature.

> Insuper dilucida voce affirmare vel potius mentire presumpsit quod omnes fatui sunt qui credunt nasci de Virgine Deum qui creavit naturam et omnia potuisse. Hanc heresim illo errore confirmans quod nullus nasci potuit cuius conceptum viri et mulieris conjunctio non precessit, et homo nihil debet aliud credere nisi quod potest vi et ratione nature probare.

> He, moreover, presumed plainly to affirm (or rather to lie), that all are foolish who believe that God, who created nature and all things, could have been born of a virgin. This heresy he confirms by the false doctrine that no one can be born whose conception has not been preceded by the copulation of a man and a woman, and that one should not believe anything beyond what can be proven by force and the reason of nature.

The pope is accusing the emperor of professing naturalistic determinism, a philosophic position associated with Aristotelian science, which challenged the Christian symbolic and miraculous reading of nature. The charge did not lack verisimilitude. Gregory continues, claiming that Frederick "endeavors to deprive [the Church] of the privilege of power granted to it by the word of God" (auferre nititur concessum verbo Dei privilegium potestatis). Of course the imperial chancery denied the accusation (see the discussion of *In exordio* below), professing belief in a God "non de potentia ordinata, sed de potentia ordinante" (not an ordered power but an ordering power).

Ascendit illustrates how the epistolary exchange has transformed the relationship between pope and emperor, at least at the level of public perception. Canon law's fortification of papal jurisdiction was stronger in the 1230s than during the pontificate of Innocent III, and the political situation was no more perilous in the later period. Nevertheless, while Gregory boldly condemns his accuser with dramatic, apocalyptic language, he remains on the defensive throughout the letter. The papacy confronts a competing, pristigious account of events that is being broadcast throughout Latin Christendom. The medium for the challenge is the epistolary narration, a traditional element of a established genre, written in an elegant Latin style.

In July of 1239, Frederick sent a letter to the cardinals, begging them to perform their office and "restrain the roaring of our adversary." *In exordio* focuses on the accusation of heresy leveled against Frederick by the papacy. Rather than prove the charges, Gregory has distorted the facts to fit them. The imperial chancery denies the charges in detail but uses it to reaffirm the claim made in *Levate,* that Gregory is not a true pope but an oppressor and a heretic who attacks one whom God elevated.

The tone of *In exordio* is authoritative and tranquil. Time-honored imagery recalls cosmic order: the sun and the moon, each pre-eminent in a clearly differentiated sphere, are analogs to the divinely ordained ecclesiastical and secular orders among men.

> In exordio nascentis mundi provida et ineffabilis Dei providentia, cui consilia non communicant aliena, in firmamento celi duo statuit luminaria, maius et minus: maius, ut preesset diei; minus, ut preesset nocti. Que duo sic ad propria officia in regione zodiaca offeruntur, ut et si se multotiens ex obliquo respiciant, unum tamen alterum non offendit: immo, quod est superius inferiori suam communicat claritatem. A simili eadem eterna provisio in firmamento terre due voluit inesse regimina, sacerdotium scilicet et imperium.[12]

In the beginning of the creation, the prescient and ineffable providence of God, whose heavenly designs are not revealed, set two bright bodies in the heavens, a greater and a lesser: the greater to be present in the day, the lesser in the night. Thus to each was conferred its own function in the heavens, so that each contemplated the other but did not offend the other: in truth the greater shone its light on the lesser. Similar to the eternal design in the heavens, He wanted there to be two governors on Earth, that is, the priest and the emperor.

The function of the two orders is different so that man, separated into two components, would be restrained by two tethers, and that there would be peace on Earth, and every excess would be curbed [ut homo, qui erat in duobus componentibus diutius dissolutus, duobus retinaculis frenaretur, et sic fieret pax orbi terre, omnibus excessibus limitatis]. But among men the natural order is threatened. The prince of prelates who currently occupies the cathedra seeks not to share light but to eclipse the brilliance of imperial splendor.

Et credit forte cum superioribus convenire, qua natura, non voluntate ducuntur; nostre majestatis jubar intendit ducere in eclipsim, veritate in fabulam commutata, plene mendaciis ad diversas mundi partes papales mittuntur epistole, de complexione, non de ratione, accusantes notre fidei puritatem.[13]

And perhaps he believes that this is appropriate to the heavenly bodies, which are guided by nature and not by will; he attempts to eclipse the splendor of our majesty when, the truth transformed into tales, papal letters full of lies are sent out to different parts of the world attacking the purity of our faith, not with proofs but with foregone conclusions.

The claim is specious, yet indicative of the imperial chancery's belief that there was a public sensitive to modes of argument. The letter continues with speculation on the man who prefers his own will to natural law—Gregory must a false pope because God would never elect such a man as his steward.

Sane, si verus esset pontifex, innocentus, impollutus, segregatus a peccatoribus heberetur, non jurgiorum victime, sed hostiarum pacificarum pacificus immolator, et poneret incensum odoris, non doloris: nec pontificum in maleficium commutaret. Si verus esset pontifex, verbum predictionis non traheret in fructum dissensionis.

Decidedly, if this man were the true pope, he would be innocent, pure, and numb to sinners; not the pawn of miscreants but a serene man who offers himself in sacrifice to the hosts of peacemakers, and he would burn the incense of sweetness, not of pain: nor would he change the papacy into a seat of evil. If he were truly pope, the word of preaching would not produce the fruit of dissension.

Obviously *In exordio* is not a comment on the corruption of Christendom; Frederick's real goal is to persuade whichever cardinals he can to support him against Gregory. The cardinals are described as the pillars of the church, and the emperor protests the passivity with which the cardinals have reacted to the present crisis.

Super quibus omnibus vehementer cogimur admirari, et nostre mentis quietem multa vexat turbatio, quod vos qui estis Ecclesie fundamenta, columne, rectitudinis assessores, Petris urbis senatores, et orbis cardines, non flexistis motum judicis fulminantis, quemadmodum superiores planete faciunt, qui ad retardandam magni corporis velocitatem contrariis motibus opponuntur.

In all these matters we are extremely amazed, and the peace of our minds is vexed with great agitation, because you who are the foundation of the church, the columns, the guardians of rectitude, the senators of the city of Peter, the linchpins of the orb, do not move with fulminating justice as the heavenly bodies do to the planets, which in order to retard the speed of a great body, oppose it with movements in the opposite direction.

The cardinals also have their natural analogs, and it their right and duty to check the mindless assault the pope is now making against the emperor.

Responding to the apocalyptic imagery in Gregory's letter, the imperial chancery offers reasons for Gregory's heresy that fall entirely within the realm of human experience: Gregory is jealous of

Frederick's success. The transparency of the situation is reinforced by a simple, anecdotal explanation.

Unde Simonides interrogatus cur invidos non haberet, respondit, "Quia nihil feliciter gessi." Et quia prospera nobis, Deo benedicto, cuncta succedunt, presertim cum Lombardos rebelles nostros ad mortem persequimur, quos ipse predestinavit ad vitam; hec est causa quare pontifex ipse apostolicus ingemiscit, et nunc de consilio vestro felicitati nostre instituerit obviare.

So Simonides, when asked why he did not have rivals, responded, "Because nothing I do prospers." And because for us, by the grace of God, all things prosper, especially when we pursue the rebel Lombards to death, which he had chosen to thrive, for this reason the pope groans, and now by your advice has sought to block our good fortune.

As in *Levate,* the focus is on Gregory, the man, the sinner, whose fall from grace is entirely comprehensible and in no way mysterious. On the other hand, *In exordio* does not hesitate to brand Gregory with Apocalyptic epithets: he is the Antichrist and the prince of the Prince of Darkness.

Again the question of intention is raised. In *Ascendit* Gregory portrays Frederick as a heretic, and explains thirty years of imperial history as an expression of the corrupt soul of the emperor. The emperor, in *In exordio,* asks to be judged on the purity of his intention. He then appeals to the cardinals to judge papal motives by the consequences of the man's actions.

At the conclusion of the letter Frederick exhorts the cardinals to exercise their reason to restore order to Christendom, thereby averting more violent intervention by the emperor.

Vos vero qui estis viri ad saniora consilia constituti, sensus et rationis excellentiam obtinentes, rugientem adversarium nostrum a processu cuius detestabile fuit initium, penitus revocetis, rerum consequentias ex causis precedentibus attendentes, alioquin, ultraque terra sentiet qualiter in persecutorem ac consequentes principes et fautores procedat Augustus, et qualiter ferro cesareas inferat ultiones.

Truly, you who are men constituted for a saner counsel, possessing sense and excellence of reason, restrain the roaring of our adversary from a course that has been detestable from the beginning, directing your minds to the consequences of things resulting from the above-mentioned causes; otherwise, all the earth will know that, in persecution and in consequence, Augustus precedes the princes and all others, and that he will strike with the sword of the avenging Caesars.

Addressed to a public of cardinals, *In exordio* does not review the details of the political struggle between pope and emperor. The letter takes the bolder position of interpreting the role of the cardinals within the hierarchy; like the emperor, it is their role to protect the church.

In 1239, when the conflict between the papacy and the imperial chancery is at its fiercest pitch, the rhetoric exchanged between the two powers reaches an impasse. In *Ascendit,* Gregory, who as pope has already positioned himself beyond the sphere of rational men, seeks to persuade Christendom that Frederick has done the same, and that he is a diabolical agent. The breakdown highlights the fact that rhetorical persuasion is predicated on a potential for the "meeting of minds,"[14] that whether an appeal is ornamental or strictly logical, there must be the presumption of a common logos and Logos, and the possibility of a shared vision on the part of the writer/orator and the public. When that presumption is denied, rhetoric degenerates into partisan broadsides, or into outright warfare, the *ultiones Cesareas.*

The correspondence of 1239 reveals the breakdown of a battle of words, and the new directions in which epistolary persuasion has moved in response to legal procedures concerning evidence, the inductive argumentation of contingent necessity, and the disassociation of the natural world and human society from the transcendent. These developments resonated far beyond their limited fields of direct application and helped to introduce a paradigm of persuasion that challenged the traditional model of epistolary persuasion. Documents like *Ascendit,* which couple Apocalyptic language to attack the enemy and detailed accountings of events, exemplify the extent of the challenge and the success of the new political rhetoric.

NOTES

1. Lomax presents the most important and informative discussion of the papal-imperial exchange of 1239. The citation is from John Phillip Lomax, *"Ingratus" or "Indignus": Canonistic Argument in the Conflict between Pope Gregory IX and Emperor Frederick II*, Diss., University of Kansas, 1987, 35. *Excommunicamus* is published in J.-L. A. Huillard-Bréholles, *Historia diplomatica Friderici Secundi* 5.1 (Paris: H. Plon, 1852-1861) 286-89, *Cum nuper* in Huillard-Bréholles, 5.1, 289-90, and *Sedes apostolica* in Huillard-Bréholles, 5.1, 290-94. The translation of *Sedes apostolica* (with some modernization) is from J. A. Giles, Trans., *Matthew Paris's English History* 1 (London: Bohn, 1852) 196-200.

2. The passage cited is in the imperial letter *Cum sit Christus*, in Huillard-Bréholles, 5.1, 282-84. The imperial text reads, "Propter quod non indigne dolemus, si pater apostolicus offendere tam graviter nos intendat; unde, dum in constantem virum tam vehemens cadat injuria, et si patienter ferre voluerimus, immanitas negotii non permittit quin ad ultiones, quibus Cesares uti solent, facti violentia nos compellat."

3. *Levate* is in Huillard-Bréholles, 5.1, 295-306. The translation is a revision of Giles, 1, 201-13. My reading of *Levate* has been greatly enriched by the meticulous research and interpretation of Lomax, who demonstrates that the entire argument is rooted in canon law.

4. Lomax's reading of the legal implications of the exordium establishes his interpretation of the document. "The emperor began by exhorting his audience to witness the fruits of Gregory's injustice: scandal, dissension, and false judgment. Frederick illustrated his point by paraphrasing Amos 6.13. He charged that the crimes of the pope 'converted judgment into bitterness and fruit of judgment into wormwood.' This accusation would have evoked a canon taken from St. Augustine who alluded to the same biblical passage. In a related canon, Pope Gregory I asserted that there were four ways in which human judgment is perverted: fear, greed, hatred, and love. During the course of *Levate* Frederick accused Gregory of perpetrating injustices for each of these reasons. The emperor would also describe the consequences of the pope's injustice, which were alleged to include scandal, schism and heresy" (440-41). Lomax continues with a discussion of the legal implications of the wording found throughout *Levate*.

5. Kenneth Pennington, *Pope and Bishops* (Philadelphia: University of Pennsylvania Press, 1984) 41.

6. The passage reads, "Illum preterea Christi vicarium habere et Petri successorem ac dispensatorem animarum fidelium indignum fatemur, non ob dignitatis injuriam, sed ob persone defectum, qui dispensationes cum fratrum deliberatione maxima faciendas, in camera sua more mercatoris cuiuslibet, in libra mercationis appendit, celatis fratrum consiliis, cum quibus secundum ecclesiasticam disciplinam deliberare tenetur, existens ipse sibi bullator et scriptor et forsitan numerator."

7. Lomax 428-29.

8. See the discussion in Chapter 2 of this book.

9. *Ascendit* is in Huillard-Bréholles, 5.1, 327-39. The text is translated in Giles, 1, 213-29. Appended to the letter sent to the English king, according to Matthew Paris, was the message, "Wherefore we have thought fit to advise and to exhort your royal highness that you cause the aforesaid to be diligently explained, so that the purity of the royal innocence may not be contaminated by deceitful words." Giles, 1, 229.

10. The passage from the imperial letter to which the papal chancery is responding reads, "Adhuc etiam tanta et superiori nequitia non contentus, Civitatem Castelle, per ipsum retroactis temporibus turbationibus occupatam, quam reddi nobis fratrum omnium consilia suadebant, receptis trecentis libris illius monete, que ad quingentarum marcarum numerum non ascendunt, nobis cum eo permanentibus in Reate, et pro eo multa marcarum milia expendentibus reddere recusavit."

11. According to de Stefano, the blasphemous doctrine of the three impostors had wide circulation and was generally attributed to Averroes. Antonino de Stefano, *La Cultura alla corte di Federico II Imperatore* (Bologna: Zanichelli, 1950), 122.

12. *In exordio* is in Huillard-Bréholles, 5.1, 348-51.

13. The accusation that Gregory has sent "papal letters full of lies are sent out to different parts of the world attacking the purity of our faith, not with proofs but with foregone conclusions" is discussed in Chapter 2, page 50 of this book.

14. The concept is discussed in Chaim Perelman and Lucie Olbrechts-Tyteca, *The New Rhetoric: A Treatise on Argumentation,* Trans. John Wilkinson and Purcell Weaver (Notre Dame: University of Notre Dame Press, 1971), 14-17.

Conclusion

In the thirteenth century, Latin Christendom was envisioned as a hierarchical, hierocratic society, a vision conceived in view of the universal salvation of mankind. Traditional epistolary form and modes of persuasion provided a fitting instrument to govern on particular issues by referring to universal ones — salvation, the necessity of the church, or proverbial wisdom. This was a rhetoric of authority and unity, a persuasive approach expressed in the elevated prose style. The institution that was principally responsible for the normalization of epistolary rhetoric in the twelfth and early thirteenth centuries was the most active chancery of Christendom, that of the Roman church. The authoritative approach to persuasion embodied in the letter served the papacy to reinforce ecclesiastical authority. Despite the tendency to recycle effective arguments over and over again, each pope assumed a unique "epistolary" persona that expressed his view of the papal cathedra and Christendom.

Why, then, the sudden appearance of a epistolary rhetoric that admitted conflict in the thirteenth century? The change was, to some extent, already anticipated in the *artes dictandi,* where it reflected the demands placed on traditional epistolography and persuasive modes by an increasingly complex society. In fact, letter-writing displayed tendencies that were at once profoundly conservative—with the embrace of a rigid structure and the recycling of arguments over and over again for centuries—and profoundly experimental—as an essentially porous art that absorbed the latest intellectual trends and responded to political pressures. Before the 1180s, the part of the letter that focused on the specific, that is, the narration, was described as brief, concise, and shorn of all detail. There was no room for debate, and the issue that had sparked the epistolary intervention was rarely treated as consequential in the overall persuasive strategy of the letter. But as the twelfth century evolved, the narration became a focus of invention, and gradually the description of a detailed, temporal narration emerged. The issue at hand became important; motives and causes were introduced to explain the evidence, and varied interpretations of events based on divergent understandings of the evidence were voiced. In the letters sent from the imperial chancery, *opinio novella* emerged. While traditional papal persuasion had treated dissension as illegitimate and sinful, and responded to opposition with cajoling, lamentation or censure, in the third and fourth decades of the thirteenth century the exchange of partisan political positions on events found a place in the prestigious genre of public letters.

Given the explosion of new voices in thirteenth-century Europe, the development of a rhetoric that justified and "legitimated" conflict was of vital importance. Merchants were demanding power that had been retained for nearly a millennium by nobles and prelates. Ecclesiastical claims based on purity of intention were challenged by claims based on the material consequences of actions. Recently encoded laws disrupted traditional practices. The Roman chancery was asserting dominion over the ecclesiastical hierarchy, and it sought to extend its control, in certain cases, to secular spheres of interest as well. Canon law provided a vibrant, progressive, functional rein for Christendom, and secular law was also maturing in the period. But in fact, many issues could not be resolved strictly on the basis of law, and in documents intended to move the public to action, legal conviction was combined with extensive rhetorical argumentation. The Roman chancery went to great lengths to gain the acquiescence of the public, whether a specific and limited public or the public at large, in order to enforce edicts and sanctions. Law and rhetorical invention, including the use and adaptation of the elevated prose style but by no means limited to it, were both powerful forces in the forging of a new society in thirteenth-century Latin Europe.

A response to traditional persuasion crystallized in the letters issued from the chancery of Frederick II. Although imperial letters from the early years of Frederick's reign were characterized by the humble recognition that its fortunes depended almost entirely on will of the papacy, later conflicts with Rome transformed the humility of the early years into a more assertive and confrontational discourse. The imperial chancery complained that its interests had been compromised by the popes, and that its ambitions were being thwarted. It took issue with the papacy by systematically focusing on specific incidents and painting them in a different light than the papacy had done, that is, in accordance with its own interests. This happened in the narration of letters.

The imperial chancery persisted, obviously, because it perceived that there was a responsive public among the cardinals and in the other ecclesiastical and secular courts of Latin Christendom. It exploited the fault line that was opened by the translation of Aristotelian scientific works into Latin, and claimed for itself a discourse that could be grasped by the rational exercise of the human mind and senses. The chancery offered a vision of society shaped by human needs and intellect which differed from and to some extent countered the papal vision of Christian society guided by transcendent laws. The imperial chancery wrote to other kings to define its interests (and theirs) in terms dictated by the contingencies of a given situation. Letters describe events in historical terms, focusing on causality accessible to the human mind, on the temporal and mutable. The chancery's way of analyzing, justifying and explaining undermined the authoritarian structure of the epistolary appeal. Although traditional epistolary persuasion did not disappear, and on the contrary, continued to be admired and imitated for centuries, the alternative represented by the imperial letters was significant because it justified conflict, the very phenomenon that traditional epistolary rhetoric was designed to exclude.

The persuasive modes of the Frederican and papal chanceries trace the political relationship between the two powers. The harmony and unity of purpose shared by both institutions was expressed in the celebratory language of the first half of the 1220s. Rigorous analysis on the part of the public was discouraged in such heavily orchestrated language; the public was invited to enjoy the words and to give its assent. The rhetorical symphony ended with a crash at the opening of Honorius's *Miranda tuis,* in which the Frederican chancery was charged with arrogance because of its reevaluation of papal policy toward Sicily during Frederick's minority, as well as its defense of recent imperial actions. Outright hostility began to find a voice in the letters exchanged by the papal and imperial chanceries in 1227, when Gregory excommunicated Frederick. Gradually that hostility was codified into two distinct persuasive modes, although it is easy to be too emphatic on this point because in practice an appeal was determined by the perceived culture of the public. Nevertheless, letters intended to shore up support for the emperor's political ambitions were generally framed by statements of the imperial mandate, and approval was sought not by claiming divine sanction or inspiration for imperial acts (except when it is particularly useful to do so)—on the contrary, the public was asked to evaluate imperial acts on the basis of their adequacy as responses to particular situations in view of the imperial mandate to restore peace and justice among men. Imperial acts, even those that stood in direct opposition to papal policy, were characterized as determined by the contingencies of the situation, the "compelling necessity of things," and consistently aimed at the fulfillment of the imperial mandate. The rhetoric is self-contained and self-referential. The papal chancery also elaborated its policies in detail when and where it was deemed effective.

We may choose to view rhetoric as superficial, purely formal and void of content, as mere window dressing for the "battle of laws" in the first half of the thirteenth century, and quite obviously persuasion was not often successful in cases of serious conflict. Yet the effort to persuade may also be read as a sign of confidence in the potential for communication, and as indicative not only of the differences that separated the two powers, but also of the vital sense of common ground, of a shared vision. The development of a new paradigm of persuasion was at once an expression of very real opposition and hostility, and a sign of affirmation, an attempt to define communality in the light of an increasingly complex political situation.

Bibliography

Abulafia, David. *Frederick II: A Medieval Emperor.* New York: Penguin, 1988.

Adalbertus Samaritanus. *Praecepta Dictaminum.* Ed. Franz-Josef Schmale. Weimar: Bohlaus, 1961.

Alessio, Gian Carlo. "Brunetto Latini e Cicerone (e i dettatori)." *Italia medioevale e umanistica* 22 (1979): 127-29; 160-69.

―――. "La Tradizione manoscritta del *Candelabrum*." *Italia medioevale e umanistica* 15 (1972): 99-148.

―――. "Brunetto Latini's *Rettorica* and the Rhetorical Trends in Thirteenth-Century Italy," Div. on *La Rettorica* of Brunetto Latini, International Congress of Medieval Studies, Kalamazoo, Michigan, May 4-7, 1989.

―――. Ed. *Bene Florentini Candelabrum.* Padova: Antenore, 1983.

Antonelli, Roberto. *La Politica culturale di Federico II.* Seminario romanzo. Rome: Bulzoni, 1979.

Aristotelis Opera cum Averrois Commentariis 6. *Ad Animalium Cognitionem Attinentes.* 1562-1574. Frankfurt: Minerva, 1962.

Aristotle. *"Art" of Rhetoric.* Trans. J. H. Freese. Cambridge, MA: Harvard University Press, 1982.

―――. *Historia Animalium 1. Books I-III.* Ed. and Trans. A. L. Peck. Cambridge, MA: Harvard University Press, 1979.

Aristotle's Physics. Ed. and Trans. Hippocrates G. Apostle. 1969. Grinnell: Peripatetic Press, 1980.

Auerbach, Erich. *Literary Language and Its Public in Late Antiquity and in the Middle Ages.* Trans. Ralph Manheim. Princeton: Princeton University Press, 1965.

Augustine. *De Doctrina Christiana; De Vera Religione.* Corpus Christianorum, Seria Latina 32. Aurelli Augustini Opera. Pt. 4.1. Ed. Joseph Martin. Turnhout: Brepols, 1962.

————. *De Mendacio. Patrologie Cursus Completus.* Series Latina 40. Ed. J.-P. Migne. Paris: Garnier, 1890. Cols. 517-47.

Aurell, Martin. *La vielle et l'épée: Troubadours et politique en Provence au XIIIe siècle.* Paris: Aubier, 1989.

Baldwin, Charles Sears. *Medieval Rhetoric and Poetic.* 1928. Gloucester: Peter Smith, 1959.

Balme, D. M. "The Place of Biology in Aristotle's Philosophy." *Philosophical Issues in Aristotle's Biology.* Eds. Allen Gotthelf and James G. Lennox. New York: Cambridge University Press, 1987. 9-20.

————. "Teleology and Necessity." *Philosophical Issues in Aristotle's Biology.* Eds. Allen Gotthelf and James G. Lennox. New York: Cambridge University Press, 1987. 275-90.

————. Ed. and Trans. *Aristotle's "De Partibus Animalium" I and "De Generatione Animalium" I.* Oxford: Clarendon Press, 1985.

Banker, James R. "The *Ars Dictaminis* and Rhetorical Textbooks at the Bolognese University of the Fourteenth Century." *Medievalia et Humanistica* 5 (1974): 153-68.

Barnes, Jonathan. Ed. and Trans. *Aristotle's Posterior Analytics.* Oxford: Clarendon Press, 1975.

Bene da Firenze. *Cedrus Libani.* Ed. Giuseppe Vecchi. Modena: Società Tipografica Editrice Modenese, 1963.

Benson, Robert L. *The Bishop-Elect: A Study in Medieval Ecclesiastic Office.* Princeton: Princeton University Press, 1968.

————. "Protohumanism and Narrative Technique in Early Thirteenth-Century *Ars Dictaminis.*" *Boccaccio: Secoli di vita. Atti del Congresso Internazionale alla University of California in Los Angeles, 17-19 October, 1975.* Eds. Marga Cottino-Jones and Edward F. Tuttle. Los Angeles: UCLA Center for Medieval and Renaissance Studies 4 (1974): 31-50.

Berman, Harold J. *Law and Revolution: The Formation of the Western Legal Tradition.* Cambridge, MA: Harvard University Press, 1983.

Beyer, Heinz-Jürgen. "Die Frühphase der *Ars Dictandi.*" *A Gustavo Vinay.* Centro italiano di studi sull' alto medioevo. Spoleto: 1977. 585-609.

Böhmer, J. F., J. Ficker and E. A. Winkelmann. *Regesta Imperii* 5. 1881-1901. Hildesheim: G. Olms, 1971.

Bolgar, Robert R. *The Classical Heritage and Its Beneficiaries.* 1954. New York: Cambridge University Press, 1974.

————. "The Teaching of Rhetoric in the Middle Ages." *Rhetoric Revalued.* Ed. Brian Vickers. Binghamton: Medieval and Renaissance Texts and Studies, 1982. 79-86.

Bolton, Robert. "Definition and Scientific Method in Aristotle's *Posterior Analytics* and *Generation of Animals.*" *Philosophical Issues in Aristotle's Biology.* Eds. Allen Gotthelf and James G. Lennox. New York: Cambridge University Press, 1987. 120-66.

————. "The Epistemological Basis of Aristotelian Dialectic." *Biologie, Logique et Métaphysique chez Aristote. Actes du Seminaire C.N.R.S.-N.S.F. Oléron June 28-July 3, 1987.* Eds. Daniel Devereux and Pierre Pellegrin. Paris: Éditions du Centre Nationale de la Recherche Scientifique, 1990. 185-236.

Brandileone, Francesco. *Il Diritto romano nelle leggi normanne e sveve del regno di Sicilia.* Rome: Fratelli Bocca, 1884.

Brandt, William J. *The Shape of Medieval History. Studies in Modes of Perception.* New Haven: Yale University Press, 1966.

Bresslau, Harry. *Handbuch der Urkundenlehre für Deutschland und Italien.* 2 vols. 3rd ed. Berlin: W. de Gruyter, 1958-1960.

Brini Savorelli, M. "Il *Dictamen* di Bernardo Silvestre." *Rivista critica di storia della filosofia* 202 (1965): 182-230.

Brundage, James A. *Medieval Canon Law.* New York: Longman, 1995.

Brunetto Latini. *La Rettorica.* Ed. Francesco Maggini. Florence: Le Monnier, 1968.

Bütow, Adolf. *Die Entwicklung der mittelalterlichen Briefsteller bis zur Mitte des 12. Jahrhunderts, mit besonderer Berücksichtigung der Theorien der "ars dictandi."* Greifswald: Hans Adler, 1908.

Buyken, Thea. *Das romanische Recht in den Constitutionen von Melfi.* Cologne: Westdeutscher Verlag, 1960.

————. "Über das *Prooemium* der Constitutionen von Melfi." *Revista Portuguesa de Historia* 14 (1941): 161-76.

Camargo, Martin. *Ars Dictaminis, Ars Dictandi.* Typologie des sources du moyen âge occidental 60. Turnhout: Brepols, 1991.

————. "English Manuscripts of Bernard of Meung's *Flores Dictaminum.*" *Viator* 12 (1981): 197-219.

————. "The *Libellus de Arte Dictandi Rhetorice* Attributed to Peter of Blois." *Speculum* 59.1 (1984): 16-41.

————. "Rhetoric." *The Seven Liberal Arts in the Middle Ages.* Ed. David L. Wagner. Bloomington: Indiana University Press, 1983. 96-124.

————. "Toward a Comprehensive Art of Written Discourse: Geoffrey of Vinsauf and the *Ars Dictaminis*." *Rhetorica* 6.2 (1988): 167-94.

Caplan, Harry. *Of Eloquence: Studies in Ancient and Mediaeval Rhetoric.* Eds. Anne King and Helen North. Ithaca: Cornell University Press, 1970.

Capua, Francesco di. "Appunti sul *cursus* o ritmo prosaico, nelle opere latine di Dante Alighieri." *Scritti minori* 1. New York: Desclée & Co., 1958. 564-85.

————. "La Diffusione del latino letterario-ritmico nei secoli XII-XIV e le scuole di *Ars Dictandi*." *Scritti minori* 1. New York: Desclée and Co., 1958. 496-499.

————. "Lo Stile della Curia Romana e il *cursus* nelle epistole di Pier della Vigna e nei documenti della cancelleria sveva." *Scritti minori* 1. New York: Desclée and Co., 1958. 500-23.

————. "Per la Storia del latino letterario medievale e del *cursus.*" *Scritti minori* 1. New York: Desclée and Co., 1958. 524-63.

————. *Scritti minori.* 2 vols. New York: Desclée and Co., 1958.

Caramella, Santino. "La Filosofia di Federico II." *Atti del Convegno Internazionale di Studi Federiciani, 10-18 December, 1950. VII Centenario della morte di Federico II, Imperatore e re di Sicilia.* Palermo: A. Renna, 1952. 103-33.

Carlyle, R. W. and A. J. Carlyle. *A History of Medieval Political Theory in the West.* 6 vols. 1903-1936. London: W. Blackwood, 1950.

Castellani, Arrigo. "Le Formule volgari di Guido Faba." *Studi di filologia italiana* 12 (1955): 5- 78.

Cessi, Roberto. "Leggendo l' epistolario federiciano." *Atti del Convegno Internazionale di Studi Federiciani, 10-18 December, 1950. VII Centenario della morte di Federico II, Imperatore e re di Sicilia.* Palermo: A. Renna, 1952. 345-49.

Charlton, William. "Aristotle on the Place of Mind in Nature." *Philosophical Issues in Aristotle's Biology.* Eds. Allen Gotthelf and James G. Lennox. New York: Cambridge University Press, 1987. 408-23.

Cheney, C. R. *Innocent III and England.* Päpste und Papsttum 9. Stuttgart: Anton Hiersemann, 1976.

————. "The Letters of Pope Innocent III." *Bulletin of the John Rylands Library* 35 (1952): 23-43.

————. *The Study of the Medieval Papal Chancery.* The Second Edwards Lecture Delivered within the University of Glasgow on December 7, 1964. Glasgow: Jackson, 1966.

Cheney, C. R. and Mary G. Cheney. Eds. *The Letters of Pope Innocent III (1198-1216) Concerning England and Wales. A Calendar with an Appendix of Texts.* Oxford: Clarendon Press, 1967.

Cheney, C. R. and W. H. Semple. Eds. and Trans. *Selected Letters of Pope Innocent III Concerning England (1198-1216).* New York: Thomas Nelson and Sons Ltd., 1953.

[Cicero]. *Ad Herennium.* Trans. Harry Caplan. Cambridge, MA: Harvard University Press, 1981.

Cicero. *De Inventione.* Trans. H. M. Hubbell. Cambridge, MA: Harvard University Press, 1976.

Cicognani, Amleto Giovanni. *Canon Law.* Trans. Joseph M. O'Hara and Francis J. Brennan. 2nd ed. Westminster: Newman Bookshop, 1934.

Conrad, Hermann, Thea von der Lieck-Buyken and Wolfgang Wagner. *Die Konstitutionen Friedrichs II. von Hohenstaufen für sein Königreich Sizilien.* Cologne: Bohlau Verlag, 1973.

Constable, Giles. *Letters and Letter-Collections.* Typologie des sources du moyen âge occidental 17. Turnhout: Brepols, 1977.

———. "The Structure of Medieval Society according to the *Dictatores* of the Twelfth Century." *Law, Church and Society: Essays in Honor of Stephan Kuttner.* Eds. Kenneth Pennington and Robert Somerville. Philadelphia: University of Pennsylvania Press, 1977. 253-67.

Cooper, John M. "Hypothetical Necessity and Natural Teleology." *Philosophical Issues in Aristotle's Biology.* Eds. Allen Gotthelf and James G. Lennox. New York: Cambridge University Press, 1987. 243-74.

Costa, Pietro. *Iurisdictio: Semantica del potere politico nella pubblicistica medievale (1100-1433).* Milan: Giuffre, 1969.

Curtius, Ernst R. *European Literature of the Latin Middle Ages.* Trans. Willard R. Trask. Bollington Foundation Series 36. Princeton: Princeton University Press, 1953.

Dalzell, Ann. "The *Forma Dictandi* Attributed to Albert of Morra and Related Texts." *Mediaeval Studies* 39 (1977): 440-65.

Dante Alighieri. *Il Convivio.* Ed. Maria Simonelli. Bologna: Patron, 1966.

Del Re, Niccolò. *La Curia Romana: Lineamenti storico giuridico.* Sussidi eruditi 23. 3rd ed. Rome: Edizioni di Storia e Letteratura, 1970.

Denholm-Young, Noel. "The *Cursus* in England." *Collected Papers of N. Denholm-Young.* Cardiff: University of Wales Press, 1969. 42-73.

Devereux, Daniel and Pierre Pellegrin. Eds. *Biologie, logique et métaphysique chez Aristote. Actes du Séminaire C.N.R.S.-N.S.F. Orléron, June 28- July 3, 1987.* Paris: Centre National de la Recherche Scientifique, 1990.

220 *Bibliography*

Dickey, Mary. "Some Commentaries on the *De Inventione* and *Ad Herennium* of the Eleventh and Early Twelfth Centuries." *Mediaeval and Renaissance Studies* 6 (1968): 1-41.

Dronke, Peter. "Medieval Rhetoric." *Literature and Western Civilization* 2. Eds. David Daiches and Anthony Thorlby. London: Aldus, 1972-1976. 315-45.

Duhamel, P. Albert. "The Function of Rhetoric as Effective Expression." *Philosophy and Argumentation.* Eds. Maurice Natanson and Henry W. Johnson Jr. University Park: Pennsylvania State University Press, 1965. 80-92.

Ehler, Sidney Z. and John B. Morrall. Trans. *Church and State through the Centuries: Collection of Historic Documents with Commentaries.* Westminster: Newman Press, 1954.

Fasoli, Gina. *Per la Storia dell'Università di Bologna nel Medio Evo.* Bologna: Patron, 1970.

Faulhaber, Charles B. "The *Summa Dictaminis* of Guido Faba." *Medieval Eloquence: Studies in the Theory and Practice of Medieval Rhetoric.* Ed. James Jerome Murphy. Berkeley: University of California Press, 1978. 85-111.

La Filosofia della natura nel medioevo. Atti del Terzo Congresso Internazionale di Filosofia Medioevale. Trent, 31 August-5 September, 1964. Milan: Vita e Pensiero, 1966.

Fleckenstein, Josef. Ed. *Probleme um Friedrich II.* Konstanzer Arbeitskreis für mittelalterliche Geschichte. Sigmaringen: J. Thorbecke, 1974.

Fliche, Augustin, Christine Thouzellier and Yvonne Azais. *Histoire de l'église depuis les origines jusqu'à nos jours* 10. *La Chrétienté romaine (1198-1274).* Paris: Bloud and Gay, 1946- 1952.

Fontaines, Jacques. *Isidore de Seville et la culture classique dans l'Espagne wisigothique.* Paris: Etudes augustiniennes, 1959.

Foreville, Raymond. *Le Pape Innocent III et la France.* Päpste und Papsttum 26. Stuttgart: Anton Hiersemann, 1992.

Franceschini, Ezio. "Ricerche e studi su Aristotele nel Medioevo latino." *Medioevo e umanesimo* 27 (1976): 377-408.

Fransen, Gérard. *Les collections canoniques.* Typologie des sources du moyen âge occidental 10. Turnhout: Brepols, 1973.

Fredborg, Karin Margareta. "The Commentaries on Cicero's *De Inventione* and *Rhetorica ad Herennium* by William of Champeaux." *Cahiers de l'Institut du Moyen-Age Grec et Latin* 17 (1976): 1-39.

———. "Twelfth-Century Ciceronian Rhetoric: Its Doctrinal Development and Influences. *Rhetoric Revalued.* Ed. Brian Vickers. Binghamton: Medieval and Renaissance Texts and Studies, 1982. 87-97.

———. Ed. *The Latin Rhetorical Commentaries by Thierry of Chartres.* Toronto: Pontifical Institute of Mediaeval Studies, 1988.

Gaudemet, Jean. "Note sur le symbolisme médiéval: Le mariage de l' évêque." *La société ecclésiastique dans l'Occident médiéval.* London: Variorum Reprints, 1970. 71-80.

Gaudenzi, Augusto. *I Suoni, le forme e le parole dell'odierno dialetto della città di Bologna.* Turin: Loescher, 1889.

———. "Sulla Cronologia delle opere dei dettatori bolognesi da Boncompagno a Bene di Lucca." *Bollettino dell' Istituto Storico Italiano* 14 (1895): 85-161.

———. Ed. "Boncompagni *Rhetorica Novissima.*" *Bibliotheca Iuridica Medii Aevi, Scripta Anecdota Glossatorum* 2. Bologna: Petri Virano, 1892.

———. Ed. "*Epistole* Magistri Guidonis." *Il Propugnatore* 6.1 (1893): 359-90; 373-89.

———. Ed. "Guido Fabe *Summa Dictaminis.*" *Il Propugnatore* 3 (1890): 287-338; 345-93.

———. Ed. "Guidonis Fabe *Dictamina Rhetorica.*" *Il Propugnatore* 5 (1892): 86-129; 58-109.

Gierke, Otto von. *Political Theories of the Middle Ages.* Trans. F. W. Maitland. Cambridge: University Press, 1900.

Giles, J. A. Trans. *Matthew Paris's English History. From the Year 1235 to 1273.* 2 vols. London: Henry G. Bohn, 1852.

Giunta, Francesco. "La Politica antiereticale di Federico II." *Atti del Convegno Internazionale di Studi Federiciani, 10-18 December, 1950. VII Centenario della morte di Federico II, Imperatore e re di Sicilia.* Palermo: A. Renna, 1952. 91-95.

Gotthelf, Allen. "Aristotle's Conception of Final Causality." *Philosophical Issues in Aristotle's Biology.* Eds. Allen Gotthelf and James G. Lennox. New York: Cambridge University Press, 1987. 204-42.

———. "First Principles in Aristotle's *Parts of Animals.*" *Philosophical Issues in Aristotle's Biology.* Eds. Allen Gotthelf and James G. Lennox. New York: Cambridge University Press, 1987. 167-203.

Gotthelf, Allen and James G. Lennox. Eds. *Philosophical Issues in Aristotle's Biology.* New York: Cambridge University Press, 1987.

Grabmann, Martin. *I Divieti ecclesiastici di Aristotele sotto Innocenzo III e Gregorio IX.* Rome: Saler, 1941.

————. "Kaiser Friedrich II. und sein Verhältnis zur aristotelischen und arabischen Philosophie." *Stupor Mundi: Zur Geschichte Friedrichs II. von Hohenstaufen* 2. Ed. Gunther Wolf. Darmstadt: Wissenschaftliche Buchgesellschaft, 1982. 134-77.

Graefe, Friedrich. *Die Publizistik in der letzten Epoche Kaiser Friedrichs II. Ein Beitrag zur Geschichte der Jahre 1239-1250*. Heidelberg: Carl Winter, 1909.

Grant, Edward. *A Source Book in Medieval Science*. Cambridge, MA: Harvard University Press, 1974.

Gregory, T. "L'Idea di natura nella filosofia medievale prima della *Fisica* di Aristotle—Il secolo XII." *La Filosofia della natura nel Medioevo. Atti del Terzo Congresso Internazionale di Filosofia Medioevale. August 31-September 5, 1964*. Milan: Vita e Pensiero, 1966. 26-65.

Guernelli, Giovanni. *Chiesa e stato nel pensiero di Gregorio IX*. Rome: Pontificia Università Lateranense, 1969.

Hagemann, Wolfgang. "La Nuova edizione del registro di Federico II." *Atti del Convegno Internazionale di Studi Federiciani, 10-18 December, 1950. VII Centenario della morte di Federico II, Imperatore e re di Sicilia*. Palermo: A. Renna, 1952. 315-36.

Hageneder, Othmar and Anton Haidacher. Eds. *Die Register Innocenz' III*. 4 vols. Publikationen der Abteilung für historische Studien des Österreichischen Kulturinstituts in Rom, 2nd ser., sect. 1. Graz: Hermann Bohlaus, 1964.

Halm, Charles. *Rhetores Latini Minores*. 1863. Dubois: Wm. C. Brown, n.d).

Haskins, Charles Homer. "Albericus Casinensis." *Casinensia* 1 (1929): 115-24.

————. "The Early *Artes Dictandi* in Italy." *Studies in Medieval Culture*. 1929. New York: Frederick Ungar Publishing Co., 1958. 170-92.

————. "An Italian Master Bernard." *Essays in History Presented to Reginald Lane Poole*. Ed. Henry W. C. Davis. 1927. Freeport: Books for Libraries, 1967. 211-26.

————. "Latin Literature under Frederick II." *Speculum* 3 (1928): 129-51.

————. *Studies in the History of Medieval Science*. 1924. New York: Frederick Ungar Publishing Co., 1960.

————. *Studies in Medieval Culture*. 1929. New York: Frederick Ungar Publishing Co., 1958.

Heller, Emmy. "Die *Ars Dictandi* des Thomas von Capua." *Sitzungsberichte der Heidelberger Akademie der Wissenschaften* 4 (1929): 1-59.

————. "Zur Frage des kurialen Stileinflusses in der sizilischen Kanzlei Friedrichs II." *Deutsches Archiv für die Erforschung des Mittelalters* 19.2 (1963): 434-50.

Hendrickson, G. L. "The Origin and Meaning of the Ancient Character of Style." *American Journal of Philology* 26.3 (1905): 257-90.

Herde, Peter. "Ein Pamphlet der päpstlichen Kurie gegen Kaiser Friedrich II. von 1245/46 (*Eger cui lenia*)." *Deutsches Archiv für die Erforschung des Mittelalters* 23 (1967): 468-538.

Holtz, Louis. "Le Parisinus Latinus 7530, synthèse cassinienne des arts libéraux." *Studi medievali,* 3rd ser. 16.1 (1975): 97-152.

Horst, Erberhard. *Federico II di Svevia.* Trans. Giovanna Solari. Milan: Rizzoli, 1981.

Hugh. *Rationes Dictandi. Briefsteller und Formelbücher des eilften bis vierzehnten Jahrhunderts* 1. Ed. Ludwig Rockinger. 1863-1864. New York: Burt Franklin, 1961. 49-94.

Huillard-Bréholles, J.-L. A. *Historia diplomatica Friderici Secundi.* 10 vols. Paris: H. Plon, 1852- 1861.

————. *Vie et correspondance de Pierre de la Vigne, ministre de l'empereur Frederic II.* Paris: H. Plon, 1885.

Hyde, J. K. *Society and Politics in Medieval Italy: The Evolution of the Civic Life, 1000-1350.* London: Macmillan Press, 1973.

Inguanez, D. M. and H. M. Willard. "Alberici Casinensis *Flores Rhetorici.*" Miscellanea Cassinese 14 (1938).

Innocent III. Registrorum sive Epistolarum Libri VI. Series Latina 214-17. Ed. J.-P. Migne. Paris: Garnier, 1890.

Isidore of Seville. *Etymologies.* Ed. and Trans. Jacques André. Paris: Les Belles Lettres, 1981.

Jakobson, Roman. *Language in Literature.* Eds. Krystyna Pomorska and Stephen Rudy. Cambridge MA: Harvard University Press, 1987.

Janson, Tore. *Prose Rhythm in Medieval Latin.* Studia Latina Stockholmiensis 20. Stockholm: Almquist and Wiksell International, 1975.

Jordan, Edouard. *L' Allemagne et l' Italie aux XIIe et XIIIe siècles. Histoire du Moyen Age* 4.1. Paris: Presses Universitaires de France, 1939.

Kantorowicz, Ernst. "An 'Autobiography' of Guido Faba." *Medieval and Renaissance Studies* 1 (1941): 253-80.

————. "Anonymi *Aurea Gemma.*" *Medievalia et Humanistica* 1 (1943): 41-57.

————. "*Deus per Naturam, Deus per Gratiam.* A Note on Mediaeval Political Theory." *Harvard Theological Review* 45 (1952): 253-77.

Bibliography

———. *Frederick the Second, 1194-1250.* Trans. E. O. Lorimer. New York: Frederick Ungar Publishing Co., 1957.

———. *Kaiser Friedrich der Zweite.* 2 vols. Munich: Georg Bondi, 1931.

———. *The King's Two Bodies. A Study in Medieval Political Theology.* Princeton: Princeton University Press, 1957.

———. "Kingship under the Impact of Scientific Jurisprudence." *Twelfth-Century Europe and the Foundation of Modern Society.* Eds. Marshall Clagett, Gaines Post and Robert Reynolds. Madison: University of Wisconsin Press, 1961. 89-111.

———. "Petrus de Vinea in England." *Mitteilungen des Österreichischen Instituts für Geschichtsforschung* 51.1-2 (1937): 43-88.

———. "Zu den Rechtsgrundlagen den Kaiserage." *Deutches Archiv für die Erforschung des Mittelalters* 13.1 (1957): 115-50.

Kehr, Paul. "Das Briefbuch des Thomas von Gaeta, Justitiars Friedrichs II." *Quellen und Forschungen aus italienischen Archiven und Bibliotheken* 8.1 (1905): 1-76.

Keil, Heinrich. *Grammatici Latini.* 1864. Hildesheim: G. Olms, 1961.

Kelly, Douglas. *The Arts of Poetry and Prose.* Typologie des sources du moyen âge occidental 59. Turnhout: Brepols, 1991.

Kelly, J. N. D. *The Oxford Dictionary of Popes.* New York: Oxford University Press, 1986.

Kennedy, George. *Classical Rhetoric and Its Christian and Secular Tradition from Ancient to Modern Times.* Chapel Hill: University of North Carolina Press, 1980.

Kronbichler, Walter. "Die *Summa de Arte Prosandi* des Konrad von Mure." Geist und Werk der Zeiten 17. Zürich: Fretz und Wasmuth, 1968.

Ladner, Gerhart. "Formularbehelfe in der Kanzlei Kaiser Friedrichs II. und die 'Briefe des Petrus de Vinea.'" *Mitteilungen des Österreichischen Instituts für Geschichtsforschung* 12 (1932): 92-198.

Lagarde, Georges de. *La naissance de l'esprit laïque au déclin du moyen âge* 1. 1934- 46. Louvain: Nauwelaerts, 1956.

Lanham, Carol Dana. *"Salutatio" Formulas in Latin Letters to 1200: Syntax, Style and Theory.* Münchener Beiträge zur Mediävistik und Renaissance Forschung 22. Munich: Arbeo-Gesellschaft, 1975.

The Latin Rhetorical Commentaries by Thierry of Chartres. Toronto: Pontifical Institute of Medieval Studies, 1988.

Lausberg, Heinrich. *Elementi di retorica.* Trans. Lea Ritter Santini. Bologna: Il Mulino, 1969.

Lavaud, René. *Poésies complètes du troubadour Peire Cardenal.* Toulouse: Privat, 1957.

Lawler, Traugott. Ed. and Trans. *The Parisiana Poetria of John of Garland.* Yale Studies in English 182. New Haven: Yale University Press, 1974.

Le Bras, Gabriel, Charles Lefebvre and Jacqueline Rambaud. *Histoire du droit et des institutions de l' Eglise en Occident. L' Age Classique, 1140-1278.* Sources et théorie du droit 7. Paris: Sirey, 1965.

Leff, Michael C. "Boethius' *De Differentiis Topicis*, Book IV." *Medieval Eloquence: Studies in the Theory and Practice of Medieval Rhetoric.* Ed. James Jerome Murphy. Berkeley: University of California Press, 1978. 3-24.

Lennox, James G. "Divide and Explain: The *Posterior Analytics* in Practice." *Philosophical Issues in Aristotle's Biology.* Eds. Allen Gotthelf and James G. Lennox. New York: Cambridge University Press, 1987. 90-119.

Leyser, K. J. "The Polemics of the Papal Revolution." Ed. Beryl Smalley. *Trends in Medieval Political Thought.* Oxford: Blackwell, 1965. 42-64.

Licitra, Vincenzo. "Il Mito di Alberico di Montecassino, iniziatore dell' *Ars Dictaminis.*" *A Gustavo Vinay.* Spoleto: Centro Italiano di Studi sull'Alto Medioevo, 1977. 607- 27.

———. "La *Summa de Arte Dictandi* di Maestro Goffredo." *Studi medievali.* 3rd ser. 7 (1966): 865-913.

Lomax, John Phillip II. *"Ingratus" or "Indignus": Canonistic Argument in the Conflict between Pope Gregory IX and Emperor Frederick II.* Diss., University of Kansas, 1987.

Luard, Henry Richards. *Matthaei Pariensis, Monachi Sancti Albani, Chronica Majora 3.* London: Longman, 1872-1883.

Maccarone, Michele. *Studi su Innocenzo III.* Italia sacra. Studi e documenti di storia ecclesiastica 17. Padova: Antenore, 1972.

Manselli, Raoul. "La Corte di Federico II e Michele Scoto." *L'Averroismo in Italia. Atti dei Convegni Lincei 40. 18-20 April 1977.* Rome: Accademia Nazionale dei Lincei, 1979. 63- 89.

Marongiu, Antonio. "Concezione della sovranità ed assolutismo di Giustiniano e di Federico II." *Atti del Convegno Internazionale di Studi Federiciani, 10-18 December, 1950. VII Centenario della morte di Federico II, Imperatore e re di Sicilia.* Palermo: A. Renna, 1952. 31-46.

Marrou, H. I. *Saint Augustin et la fin de la culture antique.* Bibliothèques des écoles françaises d'Athènes et de Rome 145. Paris: Broccard, 1938.

Martin, Janet. "Classicism and Style in Latin Literature." *Renaissance and Renewal in the Twelfth Century.* Eds. Robert L. Benson, Giles Constable, and Carol D. Lanham. Cambridge, MA: Harvard University Press, 1982. 537-68.

Matthew Paris. *Chronica Majora.* 7 vols. Ed. Henry Richards Luard. London: Longman and Co., 1872-1883.

McKeon, Richard. "Aristotle's Conception of Language and the Arts of Language." *Critics and Criticism, Ancient and Modern.* Ed. R. S. Crane. Chicago: University of Chicago Press, 1952. 176-231.

————. "Poetry and Philosophy in the Twelfth Century: The Renaissance of Rhetoric." *Critics and Criticism, Ancient and Modern.* Ed. R. S. Crane. Chicago: University of Chicago Press, 1952. 297-318.

————. "Rhetoric in the Middle Ages." *Speculum* 17.1 (1942): 1- 32.

Migne, J.-P. Ed. *Patrologie Cursus Completus.* Series Latina 216. Paris: Garnier, 1958-1974.

Miller, Joseph M., Michael H. Prosser and Thomas W. Benson. Eds. *Readings in Medieval Rhetoric.* Bloomington: Indiana University Press, 1973.

Mohrmann, Christine. "Le style de Saint Bernard." *San Bernardino: pubblicazioni commemorative nel VIII centenario della sua morte.* Milan: Pubblicazione dell' Università Cattolica del Sacro Cuore, 1954. 166-84.

Monteverdi, Angelo. "Le Formule epistolari volgari di Guido Fava." *Saggi neolatini* 9. Rome: Edizioni di Storia e Letteratura, 1945. 75-109.

Morghen, Raffaello. "Federico II di fronte al Papato." *Atti del Convegno Internazionale di Studi Federiciani, 10-18 December, 1950. VII Centenario della morte di Federico II, Imperatore e re di Sicilia.* Palermo: A. Renna, 1952. 9-17.

Morris, Colin. *The Papal Monarchy: The Western Church from 1050 to 1250.* Oxford: Clarendon Press, 1989.

Murphy, James Jerome. "Alberic of Monte Cassino: Father of the Medieval *Ars Dictaminis.*" *American Benedictine Review* 22 (1971): 129-46.

————. "Cicero's Rhetoric in the Middle Ages." *The Quarterly Journal of Speech* 53.4 (1967): 334- 41.

————. *Medieval Rhetoric: A Select Bibliography.* Toronto Medieval Bibliographies. Toronto: University of Toronto Press, 1971.

————. *Rhetoric in the Middle Ages: A History of Rhetorical Theory from St. Augustine to the Renaissance.* Berkeley: University of California Press, 1974.

————. Ed. *Medieval Eloquence: Studies in the Theory and Practice of Medieval Rhetoric.* Berkeley: University of California Press, 1978.

————. Ed. *Three Medieval Rhetorical Arts.* Berkeley: University of California Press, 1971.

Nederman, Cary J. "Aristotelianism and the Origins of 'Political Science' in the Twelfth Century." *The Journal of the History of Ideas* 52.2 (1991): 179-94.

Niese, Hans. *Zur Geschichte des geistigen Lebens am Hofe Kaiser Friedrichs II.* 1912. Darmstadt: Wissenschaftliche Buchgesellschaft, 1967.

Norden, Eduard. *Die antike Kunstprosa vom VI. Jahrhundert v. Chr. bis in die Zeit der Renaissance.* 2 vols. 5th ed. 1909. Leipzig: B. G. Teubner, 1923.

Normore, Calvin G. "Notes for Medieval Defense of Lying." Boston Colloquium in Medieval Philosophy, November 6, 1995.

Nussbaum, Martha Craven. *Aristotle's "De Motu Animalium."* Princeton: Princeton University Press, 1978.

Paratore, Ettore. "Alcuni Caratteri dello stile della cancelleria federiciana." *Atti del Convegno Internazionale di Studi Federiciani, 10-18 December, 1950. VII Centenario della morte di Federico II, Imperatore e re di Sicilia.* Palermo: A. Renna, 1952. 283-313.

Patt, William D. "The Early *Ars Dictaminis* as a Response to a Changing Society." *Viator 9* (1978): 133-55.

Pennington, Kenneth. "Innocent III and the Divine Authority of the Pope." *Pope and Bishops: The Papal Monarchy in the Twelfth and Thirteenth Centuries.* Philadelphia: University of Pennsylvania Press, 1984. 13-42.

———. *Pope and Bishops: The Papal Monarchy in the Twelfth and Thirteenth Centuries.* Philadelphia: University of Pennsylvania Press, 1984.

———. "Pope Innocent III's View on Church and State: A Gloss to *Per Venerabilem.*" *Law, Church and Society: Essays in Honor of Stephan Kuttner.* Eds. Kenneth Pennington and Robert Somerville. Philadelphia: University of Pennsylvania Press, 1977.

———. *The Prince and the Law, 1200-1600: Sovereignty and Rights in the Western Legal Tradition.* Berkeley: University of California Press, 1993.

Pennington, Kenneth and Robert Somerville. Eds. *Law, Church, and Society: Essays in Honor of Stephan Kuttner.* Philadelphia: University of Pennsylvania Press, 1977.

Perelman, Chiam. *The Realm of Rhetoric.* Trans. William Kluback. Notre Dame: University of Notre Dame Press, 1982.

Perelman, Chaim and Lucie Olbrechts-Tyteca. *The New Rhetoric: A Treatise on Argumentation.* Trans. John Wilkinson and Purcell Weaver. Notre Dame: University of Notre Dame Press, 1971.

Peters, Edward. *The Shadow King: 'Rex Inutilis' in Medieval Law and Literature, 751-1327.* New Haven: Yale University Press, 1970.

Petite-Dutaillis Charles and Paul Guinard. *L'Essor des Etats d'Occident (France, Angleterre, Peninsule Iberique).* *Histoire du Moyen Age* 4.2. Paris: Presses Universitaires de France, 1937.

Pini, Virgilio. "Summa de Vitiis et Virtutibus." *Quadrivium* 1 (1956): 41-152.

Plezia, Marian. "L'Origine de la théorie du cursus rythmique au XIIe siècle." *Archivum Latinitatis Medii Aevi* 39 (1974): 5-22.

Polak, Emil J. *Medieval and Renaissance Letter Treatises and Form Letters: A Census of Manuscripts Found in Part of Western Europe, Japan, and the United States of America.* New York: Brill, 1994.

——. *A Textual Study of Jacques de Dinant's "Summa Dictaminis."* Etudes de philologie et d'histoire 28. Geneva: Droz, 1975.

Poole, Reginald L. *Lectures on the History of the Papal Chancery Down to the Time of Innocent III.* Cambridge: University Press, 1915.

Post, Gaines. *Studies in Medieval Legal Thought.* Princeton: Princeton University Press, 1964.

Powell, James M. Ed. and Trans. *The "Liber Augustalis" or "Constitutiones of Melfi" Promulgated by the Emperor Frederick II for the Kingdom of Sicily in 1231.* Syracuse: Syracuse University Press, 1971.

Prévite-Orton, C. W. *The Shorter Cambridge Medieval History.* 2 vols. New York: Cambridge University Press, 1979.

Prodi, Paolo. *The Papal Prince.* Trans. Susan Haskins. New York: Cambridge University Press, 1987.

Pybus, H. B. "The Emperor Frederick II and the Sicilian Church." *The Cambridge Historical Journal* 3.2 (1930): 134-163.

Quadebaur, Franz. *Die antike Theorie der "Genera dictandi" in lateinischen Mittelalter.* Vienna: H. Bohlaus, 1962.

Quintilian. *Institutionis Oratoriae Libri Duodecim.* Ed. M. Winterbottom. Oxford: Clarendon Press, 1970.

Rajna, Pio. "Per il *Cursus* medievale e per Dante." *Studi di filologia romanza* 3 (1932): 7-86.

Randall, John Hermann Jr. *Aristotle.* New York: Columbia University Press, 1960.

Renucci, Paul. "Dante e gli Svevi: Alcune osservazioni e premesse." *Dante e l'Italia Meridionale. Atti del II. Congresso Nazionale di Studi Danteschi. 10-16 October, 1965. Salerno, Napoli, Caserta, Benevento, Cassino.* Florence: Olschki, 1966. 131-47.

Reynolds L. D. and N. G. Wilson. *Scribes and Scholars.* Oxford: Clarendon Press, 1984.

de Riquer, Martin. Ed. *Los Trovadores, Historia literaria y textos* 3. Barcelona: Planeta, 1975.

Robertson D. W. Jr. Trans. *Augustine: On Christian Doctrine.* New York: Macmillan, 1986.

Robinson, I. S. *The Papacy 1073-1198: Continuity and Innovation.* New York: Cambridge University Press, 1990.

Rockinger, Ludwig. Ed. *Briefsteller und Formelbücher des eilften bis vierzehnten Jahrhunderts.* 2 vols. 1863-1864. New York: Burt Franklin, 1961.

Rodenberg, C. Ed. *Epistolae Saeculi XIII e Registis Pontificum Romanorum Selectae per G. H. Pertz.* 3 vols. Monumenta Germaniae Historica. Berlin: Weidmann, 1883-1884.

Roncaglia, Aurelio. "Le Corti medievali." *Il Letterato e le istituzioni.* Letteratura italiana 1. Rome: Einaudi, 1982. 33-147.

Rubenstein, Nicolai. "Political Rhetoric in the Imperial Chancery during the Twelfth and Thirteenth Centuries." *Medium Aevum* 14 (1945): 21-43.

Rudberg, Gunnar. "Kleinere Aristoteles-Fragen." *Eranos* 9.4 (1909): 92-128.

Runciman Steven. *A History of the Crusades* 3. *The Kingdom of Acre and the Later Crusades.* New York: Cambridge University Press, 1987.

Sayers, Jane. *Innocent III: Leader of Europe, 1198-1216.* New York: Longman, 1994.

Scaglione, Aldo. *The Classical Theory of Composition from Its Origins to the Present: An Historical Survey.* Chapel Hill: University of North Carolina Press, 1972.

Schaller, Hans Martin. "Das letzte Rundschreiben Gregors IX. gegen Friedrich II." *Festschrift Percy Ernst Schramm.* Wiesbaden: Franz Steiner, 1964. 309-21.

————. "Die Kanzlei Kaiser Friedrichs II. Ihr Personal und ihr Sprachstil 1". *Archiv für Diplomatik* 3 (1957): 207-85.

————. "Die Kanzlei Kaiser Friedrichs II. Ihr Personal und ihr Sprachstil 2". *Archiv für Diplomatik* 4 (1958): 264-325.

————. "Zur Entstehung der sogenannten Briefsammlung des Petrus de Vinea," *Deutsches Archiv für die Erforschung des Mittelalters* 12 (1956): 114-59.

Schmale, Franz-Josef. "Der Briefsteller Bernhards von Meung." *Mitteilungen des Instituts für österreichische Geschichtsforschung* 66 (1958): 1-28.

————. "Die Bolognese Schule der *Ars Dictandi.*" *Deutsches Archiv für die Erforschung des Mittelalters,* 13.1 (1957): 16-34.

————. Ed. *Adalbertus Samaritanus "Praecepta Dictaminum."* Monumenta Germaniae Historica. Quellen zur Geistegeschichte des Mittelalters 3. Weimar: Hermann Böhlaus Nachfolger, 1961.

Segre, Cesare. *Lingua, stile e società.* Milan: Feltrinelli, 1976.

Segre, Cesare and Mario Marti. *La Prosa del Duecento.* Milan: Ricciardi, 1959.

Shepard, Laurie. "Rhetoric and Aristotelian Natural Philosophy." *Imagining New Worlds: Essays on Factual and Figural Discovery During the Middle Ages.* Ed. Scott D. Westrem. New York: Garland Publishing, 1991. 142-56.

————. "Rhetoric and Science at the Court of Frederick II of Hohenstaufen." *Studi di filologia e letteratura italiana in onore di M. Picchio Simonelli.* Ed. Pietro Frassica. Alessandria: Edizioni dell' Orso, 1991. 289-300.

————."Rhetorical Innovation in the Chancery of Frederick II of Hohenstaufen and Its Reception by Vernacular Poets of the Thirteenth Century." Diss., Boston College, 1985.

Smalley, Beryl. *Studies in Medieval Thought and Learning.* London: Hambledon Press, 1981.

————. *The Study of the Bible in the Middle Ages.* 3rd ed. Oxford: Blackwell, 1984.

————. Ed. *Trends in Medieval Political Thought.* Oxford: Blackwell, 1965.

Solmsen, Friedrich. "The Aristotelian Tradition in Ancient Rhetoric." *Rhetorika: Schriften zur aristelischen und hellenistischen Rhetorik.* Ed. Rudolf Stark. Hildesheim: Georg Olms, 1968.

————. Ed. *The Rhetoric and Poetics of Aristotle.* New York: Random House, 1954.

Sorabji, Richard. *Necessity, Cause and Blame: Perspectives on Aristotle's Theory.* Ithaca: Cornell University Press, 1980.

Southern, R. W. *Western Society and the Church in the Middle Ages.* 2 vols. New York: Pelican, 1970.

Stefano, Antonino de. *La Cultura alla corte di Federico II imperatore.* 1938. Bologna: Zanichelli, 1950.

————. *L'idea imperiale di Federico II.* Parma: All' Insegna del Veltro, 1978.

————. *Riformatori ed eretici nel Medioevo.* Palermo: F. Ciuni, 1938.

Steinen, W. von den. *Staatsbriefe Kaiser Friedrichs des Zweiten.* Bresslau: F. Hirt, 1923.

Sthamer, Eduard. "Studien über die sizilischen Register Friedrichs II 1". *Sitzungsberichte der Preußischen Akademie der Wissenschaften* (1920): 584-610.

———. "Studien über die sizilischen Register Friedrichs II 2". *Sitzungsberichte der Preußischen Akademie der Wissenschaften* (1925): 168-77.

———. "Studien über die sizilischen Register Friedrichs II 3". *Sitzungsberichte der Preußischen Akademie der Wissenschaften* (1930): 78-96.

Struever, Nancy S. *The Language of History in the Renaissance: Rhetoric and Historical Consciousness in Florentine Humanism.* Princeton: Princeton University Press, 1970.

———. "The Study of Language and the Study of History." *The Journal of Interdisciplinary History* 4.3 (1974): 401-15.

Stump, Eleonore. *Boethius's "De Topicis Differentiis."* Ithaca: Cornell University Press, 1989.

———. *Boethius's "In Ciceronis Topica."* Ithaca: Cornell University Press, 1988.

———. "Boethius's Works on the *Topics*." *Vivarium* 12.2 (1974): 77-93.

Stürner, Wolfgang. *"Rerum Necessitas* und *Divina Provisio:* Zur Interpretation des Prooemiums der Konstitutionen von Melfi (1231)." *Deutsches Archiv für die Erforschung des Mittelalters* 39 (1983): 467-554.

Sutter, Carl. *Aus Leben und Schriften des Magisters Boncompagno. Ein Beitrag zur italienischen Kulturgeschichte in dreizehnten Jahrhundert.* Freiburg im Breisgau: Mohr, 1894. 105-27.

Thorndike, Lynn. *Michael Scot.* London: Nelson, 1965.

Tierney, Brian. "The Continuity of Papal Political Theory in the Thirteenth Century: Some Methodological Considerations." *Medieval Studies* 22 (1965): 227-45.

———. *Crisis in Church and State. 1150-1300.* Englewood Cliffs: Prentice Hall, 1964.

———. *Foundations of the Conciliar Theory.* Cambridge: University Press, 1955.

Tierney, Brian and Sidney Painter. *Western Europe in the Middle Ages, 300-1475.* New York: Alfred A. Knopf, 1970.

Tillmann, Helena. *Pope Innocent III.* Trans. Walter Sax. New York: North-Holland Publishing Co., 1980.

Tunberg, Terence O. "What is Boncompagno's 'Newest Rhetoric'?" *Traditio* 42 (1986): 299-334.

Ullmann, Walter. "Frederick II's Opponent: Innocent IV as Melchisedek." *Atti del Convegno Internazionale di Studi Federiciani, 10-18 December, 1950.*

232   Bibliography

VII Centenario della morte di Federico II, Imperatore e re di Sicilia.
Palermo: A. Renna, 1952. 53-81.

―――. *The Growth of Papal Government in the Middle Ages: A Study in the Ideological Relation of Clerical to Lay Power.* London: Methuen, 1955.

―――. *A History of Political Thought in the Middle Ages.* Baltimore: Penguin Books, 1965.

―――. *Medieval Papalism: The Political Theories of the Medieval Canonists.* London: Methuen, 1949.

―――. *A Short History of the Papacy in the Middle Ages.* 2nd ed. London: Methuen, 1972.

―――. "Some Reflections on the Opposition of Frederick II to the Papacy." *Archivio storico pugliese* 13 (1960): 16-39.

Vallone, Aldo. "Il Federicismo." *Zeitschrift für romanische Philologie* 98.1-2 (1983): 109-28.

Van Cleve, Thomas Curtis. *The Emperor Frederick II of Hohenstaufen, Immutator Mundi.* Oxford: Clarendon Press, 1972.

Van Steenberghen, Ferdinand. *Aristotle in the West.* Trans. Leonard Johnston. Louvain: Nauwelaerts, 1970.

―――. "La philosophie de la nature au XIIIe siècle." *La Filosofia della natura nel Medioevo. Atti del Terzo Congresso Internazionale di Filosofia Medioevale. Passo della Mendola August 31- September 5, 1964.* Milan: Vita e Pensiero, 1966. 114-32.

Vaughan, Richard. *Matthew Paris.* Cambridge: University Press, 1958.

Vaux, R. de. "La première entrée d'Averroës chez les latins." *Revue des Sciences Philosophiques et Théologiques* 22 (1933): 193-245.

Vecchi, Giuseppe. "Giovanni del Virgilio e Dante: La polemica tra latino e volgare nella corrispondenza poetica." *Dante e Bologna nei tempi di Dante.* Bologna: Patron, 1967. 67-76.

―――. "Il Magistero delle *Artes* latine a Bologna nel medioevo." *Pubblicazioni della Facoltà di Magistero* 2 (1958): 7-27.

Vehse, Otto. *Die amtliche Propaganda in der Staatskunst Kaiser Friedrichs II.* Munich: Münchner Drucke, 1929.

Vickers, Brian. *In Defense of Rhetoric.* Oxford: Clarendon Press, 1988.

Wagner, David L. *The Seven Liberal Arts in the Middle Ages.* Bloomington: Indiana University Press, 1983.

Ward, John O. "The Date of the Commentary on Cicero's *De Inventione* by Thierry of Chartres (ca. 1095-1160?) and the Cornifician Attack on the Liberal Arts." *Viator* 3 (1972): 219-73.

———. "From Antiquity to the Renaissance: Glosses and Commentaries on Cicero's *Rhetorica.*" *Medieval Eloquence: Studies in the Theory and Practice of Medieval Rhetoric.* Ed. James Jerome Murphy. Berkeley: University of California Press, 1978. 25-67.

Watt, John A. "The Theory of Papal Monarchy in the Thirteenth Century." *Traditio* 20 (1964): 179-317.

Weiland, Ludwig. Ed. *Legum Sectio IV: Constitutiones et Acta Publica Imperatorem et Regum* 2. Monumenta Germaniae Historica. Hannover: Hahn, 1893-1927.

Westrem, Scott S. Ed. *Imagining New Worlds: Essays on Factual and Figural Discovery During the Middle Ages.* New York: Garland Publishing, 1991.

Wieruszowski, Hélène. "Arezzo as a Center of Learning and Letters in the Thirteenth Century." *Traditio* 9 (1953): 321-91.

———. "*Ars Dictaminis* in the Time of Dante." *Medievalia et Humanistica* 1 (1943): 95-108 (rpt. *Politics and Culture in Medieval Spain and Italy.* Storia e letteratura 121. Rome: Edizioni di Storia e di Letteratura, 1971, 359-77.)

———. "Rhetoric and the Classics in Italian Education of the Thirteenth Century." *Politics and Culture in Medieval Spain and Italy.* Storia e letteratura 121. Rome: Edizione di Storia e di Letteratura, 1971. 589-627.

———. *Vom Imperium zum nationalen Königtum.* Beiheft der historischen Zeitschrift 30. Munich: R. Oldenbourg, 1933.

Willemsen, Carl Arnold. Ed. *Friderici Romanorum Imperatoris Secundi "De Arte Venandi cum Avibus."* 2 vols. Leipzig: Insula, 1942.

Wingate, S. D. *The Mediaeval Latin Versions of the Aristotelian Scientific Corpus, with Special Reference to the Biological Works.* London: Courier Press, 1931.

Witt, Ronald G. "Boncompagno and the Defense of Rhetoric." *The Journal of Medieval and Renaissance Studies* 16.1 (1986): 1-31.

———. "Brunetto Latini and the Italian Tradition of the *Ars Dictaminis.*" *Stanford Italian Review* 3.1 (1983): 5-24.

———. "Civic Humanism and the Rebirth of Ciceronian Oration." *Modern Language Quarterly* 51 (1990): 167-84.

———. "Medieval *Ars Dictaminis* and the Beginnings of Humanism: A New Construction of the Problem." *Renaissance Quarterly* 35.1 (1982): 1-35.

———. "Medieval Italian Culture and the Origins of Humanism as a Stylistic Ideal." *Renaissance Humanism: Foundations, Forms and Legacy* 1. *Humanism in Italy.* Ed. Albert Rabil Jr. Philadelphia: University of Pennsylvania Press, 1988. 29-70.

Wood, Casey A. and Marjorie G. Fyfe. Eds. and Trans. *The Art of Falconry Being the "De Arte Venandi cum Avibus" of Frederick II of Hohenstaufen.* Palo Alto: Stanford University Press, 1943.

Wood, Diana. Ed. *The Church and Sovereignty c. 590-1918: Essays in Honor of Michael Wilks.* Oxford: Blackwell, 1991.

Worstbrock, Franz Josef. "Zu Galfrids *Summa de Arte Dictandi.*" *Deutsches Archiv für die Erforschung des Mittelalters* 23 (1967): 549-52.

Index

Terms Cited

DATE DUE

Demco, Inc 38-293